*Eddie Neville of the Durham Bulls*

# Eddie Neville

## *OF THE*

# Durham Bulls

*by*
BILL KIRKLAND

McFarland & Company, Inc., Publishers
*Jefferson, North Carolina, and London*

*Front cover:* **Eddie Neville demonstrates the form that would lead to 75 wins over four seasons with the Durham Bulls. (Courtesy** *The Herald-Sun,* **Durham, N.C.)**

**British Library Cataloguing-in-Publication data are available**

**Library of Congress Cataloguing-in-Publication Data**

Kirkland, Bill, 1940–
    Eddie Neville and the Durham Bulls / by Bill Kirkland.
      p.  cm.
    Includes bibliographical references (p. 193) and index.
    ISBN 0-89950-862-6 (sewn softcover : 50# alk. paper) ∞
    1. Neville,     Eddie.  2. Baseball     players—United
States—Biography.
    3. Durham Bulls (Baseball team).  I. Title.
    GV865.N45K57   1993
    796.357'092—dc20
    [B]                                        92-56658
                                                         CIP

Manufactured in the United States of America

*McFarland & Company, Inc., Publishers*
  *Box 611, Jefferson, North Carolina 28640*

In memory of my parents,
Helon and Buck Kirkland

# *Acknowledgments*

This book became my connection to a long line of former players who generously gave of their time to help piece together the story of Eddie Neville. The search for information started with Al Kubski, Neville's manager in winter baseball, and ended with his pitching rival in the Carolina League, Mike Forline.

Other players and managers who helped preserve the memories of that era included Wayne Ambler, Eddie Ball, Boyd Bartley, Lindy Brown, Mike Caldwell, Pete Clark, Bob Cruze, Ray Dabek, Jake Daniel, Alton Denson, Ray Dietrich, Willie Duke, Frank Fabianich, Art Ferguson, Ed Fitz Gerald, Andy "Red" Frazier, Walter "Teapot" Frye, Al Gionfriddo, Bert Haas, Pat Haggerty, Russ Hand, Howie Henkle, Ray Herbert, Ralph Hodgin, Bill Jeffries, Roy Kennedy, Ray Komanecky, Paul LaPalme, Tommy Lasorda, Walter "Buck" Leonard, George Lerchen, Carl Linhart, Connie Mack, Jr., Bobby Mavis, Eddie Mayo, John "Mickey" McPadden, Charlie Metro, Ed Mordarski, Gordon Mueller, "Rocket" Ron Necciai, Clarence "Ace" Parker, Emil Restaino, Earl Richmond, Stan Russelavage, Bill See, Ted Sepkowski, Leo "Muscle" Shoals, Lou Sleater, Walt Sorgi, Walt Streuli, Bobby Taylor, Dave Thomas, Jack Tighe, Cecil "Turkey" Tyson, Melvin Webb, Bill Werber, and Early Wynn.

Bill Deane and Gary Van Allen of the National Baseball Library in Cooperstown, New York, were diligent in tracking down numerous requests for statistical information and obscure facts about minor league players and teams. Tim Brunswick of the National Association of Professional Baseball Leagues provided leads on the whereabouts of several players.

Bill McCulloch of Chapel Hill, North Carolina, a longtime editor and writer whose ties to the game include his days as a semipro pitcher, listened to my early ramblings and helped forge a clearer sense of direction and purpose. His assistance in reviewing manuscripts was invaluable.

Four other journalists also played important roles. Jack Horner and Hugo Gemino, both retired sports editors in Durham, North Carolina, filled in gaps with facts on Neville's days as a Durham Bull. Wilt Browning, sports columnist for the *News & Record* in Greensboro, North Carolina, offered encouragement and advice after reviewing much of my early material. John Steadman, sports columnist for *The Evening Sun* in Baltimore, gave me an understanding of the Baltimore that was the backdrop of Neville's amateur years.

Janet Neville opened her heart and home in allowing me access to her late husband's papers and memorabilia. Miles Wolff, former owner of the Durham team, was a willing adviser throughout the project.

Molly Dixon, Neville's sister, and her husband, Charles, offered considerable insight into the young Eddie Neville. Information on Neville's days as a student-athlete at Mount St. Joseph High School was provided by Paul "Knobby" Harris, a Neville contemporary and a member of the school's Hall of Fame, and by Susan Reiners and Barbara Trietley of the development office.

Others who helped along the way included Burwell Allen, Wally Ausley, Terry Beasley, Anne Berkley, Pete Bock, Brent Braswell, Annie Bruce Caldwell, Lynda Caldwell, Robert Carr, Freda Collins, Leisha Cowart, Rob Dlugozima, Jim Duffy, Steve Gietschier, Lee Goodmon, Ray Goodmon, Jr., Carol Hamilton, Trecia Hamons, Victoria Hamons, Tom Harkins, Al Mangum, Carol Clayton McClancy, Hazel McDaniel, Harold Moore, Dr. Hunter Moricle, Virginia Morland, Skip Owen, Thomas "Tinker" Parnell, Lynn Perry, Monchin Pichaildo, Joe Phillips, Hester Tyson, Mary Alice Weaver, and Jake Woodall, Jr.

Family members cheered me on to the finish. My wife, Ann, trained me on the computer and encouraged me during periods of frustration. My daughter, Elizabeth Sickles, proved to be a top-notch copy editor. And my son, Kirk, peeked at a couple of chapters during his senior year at Randolph-Macon College and responded with a thumbs up.

# Contents

# *Prologue*

*He spent some of his days wandering a golf course picking up lost balls. He sat as a stranger in a park that he once ruled. And nobody asked any more about his crumbling scrapbooks and his yellowing baseballs and his uniforms that hadn't been worn since orange-colored grease propped up flattop haircuts. Was it really that long ago?*

---

The front stoop—there it stood, the very heart of a baseball fantasy, its three steps leading up to the front door of a two-story white frame house just a mile and a half from the park where they played the real game.

It was the summer of 1949, a time when a boy could spend a lazy day firing a balding tennis ball against the stoop and watching it ricochet toward an imaginary field that was really just a little front yard bordered by tree-lined Englewood Avenue. The pitcher's mound rested on a stone sidewalk. Thirty feet away stood a low-lying outfield fence that others recognized as a street curb neatly marked by house numbers painted by the local Jaycees.

Any ball eluding the pitcher's grasp was considered a hit. Balls reaching the street were scored as doubles. They turned into triples if they caromed off the curb, home runs if they jumped it. The field was anchored by unsightly bushes that served as first and third base. Clover and dandelions decorated the field; bees on a bridal-wreath shrub hummed like an excited crowd. Rain never halted a game, but foul balls often did. The limit of fouls behind home plate varied with human tolerance. When the ball struck the top edge of a step, sailed backward, and banged against the front-door screen one time too many, an angry parent usually postponed play until the next day.

Alone with the stoop, you could be any pitcher who ever played the game. For me, the choice was clear: "And pitching for the Bulls, Number 7..."

Eddie Neville arrived in Durham, North Carolina, that year, suited up for the Durham Bulls, and became a local hero over four glorious seasons. Neville was 26 years old and I was 8, almost a generation apart. Yet our lives followed similar patterns as the innocence of post–World War II baseball paralleled the innocence of youth.

The lefthander was to enjoy an outstanding season that resulted in his promotion in 1950 to a team one step removed from the major leagues. Life for me was never better: velvet-voiced Wally Ausley broadcasting the Bulls on the radio, neighborhood games lasting until sunset, a grandfather willing to watch western movies every Saturday, a pitcher for a hero.

The next spring, after learning that Neville had been promoted to the Toledo Mud Hens, I soothed myself by writing the first letter of my life. My mother addressed the envelope to the Ohio club's spring training camp at Bartow, Florida.

The words went down slowly, almost painfully. "I am a loyal follower of yours," I wrote, "and I would like very much for your autograph. If you would send it to me I will give you my name, address and city and I will print it." I did all those things and more. In a final burst of genius, I taped in a nickel to pay for the return postage.

Although the address was incomplete, my plea somehow made it through the postal system to Toledo's Tropical Court Hotel headquarters. Neville and the rest of the team had taken over the U-shaped, 22-room motor court that sat off Route 60 in the shade of scraggly palm trees.

I was sick with a spring cold when the little box in the brown wrapper arrived by mail. I discovered my genuine Eddie Neville autograph—a fancy one that leaned to the left—on the milk-white hide of an American Association baseball. Prodded by my parents, I rushed out a letter of thanks. "I used to go with my daddy to see you play for the Bulls," I wrote. "I think you are a fine player."

Neville would not return to Durham for two years. I passed the time staring at the autographed ball, reading Joe Palooka comic books, and playing a year of midget league baseball.

Billy Cox, Duke University's All-American tailback from Mount Airy, North Carolina, rented a house near our neighborhood and spent the summer of 1951 coaching the Durham Rotary Club's midget team. When he issued an announcement of the first practice to the boys at George Watts School, I grabbed my cheap, unpadded infielder's glove, and joined two others as we attempted to be the first boys on the block to become bona fide baseball players.

Neighbors Joe and Louis made the team easily. After Cox handed out 14 uniforms, one slot remained as two of us auditioned for the final spot on the team. "Please, Billy; please, Billy," we took turns saying. I was the better beggar. The loser was more successful in later pleas; he turned out to be a lawyer.

We played on a field bordered by a cotton mill and railroad tracks. A blond-haired mill boy from down a dirt street toughened up a team composed mostly of youngsters who led a softer—although hardly privileged—life.

We lost the first game when I missed a throw at second base. The throw was wide, but not that wide. I threw my glove and cried a lot. I vowed it would never happen again. Cox probably did the same; he played me very little after that.

I bought a new first baseman's glove, then warmed the bench for weeks, relegated to emergency duty in what would be my first and final season. The emergency came when Joe, our regular first baseman, suffered an early morning attack of diarrhea. After finishing four innings with only two errors, I was disappointed to see Joe trotting toward the field. Paregoric had cured his distress and ended my hopes of stardom. They told me later that it was the best game I had ever played.

Neville returned to Durham in 1952, and our passion for baseball continued on a pleasant little street called Dollar Avenue. Instead of baseballs, we swatted tennis balls to avoid smashing car windows.

The two oldest—Simp and Jack—led the charge, along with the remarkably talented Joanna, who became a star in girls' tennis after her father advised her to give up tackle football. The midget league's one-time threesome took to the street along with Dewey, Rhodney, Sammy, and the three Dominick boys. We welcomed anyone else with the ability to chase down the fly balls struck with gusto by Simp's father, a lanky college professor we sometimes referred to as "Suitcase."

As we outgrew the narrow confines of the street, we searched for other sites. Louis's father, electrical contractor Jim Vaughan, suggested an empty lot near his house as a suitable spot for both baseball and football. We cleared the lot with sickles and hand mowers. We built a backstop and dugout with used lumber and chicken wire. In the fall, a rickety goalpost went up in right field for the football season.

We called the little park Vaughan Field in honor of our benefactor. Teams from other neighborhoods would challenge us just for the chance to play there. When it rained, we would sit under trees near the field, listen to the falling rain, and wait for another day.

On mornings before the games began, I read about Neville and the Bulls in the *Durham Morning Herald*, following them so closely that my father was forced to have two copies of the newspaper delivered to our front stoop every day. He would retire to one bathroom with his copy; I would go to the other bathroom with mine.

Despite my early desire to read the sports pages, my comprehension level matched my age. When over 4,000 fans turned out the night Neville faced "Rocket" Ron Necciai in the pitching duel of the year, I was convinced that most of the crowd came to see a cow-milking contest matching my father, who headed the Durham Merchants Association, against a banker and the executive director of the Chamber of Commerce. I could see the next day's headline: "Buck Kirkland Wins Cow-Milking Contest As Neville Cheers." But that was not to be. Stuck with a dry cow, my father came in a distant third.

By the time Neville's career started winding down, all of us had left the nearby elementary school and had become classmates in high school or junior high on the edge of downtown. The boys who once wore striped polo shirts had entered puberty; the biggest game now was dropping water-filled condoms out of second-story windows.

Vaughan Field, after becoming engulfed in weeds, disappeared under a monotonous series of brick ranch houses. The street where we struck tennis balls suddenly lost its magic. The front stoop became little more than a convenience for the mailman and milkman. Eddie Neville left the Bulls, gave the game one more shot in Albany, New York, then retired. We lost Neville and our childhood at the same time, but what a run we had.

The years passed. The youngsters of Vaughan Field and Dollar Avenue would have sons and daughters who would grow up in other places in a more sophisticated time. The park where Neville played would become a baseball landmark. The players of the modern era would come and go, but no one would love the place as much as Neville and Claude "Buck" Weaver, a Durham pitcher from the same era who left instructions that his ashes be scattered over the mound after his death in 1967.

Nearly 35 years after I wrote Neville, I received a letter from the pitcher I had almost forgotten. "I was going through a lot of things that I never throw away," he wrote in February of 1985. "Among them, I had two letters from a young boy. That boy was you." The Bulls' all-time winning pitcher had tracked me down at my newspaper office in Charlottesville, Virginia, through a mutual friend, Jack Horner, the former sports editor of the *Durham Morning Herald*. He invited me to visit him in Durham, where he worked for Duke University. He suggested his favorite bleacher seat at Durham Athletic Park as a possible meeting place.

We visited Durham that September, staying with my wife's parents only two blocks from Neville's house on Hammond Street. I called and asked if I could stop by, but his response was unsettling. He didn't remember me, or his letter, or his invitation to see him. He sounded lost and confused. He turned over the telephone to his wife, Janet, and she encouraged me to come over, although by this time it no longer seemed like a good idea. Still, I took my 15-year-old son, Kirk, and told him he would learn what heroes are all about.

We arrived at the front door of a two-story brick house and met Neville for the first time. He was no longer a pitcher with a relentless left arm that helped him win 184 professional games, no longer an athlete with movie-star looks. His haggard appearance and problems with his memory accelerated his age far beyond his 63 years.

We shared his dreams for more than an hour that Sunday afternoon. Neville said little, but showed us his scrapbooks. Pictures and clippings told the stories of when he rode buses through the bushes of Class D and boarded steamships bound for games the week before Christmas. He seemed mystified, however, when I asked about my boyhood letters. They had vanished from his memory, perhaps only briefly, perhaps forever.

We headed back to my in-laws' house and prepared to return to Virginia. An hour later, as we packed the car, Neville showed up in the driveway. He had a silly kind of a smile, and I knew why he was there. When he turned over the letters, the clock turned back ever so briefly to 1950. Even my old nickel was there, taped to the bottom of the note I had mailed to his spring training camp.

We posed for a picture in the driveway, the old pitcher with a father and his son. Kirk's smile was more of a reflex than anything else; it would be years before he understood what the day was all about. I promised to stay in touch with Neville, but I never did. I preferred the memories of a proud little pitcher who confounded a lot of guys in gray uniforms. He died in 1989, the victim of a dementia that stole his mind with the same cruelty as Alzheimer's disease.

His life story would show that he never reached the highest point that some say makes a baseball career count. He never made it to Detroit with Newhouser and Houtteman and Hoeft. He never became immortalized by having his name inscribed in a baseball encyclopedia that lists every player who ever made an appearance in a major league game.

He did smash a memorable home run that made champions out of his high school team in Baltimore. He heard cheers from Tarboro to Toledo, from Butler to the "Bull City." He became part of a winter league baseball dynasty. He won two of the most extraordinary extra-inning games in minor league history. He pitched so many games in such fast times and picked so many runners off first base that he became a legend at the game's grassroots.

Newspaper obituaries recalled Neville as a great minor league player. He would have liked that. Until the day no team really wanted him, he came ready to play—a symbol of all those players who became local heroes and then slipped into obscurity once they passed the town line.

The thousands of fans who saw Eddie Neville play would tell you this about the man: his baseball career counted. And he could pitch. God, how he could pitch.

*Of course you want to be a star in the big leagues. Who doesn't? But you can still be a tremendously fulfilled athlete and suffer the disappointment of only having gotten to Triple A and still have done something quite remarkable.*

A. Bartlett Giamatti (1938–1989)
Commissioner of Baseball

# The Baltimore Kid

*I never really thought about Baltimore until the St. Louis Browns moved there in 1954. Then we recognized the born-again Baltimore Orioles as a rival of the beloved Washington Senators, a hopeless team that we saw once a year as we sat across from the National Bohemian Beer sign in the swampy heat of Griffith Stadium. The closest we came to Baltimore was listening to the names of Larsen and Turley breaking through the static of a faraway radio station.*

It was a home run of Ruthian standards, struck to the same spot in the same Oriole Park where the Babe had pounded it out in New York Yankee exhibition games. Only this time the batter was not Ruth, not even a Baltimore Oriole, but a 17-year-old high schooler who until this May afternoon had played in the park only as a participant in a summer instructional program. The left-handed schoolboy slammed the ball over the fence in right center field, then trotted around the bases in a flat-footed style hardly reminiscent of the pigeon-toed Ruth. As he headed for the dugout with another base runner ahead of him, cheers erupted from his Mount St. Joseph teammates who were on their way to a 5–1 victory and Baltimore's high school championship.

The year was 1940, the batter was Eddie Neville, and the game matched Mount St. Joseph against City College in the finals of the Maryland Scholastic Association playoffs. More than 50 years later, Neville's blast remains part of Baltimore's rich baseball lore that started with stories of Ruth and expanded to include the feats of other native sons.

Al Kaline's Detroit career was worthy of the Hall of Fame. Another Tiger, Johnny Neun, would be remembered for his unassisted triple play against Cleveland in 1927. Tommy Byrne had a shot at being a Yankee World Series hero, only to lose the seventh game of the 1955 series to the Dodgers.

And then there was Eddie Neville.

I

Neville literally walked into baseball through his front door, bounding down the steep steps of his family's row house in West Baltimore, then running across the street and down an alley to a field that served as the site of neighborhood games. West Mulberry Street was really just one long dugout, the neatly kept row houses a locker room for players, umpires, and fans who would trot out for a game as quickly as you could shout a challenge across the narrow street or egg on youngsters in the house next door.

The Neville house at 2840 West Mulberry stood squat in the middle of a block of working-class people who would rush through meals to join in a game of baseball or softball. Fathers played alongside sons. Mothers and daughters cheered from the sidelines. At night, they would play under dim lights at nearby barns that housed the city's fleet of trolley cars.

Without that environment, without a blue-collar Baltimore that was as crazy about baseball as the San Francisco that produced the DiMaggios and the St. Louis that gave birth to Berra and Garagiola, it is unlikely that Neville and baseball would have become so intertwined.

His heritage hardly involved athletics. His father, Ed Neville, did play baseball as a teenager on the same grounds as Ruth. He was sent to St. Mary's Industrial School after his father, a stonemason and French-Irish immigrant who had seen six of his nine children die, abandoned the family. Although records were destroyed in a fire at the school in 1919, Ed Neville is believed to have been at St. Mary's from 1911 to 1914, departing the same year as Ruth. Neville was five years younger, however, and it is very unlikely they played on the same team.

Although Ruth's brute strength became legendary at St. Mary's, physical ability was not one of the requirements to play. The Xaverian Order, which supported the school along with the City of Baltimore, saw baseball as a morale-building force amid the grim surroundings of an institution that bore the official name of St. Mary's Industrial School for Orphans, Delinquent, Incorrigible, and Wayward Boys. If you were among the more than 1,100 boys confined there, it was assumed you would play on one of 43 teams competing at various levels. Young Ed Neville chose to be a catcher.

Two years after leaving St. Mary's, Ed Neville enlisted in the U.S. Army. He fought against Pancho Villa in Mexico and drove an ambulance in France during World War I. In 1918, he returned to Baltimore and married a local girl with Irish ancestry, Helen McCain. Edward Joseph Neville was born September 25, 1922, the same year that his father signed on to work in the yards of the Baltimore & Ohio Railroad. His arrival made it a family of four, Cecilia (later called Molly), having been born two years earlier.

For the Nevilles, it was a marriage of opposites. Ed Neville was quiet, almost solemn. He was content to stay with the railroad for 41 years,

returning home to a good meal and spending his spare time with an assortment of house repair and remodeling projects. Helen Neville was outgoing
and energetic with a deep, booming voice unopposed by her husband's
silence. She used her energies to run the household, raise her two children,
and see the family through difficult financial times.

During the Depression, Ed Neville found himself at home on fur-
lough more often than not, sitting close to the telephone he couldn't afford
and hoping to be called in for periodic work assignments. It was then that
Helen Neville started going door to door peddling household products to
accumulate enough nickels and dimes to keep the family one step ahead
of eviction. Far more energetic than athletic, she did possess one trait that
would serve her son well when he pursued a career throwing baseballs from
the wrong side. She was a lefthander, a motherly sort of southpaw whose
only curves would be thrown at umpires and coaches with shouts that
made them shudder.

Helen and Ed Neville both were perfectionists—Ed demonstrating it
with his precise handiwork and handwriting, Helen with a well-organized
household where even the dustcloths were ironed and neatly folded. Their
son would carry that legacy the rest of his life.

By the time he was a teenager, Neville had moved from the makeshift
field on West Mulberry to the Bloomingdale Oval, a sandlot that was the
very heart of West Baltimore baseball. His wide-sweeping swing and enthusiasm for the game often earned him spots on teams with boys who
were at least two years older.

Until he entered the service at the age of 20, Neville was primarily a
first baseman and outfielder. He pitched rarely in high school, less than
half the time in the sandlot leagues. Despite his fascination with the
mechanics of pitching, he preferred positions that made it possible to start
every game.

Eventually, Neville's bedroom closet would be jammed with uniforms representing teams in just about every amateur and semipro league
on his side of the city. His mother, who often listened to Oriole games
on the radio while she washed clothes, watched him play as often as five
times a week for an assortment of teams ranging from the Calverton
Pleasure Club to the Fitzberger All-Stars. One Saturday league for
younger players even banned him after learning he played with the older
boys on Sunday.

It was natural that Neville found his way to Mount St. Joseph. He was
Catholic; he could play baseball. The Xaverians who supervised the school
saw to it that tuition costs remained modest despite its excellent academic
reputation. And when working-class families sometimes found it difficult
to make payments, there was always forgiveness or even a scholarship, particularly if the boy was an athlete.

Mount St. Joe had been founded as a college by the Xaverians in 1876, but declining enrollment forced the closing of the college program in 1918 and led to a rebirth as a secondary and college preparatory school. Although Mount St. Joe had claimed a city championship in 1931, its strongest link to Baltimore baseball history dated back to the days of Babe Ruth. In 1913, the Mount team took the mile and a half trip to St. Mary's for a game that would give Jack Dunn, owner of the Baltimore Orioles, a chance to see Ruth pitch against the supposedly tougher competition of a college club.

Ruth was matched against Bill Morrisette, whose credits included a no-hitter over Georgetown, a one-hitter over Holy Cross, and a 15-strikeout performance against Seton Hall. Morrisette, a righthander who would record three American League victories in four decisions with Philadelphia and Detroit, would not be as fortunate against the wayward boys from the corner of Wilkens and Caton avenues. Although there is more than one version of the game, Ruth biographers agree on one point: the Babe pitched a shutout. Dunn eventually signed both Ruth and Morrisette to Oriole contracts.

Neville would play his first game for Mount St. Joe 22 years later as a first baseman on the junior varsity. He was a quiet, singularly focused, good-looking kid, baby fat still present on a face that was anchored by a cleft chin and topped off by curly, dark brown hair. He was squarely built, with legs resembling tree trunks and arms to match. While most students took the trolley, Neville built up his strength by pedaling a bike or walking the five-mile round trip from his house to the campus on Frederick Avenue.

In the classroom, Neville and other students walked a straight line. They wore coats and ties and made every effort to stay clear of Brother Bertin Manning, the no-nonsense prefect of discipline who stood six-foot-three and projected even larger dimensions to the unfortunates summoned to his office. For the most part, the Xaverians ruled in a benign sort of way. When Brother Martin John whacked students on the hand with a ruler, the discipline was accepted and instruction resumed without further interruption. In the spring, the Brother often headed for the baseball field and cheered on some of the same boys he whacked on a regular basis.

Neville, who had an above-average IQ of 120, joined more than half of his class in advanced studies. He excelled in history and math, struggled in English and Latin, and flunked German. He was ranked eighty-first among the 111 seniors earning diplomas in the academic program.

The ranking reversed itself on the field. As a junior, the first baseman they called "Lefty" and "Flash" broke into the starting lineup in what would be a disappointing .500 season for the Gaels. An American Legion All-Star the summer before his senior year, he became captain of a potentially powerful 1940 Mount St. Joe squad built around seven top returnees.

The Gaels bordered on being unbeatable, but still finished second in the conference after winning eight of nine games. The one loss was to a McDonogh team that would be seeded first in the playoffs after an unbeaten regular season.

In the opening playoff game against Polytechnic, Mount St. Joe trailed 3–0 in the fourth when Neville, who was touted in the school's annual as "another Lou Gehrig," tripled and scored on a single. In the fifth, with two out and a runner on first, he drove the ball over the center fielder's head on a fenceless field and rounded the bases with a game-tying home run. Mount St. Joe broke the tie in the seventh to post a 4–3 victory and move into the finals against a City College club that had eliminated McDonogh in a first-round upset.

In the championship game at the home park of the International League Orioles, Neville, as Baltimore's *Sun* described it, "picked out a pitch in the fourth ... and slammed it over the fence in right center, a favorite spot for Babe Ruth when he visited here with the Yankees. That blow, as matters developed, was the crusher."

Neville's home run, believed to be the first one ever hit by a high schooler in Oriole Park, gave Mount St. Joe a 3–0 lead en route to a 5–1 victory. In the first inning, he had singled and scored all the way from first on a hit-and-run play, sliding across home plate just ahead of the tag. In the bottom of the fourth, he followed up his home run with an unassisted double play.

Celebrating its first championship in nine seasons, the school treated the team to a victory dinner featuring oxtail soup, creamed chicken, and candied yams. After the players sipped soup and their fathers puffed on the cigars placed at each table, the festivities took on a more serious tone with the singing of the alma mater. The song should have signaled an end to Neville's high school baseball career, but he decided to take postgraduate courses since he had another year of athletic eligibility. In addition to brushing up on academics, he hoped to attract the attention of the Baltimore Orioles.

Neville had been contacted his senior year by the Cleveland Indians, but never answered a letter from scout Charles Draper of Pomona, New Jersey. Draper wrote again in November of 1940, asking for a meeting with his parents to discuss a contract. Neville ignored the second letter as well. He stayed at Mount St. Joe, pulled off high grades in chemistry and physics, and captained the baseball team for the second straight season. This time, there would be no soup and cigars; the team finished second behind Polytechnic in division play.

Oriole officials, who first had noticed Neville at the club's summer instructional school in 1939, were impressed enough to offer a contract after scouting him the summer after his final high school game. His outfield play had been a key to the success of two teams: Spring Grove, second-place finisher in the Maryland Amateur Baseball Association, and Glen Burnie, runner-up in the playoffs of the Baltimore Semipro Baseball League.

This time, he signed. On March 5, 1942—with the future of professional baseball clouded as General Douglas MacArthur stepped up bombing attacks in the Philippines—Neville and nine other prospects from Baltimore schoolyards and sandlots left by train for the Oriole camp in Hollywood, Florida.

The Orioles were no longer the magic team of the 1920s when owner Jack Dunn turned the franchise into one of the best in baseball. Even so, signing with a hometown team whose history included Babe Ruth and a long string of pennants was at least the match of a South Bend Catholic schoolboy landing a scholarship to Notre Dame.

Dunn had signed Ruth in 1914, but sold him that same season to the Boston Red Sox for $10,000. The sale had been forced by the financial trouble triggered by the new Federal League, whose Baltimore Terrapins stole most of the Orioles' fans after building a park across the street. The Federal League claimed major league status; the more talented Orioles could boast only that their Class AA designation was the highest at that time in minor league baseball.

Dunn shifted the club to Richmond in 1915 and sold out after the season. He then acquired the International League's Jersey City franchise and returned to Baltimore in 1916 after the Federal League went out of business. He bought the Terrapins' park for $25,000, renamed it Oriole Park, and started shaping a baseball dynasty.

Starting in 1919, the Orioles won seven consecutive pennants with teams of major league caliber. Dunn would sign and develop gifted players, pay them top dollar for several years, then sell their contracts when the price was right. Lefty Grove, who signed for $3,500 and stayed with the Orioles five years, commanded the highest price of all when Dunn sold his contract for $100,600 to Connie Mack of the Philadelphia Athletics.

After Toronto snapped the pennant streak in 1926, the Orioles suffered a reversal that continued into the year of Neville's signing. Dunn had died of a heart attack in 1928. His widow still owned the team in 1942 (she would die the next year), but she left the running of the club to baseball men such as Manager Tommy Thomas, an Oriole pitcher from the glamour days.

Thomas welcomed Neville and two others who had played in the 1940 championship game: Mount St. Joe infielder Ted Sepkowski and City College pitcher Gordon Mueller. The home run to Neville aside, Mueller had struck out 15 Gaels that afternoon after pitching 12 innings in the playoff opener only two days earlier.

Neville would see his two Oriole teammates and a third player from the championship game go on to brief stays in the majors. Sepkowski would play in 19 games for the Cleveland Indians and New York Yankees; Mueller would relieve eight times for the Boston Red Sox. The winning pitcher in the game, curveballer Johnny Fick, was passed up by the Orioles, but was talented enough to appear in four games with the Philadelphia Phillies.

In Hollywood, Neville joined a roster that included future Hall of Famer Bob Lemon, a left-handed hitting third baseman who would switch to pitching and would be such a workhorse in winning 207 games for the Cleveland Indians that his loose shirttail became something of a signature. The Orioles also were boosted by first baseman Eddie Robinson, who would bat .268 in 13 major league seasons and would return to Baltimore in 1957 for the final four games of his career. Untested youngsters far outnumbered future stars, however, and press reports out of Florida—sometimes referring to the once-proud Orioles as "Birdlets"—were generally unfavorable.

Neville injured an ankle in early March, saw limited duty, and failed to impress Tommy Thomas. Columnist C. M. "Abe" Gibbs, in a March 27, 1942, interview in Baltimore's *Sun,* reported the Oriole manager's observations on all 20 players in camp. Thomas summed up Neville's chances in a single word: "No."

Neville fizzled the final two weeks of spring training. He substituted in the outfield briefly in three games and went hitless in five trips. On April 11, after failing as a pinch hitter against the Savannah (Georgia) Indians of the Class B South Atlantic League, Neville stripped off his Oriole uniform for the last time.

Two summers later, the landmark that assured his place in Baltimore baseball history burned to the ground. There never would be another game in front of the wooden stands at Greenmount Avenue and 29th Street.

Oriole Park had been considered so incendiary that groundskeeper Mike Schofield hosed down the stands after every night game. After a July 3 contest against Syracuse, Schofield thought he smelled smoke but failed to find the source. He soaked the stands twice, the last time at 2 A.M.

At 4:15 A.M., a neighborhood resident looked out her window and saw the grandstand in flames. Within an hour, the park and its 11,000 seats had been destroyed.

In center field, a manually operated scoreboard billed as the biggest in baseball remained untouched by the fire, as did the Gunther Beer sign that trimmed its top. It was to the right of that scoreboard, at a point some

**In spring training with Baltimore in 1942, Neville takes his cuts at the Orioles' camp in Hollywood, Florida. (Courtesy Janet Neville.)**

300 feet from home plate, that Neville's home run had cleared the fence and bounced into the bleacher seats.

John Steadman, a prep baseball player and minor leaguer from Neville's era who became a widely read sports columnist for *The Evening Sun* in Baltimore, recalled that two other high schoolers followed up with home runs of their own despite warnings from their coach not to swing for the fences and "try to be another Eddie Neville." The fire assured there would be no future attempts.

The Orioles moved into Municipal Stadium, a 60,000-seat football arena, and played on a makeshift field with a layout resembling the one the Dodgers would use 24 years later in the Los Angeles Coliseum. Drawing record crowds, the club won its first pennant since 1925, then captured the league playoffs and the Junior World Series over the Louisville Colonels of the American Association.

Neville remained in the Oriole organization even after his disappointing spring training in 1942. He no longer wore the uniform, but he was still under contract when he reported on a 30-day option basis to the Wilmington (Delaware) Blue Rocks of the Class B Inter-State League. One day after his departure from the Oriole camp, he played in an exhibition game at Rock Hill, South Carolina, and went three for five.

As a center fielder, Neville batted .304 in ten straight exhibition games that took the club from its Rock Hill base, through North Carolina and Virginia, and finally to Wilmington Park for a preseason finale against in-state rival Williamsport of the Class A Eastern League.

Manager Herb Brett, a one-time submarine pitcher for the Chicago Cubs, had to be impressed with his 19-year-old prospect. Neville's chance to make the team, however, hinged more on the fate of another outfielder not even on the roster. Felix Mankiewicz, a former Blue Rock, was on option to the Philadelphia Athletics and hoped to reach the majors with a successful spring.

The Blue Rocks were in North Carolina when Brett announced that Mankiewicz would be returning. Neville promptly hit Wilmington's first home run of the exhibition season in a rout of Statesville's Class D club of the North Carolina State League, but his days were numbered. Even a utility spot was ruled out after he made an unforgivable three errors, including one before the home fans in the Williamsport exhibition.

Neville made one start in the regular season, going hitless in four trips against the Hagerstown Owls. His only success in nine trips was a pinch-hit, two–RBI single at Trenton.

One day before the 30-day option expired, Wilmington returned Neville's contract after he struck out in a final pinch-hitting appearance. Since ten games were required to be listed in official statistics, his name never made the record books. About the only evidence that he ever wore a Blue Rock uniform came in the form of snapshots his family had taken when they drove up one Sunday from Baltimore.

Herb Brett, however, had not seen the last of Neville. They would meet once again in the Carolina League with Brett on the opposite side as a manager and front-office official.

Optioned to Butler of the four-team Class D Penn State Association, Neville arrived in the western Pennsylvania city and signed a contract May 18 for $100 a month. He played for the Butler Yankees that same day.

If nothing else, Butler was an interesting place to be in that wartime summer of 1942—a sort of minisized Pittsburgh where the working folks topped off French fries with chili and gravy. At the American Bantam Car Company, workers turned out 30 Jeeps a day for the U.S. Army. At the Pullman-Standard plant, where railroad passenger cars were manufactured in peacetime, high-explosive shells, rockets, and 500-pound bombs rattled down the assembly line.

A week after Neville's arrival, Butler played its first night game after installing transformers purchased on the black market for $2,000. The high price nearly wiped out the team treasury, but the investment seemed reasonable since day games were attracting crowds of less than 200 in a city of more than 24,000.

Crowds picked up considerably, but in wartime, night baseball could be guaranteed only one game at a time. Earlier, night games had been banned in New York City because of an ever-widening coastal dim-out to protect ships from submarine attacks.

One month after the lights went on, Butler staged its first blackout as a precaution against future bombing attacks. When fire sirens and factory whistles sounded at 9:45 P.M., the city of Butler, including the little park blessed with the blown-up name of Yankee Stadium, went dark for 30 minutes. Washington's Red Birds, trailing Butler by a dozen runs after eight innings, agreed that a ninth would be unnecessary and slipped out of the park.

After the season, the lights would not shine again on Butler baseball until 1946 when the club joined the Class C Middle Atlantic League. A 19-year-old lefthander on that team eventually would reach the real Yankee Stadium as well as the Hall of Fame. His name was Whitey Ford.

Ford continues to be remembered in Butler, but Neville became nothing more than just another name on newspaper microfilm after re-injuring his ankle. The closest he came to fame was chasing a triple off the bat of Oil City outfielder Al Gionfriddo, a future Brooklyn Dodger.

Manager Dallas Warren, a 17-year veteran who doubled as a catcher, started Neville in 22 straight games before the injury put the outfielder on the disabled list and led to his release by the Oriole organization on June 20. Neville closed this chapter of his career with a batting average of .304, his 24 hits including a grand slam home run that helped lift his runs batted in total to 20. He made two errors patrolling a center field where the fence reached 424 feet, but received praise in the *Butler Eagle* for racing "back almost to the fence ... to haul in a powerful drive."

When the season ended, Butler players split a playoff pot amounting to just under $50 per share. The batboy and bus driver each received half a share, but no one remembered the kid from Baltimore.

Neville and the minor leagues were struggling at the same time. The number of leagues had dropped to 31 that season and would decline to 12 before the end of the war as more young players were called into service. The impact of World War II was never clearer than on October 30, 1942, when a Navy enlisted man became the first professional baseball player to lose his life in combat.

Neville returned to the security of West Mulberry Street and awaited the military draft. On January 12, 1943, he reported for Army duty at Fort Meade, Maryland. Assigned to recreation and athletics, he resumed playing the outfield at Fort Meade and hit the ball with such authority that resuming his pro career after the war appeared to be a likely option.

In the fall, he was assigned to an Army training program in basic engineering at the College of William and Mary in Williamsburg, Virginia. He took a shot at another sport, returning to the football field for the first time since the ninth grade. Trying out for the freshman team as a blocking back, he ended up with a damaged left knee. Three operations would be required to remove the torn cartilage—operations serious enough that Neville would be granted ten percent disability pay when he left the service.

Neville, who was never fast afoot, knew then that he would never play the outfield again as a pro. As he studied in Williamsburg, taking 24 courses over eight months, he likely recalled his sandlot days when he was a pitcher on several amateur teams. By the time he arrived at Camp Beale, California, in the summer of 1944, he discovered there could be life after the outfield. In a game that few people saw, Neville ignored his banged-up knee and struck out 21 batters in nine innings.

Assigned to the Philippines in 1945, Staff Sergeant Neville continued pitching on Fenton Field, a facility built and maintained in part by Japanese prisoners of war. He struck out 16 and scored the winning run in a no-hit, 2–1 game that went 11 innings.

He also had a close call with the real enemy. "It wasn't too bad over there for me except the time I almost walked into a nest of Japs," he once recalled. "Luckily they didn't see me and I backed out to safety again. Those Japs in the jungles were cagey. You could hear them and feel them, but you couldn't see them."

"Eddie was my best pitcher over there," said Boyd Bartley, who was the lieutenant in charge of recreation and athletics. "He was a tough, hard-nosed kid."

Bartley, a shortstop who played briefly with the Brooklyn Dodgers in 1943, also saw another side of Neville. "He was a real lefthander, and by that I mean if you wanted him to do something, he would do just the opposite," said Bartley, who would serve as a Dodger scout and minor league manager for 37 years before retiring in Fort Worth, Texas. "He would be in the ballgames all the way, but he would do anything to get out of kitchen duty or working on the field."

For someone who had pitched only at the amateur and semipro levels, Neville would face the ultimate pitching challenge before returning home. After the Japanese surrendered on September 2, 1945, the military staged a Philippine "Olympics" in several sports and paired Neville's Base M Dodgers against a Manila club loaded with nine past and future big leaguers.

Besides Bartley and Neville, Base M's best included Loy "Cowboy" Hanning, a tall pitcher from Missouri who had thrown ten innings for the St. Louis Browns in 1938; Fred Caliguiri, who had pitched briefly for the Philadelphia Athletics in 1942–43; and three players with experience in the lower minors.

The team was overmatched in equipment as well. "We traded Ping-Pong balls to the Filipinos for some of our stuff," said Bartley. Neville later claimed that the original equipment supplied by the Army included 40 gloves, all of them left-handed.

Surprisingly, Base M won the opener behind Hanning's pitching and second baseman Bob Helmick's grand slam home run off the Brooklyn Dodgers' Kirby Higbe. Neville, who played center field in the opener, switched positions with Hanning in the second game.

His pitching opponent that Saturday afternoon, he later recalled, was Early Wynn, the son of an Alabama auto mechanic. Wynn at 25 was a thrower with a single pitch, a wicked fastball that had been good enough to produce 39 wins in four seasons with the Washington Senators.

It would be four years before Wynn would be traded to the Cleveland Indians and learn the finer points of pitching under coach Mel Harder. And it would be 18 years before he would leave the mound in Kansas City after five innings and watch as reliever Jerry Walker preserved his three hundredth and final major league victory.

Wynn, who played shortstop most of the time in the service, was a long way from the Hall of Fame when he faced Neville in the Philippines. But even in those early years, he had a reputation as an intimidator who was not afraid to brush batters back. Neville was just as competitive, though hardly intimidating at five-foot-ten, just a cocky sort who assumed every game was his to win despite his inexperience.

With servicemen packing the bleachers and Filipinos sitting on the ground in center field, Wynn and Neville went after each other for 11 innings before finishing up in the shadows of hills that formed a backdrop behind home plate. Bartley recalled seeing Manila's 19-year-old catcher, future St. Louis Cardinal Joe Garagiola, thrown out for arguing with an umpire before the game even started. "Joe had something else to do, and that was the quickest way to get out of there," said Bartley. "He was too easy-going a guy to get in a real argument."

Neville wrote in later years that he came within one out of beating

Wynn. "We were winning by 2 to 1 with two outs in the ninth inning," he said in a letter to a friend. "Roy Partee [a Boston Red Sox catcher] hit one in dead center and the Cowboy [Loy Hanning] ran in toward us to catch it. He dove toward it, but could not catch it or stop it, and the ball kept moving away. In the eleventh inning, I walked one and Early Wynn hit a triple for a run," he continued. "They got no more. We didn't either."

Base M lost the final game by a dozen runs, but still could claim one out of three. "Because they were so loaded, we think that we did a good job," Neville wrote. Neville himself had taken his ability to a new level. The war that spoiled promising careers for many players became his launching pad.

Bartley recommended Neville to the man who started baseball's farm system, Branch Rickey of the Brooklyn Dodgers. Fresco Thompson, who later would head the Dodger minor league organization, asked Bartley in a December 14, 1945, letter to check out Neville's interest in playing for a Dodger farm club.

Neville apparently felt the timing was wrong for a return to professional baseball and elected to remain a free agent. Released from the service on February 24, 1946, he headed for Baltimore and the Bloomingdale Oval instead of the Dodgers' training camp.

He returned to his home town three years older, a few pounds heavier, and wise enough to continue developing his pitching skills. He signed on with the Bloomingdale semipro club for the summer and hurled a no-hitter, two-hitter, and three-hitter. He also pitched for a Spring Grove team that qualified for the All-American Amateur Baseball Association Tournament at Harrisburg, Pennsylvania, after back-to-back titles in the North Baltimore Major League and the Maryland Amateur Baseball Association. Spring Grove claimed another championship at Harrisburg, winning six of seven in the 12-team, double-elimination tournament as Neville went the distance against a Washington, D. C., club in the finals.

The twisted ankle at the Oriole camp, the disappointment of Wilmington and Butler, and the injured knee at Williamsburg had failed to stop Neville. The lefthander still had a strong pitching arm, the war was over, and at age 23 he was ready to resume his pro career from a hill just 60 feet and six inches from home plate. He would pitch almost nonstop for the next eight and one-half years.

# Pitching in Paradise

*Neville's dark features defied his French-Irish ancestry. I realized later that he wasn't born that way; his skin had been baked by all those winters near the Equator.*

---

It was the stuff of dreams, only this time the setting wasn't a cornfield in Iowa that served as the heavenly home of Shoeless Joe Jackson and the Chicago Black Sox. Emerging from the warmth of the Atlantic Ocean were Stanky, Furillo, Walker, and Lavagetto, Brooklyn Dodgers all, their pant legs rolled up to protect their uniforms from the salty surf.

In a nearby raft bobbed Reese, Reiser, Miksis, and Minner, with Durocher paddling away at the fore. A little Xavier Cugat music, please, the Dodgers are barnstorming through the Panama Canal Zone.

Eddie Neville is tossing on the bed—or is it a mound?—emerging from a baseball player's dream, the chance to go man to man against a team that would come within pinstripes of winning the World Series, pinstripes worn by that hated team from the Bronx.

The year was 1947, the month was March, and this was no dream. Eddie Neville, the Most Valuable Player in the Canal Zone League, would start that afternoon against the Dodgers, far from the sandlots of Baltimore, far from Flatbush and Ebbets Field. The scene shifts to little Mount Hope Stadium, home of Neville and the Cristobol Mottas (pronounced Cris-TOE-bal MOE-tas). As game time approached, Neville—all 170 pounds of him—trotted out before 1,575 fans to receive his MVP certificate in full view of the Dodgers who lined the dugout.

It would be a somewhat rattled Brooklyn team this day. Earlier, Coach Ray Blades had been knocked out after being struck on the right side of the head by a line drive off the bat of rookie outfielder Marvin Rackley in batting practice. Blades spent the afternoon resting at a nearby USO location, then returned with the Dodgers to their head-quarters at Fort Clayton near Panama City.

Neville had troubles of his own in the first inning, but not before an incident that reminded fans of the days when the Dodgers were far more laughable than competitive. Carl Furillo, who had doubled to drive in the first of two Dodger runs in the opening inning, pumped around third after a single to left by catcher Bruce Edwards. Flagged down from the third-base coaching box by Manager Leo Durocher, Furillo came to an abrupt halt, wheeled, and returned to the base head first. In the process of turning, he ripped a portion of the leather off his right shoe. Furillo removed both shoes, handed them to Durocher, and remained at third in his socks as Neville retired an even more distracted Rackley on a force play.

For the next five innings, Neville baffled the Dodger squad despite unusual wildness as he drew too fine a line in attempting to hit the corners against a powerful lineup that would score 774 runs in winning the National League pennant by five games. He limited Brooklyn to one run and two hits during that stretch, picked shortstop Eddie Miksis off at first, and moved into the seventh with the game tied at 3–3. Four runs and one inning later, Neville watched from the dugout as the Dodgers scored a final run and sealed an 8–4 victory. It surely was not the stuff of dreams, but for a time he had mastered the Dodgers as well as any pitcher in the National League.

Brooklyn, on a ten-day swing through Panama and the Canal Zone before returning to its spring training camp in Havana, won the second game of the All-Star series 4–3 before running into Neville again in the finale. In relief, the lefthander allowed two earned runs and two hits in three and one-third innings. In the bottom of the eighth, with the Dodgers ahead 6–5, Neville walked on six pitches and scored the tying run as a drive to right bounced over the head of Arky Vaughn, the one-time Pittsburgh Pirate shortstop who was near the end of a career that would lead to his induction into the Hall of Fame.

The game ended in a 6–6 tie as the darkness that comes early to the equatorial region made play impossible shortly after six o'clock. Until lights were installed a year later, weekday games had to be completed in a limited time frame because of a late four o'clock start that allowed government workers to attend.

The Dodgers headed back to Cuba to continue what would be a land-mark season. A month later, Durocher would be replaced by Burt Shotton after being suspended for the season by Commissioner A. B. "Happy" Chandler for off-the-field conduct that included his association with gamblers. Another Dodger who made the Panama and Canal Zone trip as a member of their Montreal farm club would rate even larger headlines:

Jackie Robinson, who broke modern-day baseball's color line and batted .297 in 151 games as the Dodgers' first baseman.

Robinson, who hit .349 at Montreal in his rookie season of 1946, was matched against the Dodgers in a March 18 exhibition game at Panama City. *New York Times* writer Roscoe McGowen, referring to Robinson as the "dusky Robbie," described one of his 13 putouts as "a brilliant bit of collaboration with Kehn [pitcher Chet Kehn] in which Jackie took a quick throw while falling forward to nail Carl Furillo." Robinson collected two of Montreal's six hits and scored the Royals' only run after leading off the fourth with a single.

Programs distributed at the game made it apparent to the 6,000 fans that Robinson, at 28, was not considered a typical second-year performer. He was the only Montreal player to have his first name listed on the roster and his surname printed in capital letters.

The Canal Zone All-Stars discovered why when they took a 25–7 licking from the Royals three days later as Robinson went four for five to boost his spring exhibition batting average to .519. A Montreal newspaper account did not give specifics as to how Neville fared against Robinson, but the lefthander reported in his diary that he escaped with two earned runs in two innings. "What a game," he wrote.

Had it not been for a Baltimore connection, Neville probably never would have traveled to the Canal Zone and faced major league competition with a pitching arm yet to be tested in the minors. His contact would be a minor league infielder by the name of Al Kubski, who in December of 1945 worked out daily at the YMCA in downtown Baltimore in preparation for spring training with the St. Louis Cardinal organization.

Four years away from organized baseball after serving with the Army in World War II, the 25-year-old Kubski would circle the wooden track in the upper reaches of the gymnasium, play basketball and volleyball, toss a medicine ball, or simply whack a tennis ball against the wall with his favorite baseball bat.

His indoor training schedule ended abruptly when he made a Canal Zone connection through another minor league infielder from Baltimore, Mike Sabena, who planned to play that winter for the Cristobol Mottas. Kubski soon received a contract offer from Gilbert Morland, a personable 44-year-old Englishman who served as a director of the Cristobol club and later would become its president.

Morland, a pipe-smoking shipping agent whose dapper dress and deep tan gave him the look of a native Panamanian, arranged for Kubski's expense-paid trip to the Canal Zone via a government-operated steamship out of New Orleans. Before New Year's Day, Kubski found himself astride third base as trade winds and a tropical sun replaced the drabness of the sweaty YMCA.

**Al Kubski, manager of the Cristobol Mottas, in front of the grandstand at Mount Hope Stadium. (Courtesy Janet Neville.)**

His timing could not have been better. Late in the season, pitcher Al Jarlett vacated the manager's post to report to spring training with Sacramento in the Pacific Coast League. Morland liked Kubski's spunk and gave him the job. For that season and ten more, there would be no better manager in the winter leagues than the tall, slender infielder with a baseball mind as broad as his smile.

In a short time, Kubski would develop a reputation as a tough-guy manager who understood his players. He talked about his favorite sport in gushes. He studied the nuances of the game through the glasses that he first wore after realizing he couldn't read the outfield billboards. He was so spirited on the field that he earned the right to push the best players with the same intensity as the worst. He was, everyone agreed, the boss.

Kubski won the league championship his very first year. After that, he also became the team's chief scout as he tried to sign American players in the face of opposition from most major league organizations. He recruited most of his players from the farm systems of the St. Louis Cardinals, Brooklyn, and Pittsburgh, running into brick walls when he sought to sign others whose parent clubs vetoed year-round play. One of his greatest disappointments came when the Cincinnati Reds refused to approve winter league play for Roy McMillan, a future All-Star spotted by Kubski in 1948 when the smooth-fielding shortstop was an 18-year-old prospect in the Class C Lone Star League.

Kubski's assignment was to round up a dozen minor leaguers in the United States and recruit another four in the Canal Zone and Panama — most of them either old pros with government jobs or raw-talent Panamanians just out of high school. Looking for a left-handed pitcher as the 1946–47 season neared, he contacted Neville on the recommendation of Ernie Gardner, who had been a teammate that summer on the championship Spring Hope club. The Mottas agreed to sign both Neville and Bob Young, another Baltimore product who, like Kubski, was an infielder in the Cardinal organization.

Young, who played with Neville for two seasons, later gained the distinction of performing for his hometown team in both the major and minor leagues. After two seasons with Baltimore in the International League, the lean, lantern-jawed second baseman moved up to the St. Louis Browns in 1951. Three years later, the St. Louis franchise was shifted to Baltimore, and Young wore an Oriole uniform until being traded to Cleveland in 1955.

Neville had ignored Brooklyn's feeler a year earlier, but he saw the Canal Zone as a final step in his development before returning to the minors as a pitcher. He also knew that the league's small rosters would allow him to play the outfield or first base between pitching assignments, a side benefit just as important as his monthly salary of perhaps $200 a month.

Neville received a Pan American Airways ticket to the Canal Zone from Morland in mid-December. Shortly before Christmas, he boarded a flight in Washington, stopped over at Miami, and arrived at Balboa on the Pacific Ocean side of the Canal Zone the next day. His trip from Balboa to Cristobol gave him his first look at the 500-square-mile zone established under the same treaty that cleared the way for the United States to build and operate a canal linking the two oceans. (Under two 1977 treaties, Panama took control of most of the Canal Zone in 1979 and will take complete control of the canal on December 31, 1999.)

To a former high school hero who had seen his first career as an outfielder die in a park at Butler, Pennsylvania, the Canal Zone offered an extraordinary busman's holiday in a baseball paradise complete with banyan trees and government privileges. Neville was there strictly as a player, but each season he would receive a certificate listing him as a "welfare worker" for the Canal Zone League. The document was a loophole that allowed him to stay in a government-owned apartment complex at a low rate ($21.50 a month that first season) and to spend up to $50 a month at the commissary.

For extras, a nearby golf course offered free greens fees and the use of complimentary clubs. Players also could fish at several fresh and saltwater sites, the top prize being tarpon whose texture was so coarse that they were either thrown away or given to poor Panamanians.

The setting was spectacular. Massive walls of red stone could be observed along a nine-mile canal stretch where engineers had sliced through two hills. Orchids covered branches jutting above a manmade lake that had swallowed up what once was a jungle. At Cristobol, Neville could see ships sailing the Atlantic stop along a bay to refuel before entering the canal.

At first, neither privileges, nor recreation, nor sightseeing, nor even baseball mattered most to Neville. What he really wanted was mail from home. On January 7, 1947, he recorded one of the first entries in a pocket-size diary: "Nothing doing today. No practice; no mail; no date; no movie; no bowling. Nothing."

Neville would keep diaries of his baseball career for the next six years. Because of the limited amount of space—six short lines a day—most of the information was limited to game scores, statistics, and his social life.

He soon recorded an increase in both mail and dates. With his life more complete, Neville could concentrate on baseball Canal Zone–style, where league play started in late December after the rainy season and continued into March. In the daytime, players beat the humidity by shedding their shirts and working out in their shorts. It was a carefree kind of practice with an atmosphere allowing the players to turn their caps backwards and clown it up in a game of pepper.

The informality applied off the field as well, the players being welcomed into many local homes by admiring American families. Neville and Bob Young often gathered around the dining room table at the house of the Maloney family, where Young soon learned that food was not the only attraction. On March 7, in the middle of the Isthmian Championship series, Young took one of the Maloney daughters, Phyllis, as his bride.

Romances linking baseball players and island residents dated back to the league's first game in 1914, the same year the U.S. government completed construction of the canal. By 1946, more than 35,000 people held government jobs in the Canal Zone. At Fort Davis, the largest of 14 military bases, some 4,000 soldiers had been assigned to guard the canal and protect American interests.

Canal Zone residents, most of them Americans, followed the fortunes

**Neville, right, in the attire that helped him survive the humidity of the
Canal Zone. He's joined here by Cristobol outfielder Bob Vorell, left, and
second baseman Bob Young. Like Neville, Young was a Baltimore product.
He played for his hometown club both as a minor and major leaguer.
(Courtesy Janet Neville.)**

of four teams, the Mottas and the Colon Lucky Strikers from the Atlantic
side of the canal and the Balboa Brewers and Diablo Heights Devils from
the Pacific side. Cristobol credited its unusual nickname to the Motta
brothers, who sponsored the team as a sideline to their import business.

Cristobol and Colon shared Mount Hope Stadium as a home field.
Nearby was a reminder of the canal's most tragic days, a cemetery where
hundreds who helped build the waterway were buried after dying in construction accidents or from malaria, yellow fever, and the bubonic plague.

Pacific-side games took place at Balboa Stadium, where home runs
produced more than a shot at stardom. Thanks to Julio Canavaggio, a
local liquor dealer, every home run at Balboa earned the batter a bottle of
Lord Calvert whiskey. It became a promotion of staggering proportions,

with many of the blasts being labeled in Panama's English language newspapers as Lord Calvert home runs.

The bonus so inspired Diablo Heights' outfielder-manager Joe Cicero that all six of his home runs were hundred-proof bombs out of Balboa. The six gave the 36-year-old Cicero over 20 percent of the league's 29 home runs and twice the number of the second-leading producer, Bob Young. In 40 games as an American Leaguer, dating as far back as 1929 when he made his debut with the Boston Red Sox, Cicero never hit one over the fence.

Cristobol entered Neville's first season as the defending league champions despite losing both games in the championship series to Colon. The Mottas, managed by Kubski in the final weeks, were awarded the title after the league office ruled Colon outfielder Bill Hartman had signed a contract after the deadline for eligibility.

Neville would enjoy a record season, but he achieved more in practice than in actual competition. With four days off every week (most games were played Wednesdays and weekends), he spent hours under the sun refining a pitching style stamped with his personal trademark.

His modest fastball came in three speeds, his curve in two. His money pitch was a knuckleball; his salvation was a blend of control and savvy. He would learn to outguess guess hitters and outthink the rest.

At the start, he was so raw in his new trade that he virtually ignored base runners. With Kubski as his teacher, he developed a pickoff move that by March was quick and clever enough to trap Eddie Miksis of the Dodgers. By 1949, it was downright mystifying; he picked off 32 Carolina League runners that season and kept countless others from even thinking about stealing second.

His first professional win came in Cristobol's opening game against Diablo Heights. He capped his ninth-inning relief effort by striking out Roy Kennedy, a quick-footed outfielder who would win the batting championship with a .385 average. The win represented the first leg of Neville's chase to match the record of nine consecutive victories in a single season, a mark set two years earlier by a Balboa Brewer lefthander who almost blew his shot at the pros when he was being scouted by the Boston Red Sox.

The record holder was Maurice "Mickey" Harris, who pitched in the Canal Zone when he was a serviceman stationed in Panama during World War II. The New York City native had attracted the attention of Red Sox scout Jack Egan as a semipro pitcher, but on the day Egan was prepared to offer a contract, Harris gave up a bases-loaded homer and lost the game.

Egan still offered Harris a contract for $100 a month plus another $100 for signing. Harris won a dozen games for the Red Sox before the war, then followed up his record-setting Canal Zone performance by winning 17 in the Red Sox pennant season of 1946.

Neville made a run on the Harris record from start to finish, going undefeated in eight straight starts after that first victory in relief. His bid to break the record ended on the final day of the season in a 4–0 setback to weak-hitting Balboa.

One loss or not, no one could challenge Neville's selection as the league's Most Valuable Player. His first statistics as a pro pitcher were in; he had surrendered an average of nearly eight hits per nine innings, but his earned run average was a lean 1.98. At the plate, he posted a .321 average with 17 hits in 24 games, including a homer, triple, and three doubles.

The other two members of the Baltimore contingent finished with even higher batting averages. Kubski, who for the next four seasons would terrorize pitchers in the Class C Lone Star and East Texas leagues, led all batters with a .394 average, but failed to qualify for the batting title since two weeks of illness kept the player-manager from reaching the required number of times at bat. Young actually led the batting race until the final day of the season when a one-for-six showing in two games against Balboa dropped him to .382, three points behind Diablo Heights' Kennedy.

Cristobol finished with a record of 19–8, winning both halves of a split season. In the first Isthmian Championship against the winner of the Panama Professional League pennant, the Mottas took the opener over General Electric, but scored only three times in the next three contests to lose the series three games to one. The third game was a disaster for Neville as he gave up seven runs and nine hits in five innings.

Neville received overtures from major league organizations long before the championship series. Two clubs, the St. Louis Cardinals and Philadelphia Athletics, made firm offers. St. Louis, on Kubski's recommendation, invited Neville to its Daytona Beach, Florida, minor league base to seek a spot on the Rochester and Columbus (Ohio) Class AAA clubs or the Columbus (Georgia) and Omaha Class A clubs. Philadelphia farm director Arthur Ehlers offered Neville $250 a month, without requiring a tryout, to sign a Class A contract with Lincoln (Nebraska) of the Western League.

At this stage of his career, the lefthander preferred to aim low. Repeating his rebuff of the Dodgers in 1945, Neville steered clear of both Daytona Beach and Lincoln. Along with batting champ Roy Kennedy, he was lured to a small eastern North Carolina town by the colorful manager of an independently owned Class D team. He could pitch all he wanted, play a little first base and outfield, and — thanks to payments made under the table — earn more than he could for any Class A club with a major league affiliation.

In the final Canal Zone exhibition game against Brooklyn, Kennedy drove in all six All-Star runs, four of them with a grand slammer off the same Ralph Branca who would serve one up to the New York Giants' Bobby Thomson four years later in the decisive playoff game for the National League pennant. He then headed stateside to join Neville on the 1947 edition of the Tarboro Tars. Teamed up, the Canal Zone's best hitter and best pitcher could tear the Coastal Plain League apart.

# Welcome to Tarboro

*Until Neville arrived in Durham, baseball wasn't very important in our neighborhood. We became cowboys hiding in holes next to the basement or engineers operating electric trains. We kicked footballs over a wooden swing in a yard that three years earlier had been the wartime home of chickens and goats. None of us had ever heard of Tarboro.*

---

It resembled the set of an Andy Hardy movie, this North Carolina town of just under 8,000 souls where Eddie Neville came to pitch in 1947.

Right smack in the middle of Tarboro's downtown stood the Soda Shop, where they dipped into frosty cardboard containers and served up ice cream sodas and milk shakes and things like that.

A little to the west stood the Southern-style town common, an expansive stretch of space full of oaks and magnolia and lots of lush grass. Victorian houses stood guard along the common, their massive white frames fronted by sweeping porches where people sat and socialized and sipped out of big glasses brimming with ice and sweet tea.

Tarboro was really like that, at least to the eye, only Mickey Rooney didn't appear as Andy Hardy, and the plays took place in a baseball park instead of a barn filled with kid actors.

The townspeople needed that ballpark after World War II, having grown weary of the fighting and perhaps not fully satisfied with lives that for many of them meant coming home after a day at the cotton mill with lint still clinging to their hair and clothes. Others went to the park to escape the tobacco fields, their sore backs soothed by occasional snorts of whiskey from a bottle tucked away in someone's coveralls.

They were a rowdy bunch, these fans of the Tarboro Tars. Daisy Bardin, the doll-like wife of the sheriff by day, turned into a terror at night. Even more reserved fans, such as Father Timothy Shannon and Mabel Fountain, a spinster who walked with the aid of a cane, cheered mightily

24

as the boys in white uniforms trimmed in navy blue fought it out on a field far removed from Bataan and the Burma Road.

Home games took place in a park that had been built in a hurry just before the 1946 season after the wooden stands of old Bryan Park burned to the ground on December 22, 1945. Nash Memorial Park stood on the same site, an impersonal but fireproof structure consisting of nine rows of concrete that stretched from home plate to just past first and third. It was an uncomfortable place, without a roof in its early days, and it turned into a sea of sweaty, short-sleeve white shirts on Sunday afternoons when spectators gathered after church and chicken dinners.

Not that night games were much better. When an attendant cranked up the boiler to heat the water for postgame showers, so much smoke came pouring out that it sometimes settled over the field and made ordinary fly balls as exciting as a parachutist plunging through a cloud. And on at least two occasions in Neville's time, the field became shrouded in a late evening fog that forced the umpires to halt play once the outfielders disappeared from view.

On clear nights, the park's low-wattage bulbs provided a dim setting even when the town's electric plant operated at full efficiency. At peak periods, power was reduced because of a coal shortage, and the playing field was bathed in lights flickering like a silent movie.

Still, it was baseball and the team was Tarboro's own. Even if the seats were painful and the lights flickered and the field resembled a souped-up cow pasture, it was the team and players that really mattered.

And in the Coastal Plain League, one of the strongest Class D circuits in the country, they wore their flannel uniforms proudly, the streaks of Carolina dirt and clay a badge of courage and honor. They drank out of the same dipper from the same dented bucket and swished the cool water inside ruddy cheeks often plugged with tobacco.

They had nicknames like "Bull" and "Turkey," "Spike" and "Pap," "Little Joe" and "Gashouse." They came from farms and cities, from distant states, and from just around the curve down a country road. Some young, some old, some scaling the hill for the first time, some who had risen and fallen and were trying to climb their way back.

They played in small eastern North Carolina towns and cities such as Greenville and Goldsboro and New Bern, riding rickety buses and running across rocky infields in the name of the Greenies, Goldbugs, and Bears. They were so full of fire that three quarters of a million people came out of nowhere to see them that season of '47.

They scrapped for wins and every nickel they could make. Most of them signed contracts for an average of $125 a month and slugged it out to earn another $40 for winning a pennant.

For a chosen few, including Neville, owners ignored minor league

**An outfielder's view of the concrete stands at Nash Memorial Park, home of the Class D Tarboro Tars. (Courtesy Janet Neville.)**

contract requirements and passed cash under the table in amounts that jacked up total monthly pay as high as $500. The rest remained grateful for leftovers and the $25 or so they pocketed when fans passed the hat at the end of the season.

The players pursued their dreams with spikes held high and tempers on the edge. They survived 15-man rosters and grinding, five-month seasons with bandages, guts, and the love of a game that for many was the only way they knew to make a living.

It surely was not a game for boys in short pants. Without a strong manager in command, the players often pursued their off-field exploits with the very same passion.

That was the case in 1946 when a reasonably talented Tarboro club plunged into last place under still another Baltimore sandlot graduate, Mike Kardash. In July, owner Charles Allen fired the easy-going infielder, and the Tars finished the season in a far more respectable fifth place after winning 22 of their last 32 games.

Allen, who also owned another North Carolina team, the Durham Bulls of the Class C Carolina League, replaced Kardash with a journeyman pitcher whose hard-nosed approach to the game had been fashioned in the cotton mill leagues of LaGrange, Georgia. Frank Hamons' explosive temper and body language backed up his nickname of "Bull," and his reputation as a gruff, no-nonsense pitcher had grown as he snorted on the mound and kicked at the dirt in a career that carried him to the top of the minors with Buffalo of the International League.

Hamons answered to both Frank and his middle name of Lowell in his first trip through the league when he pitched at New Bern in 1937, but the manager and his nickname were inseparable the second time around. A 31-year-old country boy who looked at least 40, Hamons was a fireplug of a fellow whose sideline antics once inspired rival fans to plant a bale of hay beside the third-base coaching box. His next-to-nothing neck—the anatomical feature that first inspired someone to call him "Bull"— supported a head so round that he cocked his cap a full two inches above his ample ears, fully exposing squinting eyes that were softened by a puckish turn of the lips.

Realizing that virile athletes on the loose in a small town could spell trouble, Hamons established ground rules to keep his club in harness once the park lights went out. The rules were simple: be in bed 90 minutes after home games and one hour after reaching the town limits after a road game. To assure compliance, Hamons would patrol the town in a light blue Ford complete with a rumble seat. If he caught a player breaking curfew, it meant a $10 fine—or eight percent of a month's pay for many of the Tars.

Pitcher Pete Clark, the only Tarboro native on the team, was one of three players spotted by Hamons after eating at the Hollywood Drive-In and cruising Main Street nearly two hours after the park lights went out. Clark, accompanied by teammates Nate Saxon and Ralph Caldwell, attempted to elude the manager by heading for the Clark family home where he lived in a renovated garage.

On this night, Clark's parents slept soundly as their son and his two playing partners crept into a single bed and feigned sleep as their manager pulled into the driveway with his car lights off. Hamons opened the door without invitation, Clark recalled, and stood silently as he waited for the three players to admit their escapade.

Hamons could see the three only from the neck up as he listened to them insist they had been in bed within the obligatory 90 minutes after the game. But as Caldwell pleaded his case, smoke from the cigar he had hidden under the cover began to curl around his neck. Hamons abruptly pulled down the cover and discovered three fully dressed players and a half-lit cigar. "Bull went out the door singing," said Clark. And each of the players discovered $10 missing from his next paycheck.

Hamons also had a violent side. Russ Hand, a catcher on the 1947 club, recalled seeing him batter the head of a Marine against the concrete stands at New Bern, then smash out the headlights of his adversary's car with a soft-drink bottle. In a later incident at a restaurant, Hamons drove a fist into the face of a bespectacled diner. Both incidents, said Hand, came amid losing streaks and Hamons' belief his players were being badgered.

Another player recalled that Hamons expressed his bigotry openly. When he spotted blacks from his seat in front of the team bus, he reportedly would aim an imaginary rifle and pretend to gun them down one by one. Still another story had the manager baiting a Jewish pitcher by waving a dollar bill from the dugout and deriding him as a "no-good son of a bitch."

Protected by male camaraderie and softened at times by an understanding wife, Hamons endured despite his weaknesses. Just the mention of his name generally brings a smile to those he touched as he took the Tars from town to town in search of nothing more than a higher spot in the standings.

Hamons had played in so many places, including the Canal Zone, that his network of contacts was wide enough to turn up blue-chip players such as Neville and Roy Kennedy. The courtship ended as soon as they signed; he was toughest on those he thought had a shot at moving up. Neville recorded that Hamons "nearly ran my legs off" before a Sunday exhibition game against a punchless bunch known as the West Durham Athletics. Tarboro won 29–1 as the lefthander, making his first appearance, toyed for two innings and gave up three hits.

Neville soon found a place to live after meeting Charles "Vet" Clayton, a printshop operator and diehard fan who invited him to stay at his five-bedroom house on St. Patrick Street, just nine blocks away from the Panola Street park. Clayton's wife, Frances, expressed concern at first, not exactly welcoming a baseball player into the family of four that included a son and a 16-year-old daughter, the very blonde and attractive Carol Clayton.

Neville rented a second-floor room for a dollar a day. Before long, the rate also included refrigerator privileges and a standing invitation to join the family for meals. The landlady was at last convinced that the baseball player was more of a big brother than a suitor to her only daughter. Besides that, Neville had started dating Carol's best friend and territorial rights had been drawn. Neville charmed most women, whatever their age, disarming them with a quiet, almost gentle approach not expected from an athlete. Mabel Fountain baked him cakes and later would send Christmas cards; Carol Clayton anxiously awaited his return from home games. To Neville, Carol would always be "the princess" who joined him in listening to popular songs on 78 r.p.m. records.

On the morning of the opening game, the team gathered at the Soda Shop before boarding a bus to Greenville. A studio photographer rounded up nine of the new players and one of the fans, and they headed outside for a snapshot that would freeze the moment forever. Five sat on the sidewalk; five stood behind. They posed in pleated pants and T-shirts and sweaters with shirt collars flapping at the top, most of them war vets in their midtwenties and still a little uncertain about how it was all going to turn out. Neville sat bright-eyed on the front row, complete with striped

**Tarboro players and a fan gather in front of the town's Soda Shop before leaving by bus for the opening game at Greenville in 1947. Seated, left to right, are fan Sammy DeRosa, Ray Dietrich, Ray Komanecky, Leroy Carlton, and Eddie Neville. Standing, left to right, are Stan Russelavage (who would change his baseball name to Stan Russell shortly after the season started), Jerry Kavanaugh, Art Ferguson, Charles McNay, and Bill Elkins. (Courtesy Janet Neville.)**

socks and Popeye arms. They may not have known it then, but the new boys on the block had signed up to play in a rough-and-tumble league that by 1947 could claim to have been the starting point for more than 30 major leaguers. Most of the graduates to the majors were college players who performed in the league during its days as a semipro, summer-only circuit. In that era, regulations did not prohibit paying amateurs who played in leagues outside organized baseball, and the collegians welcomed weekly checks that averaged $4 to $5 a game.

Foremost among the semipros was Charlie "King Kong" Keller, an outfielder for Kinston in 1935 and 1936. Keller, who also starred at the University of Maryland, ripped the league apart in 1936 when he batted .468 and hit 20 homers in 76 games. In 11 seasons with the New York Yankees and two with Detroit, he compiled a lifetime batting average of .286, was an All-Star three times, and played in four World Series.

The most notorious alumnus was West Virginian Bob Bowman, who pitched for the semipro Snow Hill Hillbillies in the early 1930s. Bowman, as a St. Louis Cardinal in 1940, beaned former teammate Joe "Ducky" Medwick of the Brooklyn Dodgers and became the focus of two investigations. Both the district attorney of New York and National League President Ford Frick cleared Bowman of deliberately hitting Medwick, who suffered a concussion and was said by some to be gun-shy in the final eight years of a career that led to the Hall of Fame.

Connie Mack, owner and manager of the Philadelphia Athletics, was the chief beneficiary of the collegiate pipeline. Many of the players had been groomed by one of Mack's former pitchers, Duke University Coach John Wesley "Jack" Coombs.

Two players signed by Mack—Clarence "Ace" Parker and Eric "The Red" Tipton—not only played under Coombs but also starred on Wallace Wade's great Duke football teams. Had it not been for Wade, fans would have called Wallace Wade "Wally" Moon by another name when he played the outfield for the St. Louis Cardinals and Los Angeles Dodgers. Moon's father never knew the coach, but he was a big fan when Wade coached at the University of Alabama.

When the Coastal Plain became affiliated with organized baseball in 1937, rosters included 17-year-old outfielder Johnny Wyrostek of Kinston and 18-year-old catcher Aaron Robinson of Snow Hill. Wyrostek became a two-time All-Star with the Cincinnati Reds; Robinson saw action in the 1947 World Series as a New York Yankee.

One of the last Coastal Plainers to reach the top, lefthander Bill Kennedy of Rocky Mount, burned up the league in 1946 after play had been interrupted for four seasons by the war. Kennedy finished at 28–3 and struck out 456 batters, or nearly 15 a game. When he set a new strikeout record, famed band leader Kay Kyser of Chapel Hill was among the first to offer his congratulations.

Kennedy never struck out more than 144 in any season after that, reaching that mark in 1950 with Baltimore in the International League. In four seasons with the Cleveland Indians and St. Louis Browns, he would win only 15 of 43 decisions.

Another Coastal Plainer in Neville's era had a famous name but never rose above the lower minors. Although outfielder Ed Musial enjoyed outstanding seasons at Fayetteville in 1946 and Rocky Mount in 1947, he will be remembered primarily as the brother of Hall of Famer Stan Musial.

Despite its designation, Class D baseball often produced Grade A excitement. The classification system was based on the breakdown of veterans with at least three years experience, limited service players with less than three years, and rookies. Class D leagues could allow up to four veterans, and the number increased with each jump in classification.

When interest in minor league baseball reached its peak in 1949, the country could claim 59 minor leagues in 464 cities and towns. Over 9,000 players performed that season before crowds totaling nearly 42 million people. Nowhere was interest greater than in North Carolina, which over the years had fielded 70 teams in the lower minors.

In 1962, with the number of leagues reduced to 20 and attendance down by more than 75 percent, the majors revamped the classifications and established a player development plan that favored farm systems over independently owned clubs. Class AAA remained the same; Class AA absorbed Class A; the new Class A merged the B, C, and D clubs; leagues with a "rookie" classification were established for first-year players.

The Coastal Plain League would disappear in 1953, nine years before the new classification system swallowed up what remained of the once proud bush leagues. In 1947, however, fans in every little town thought it was going to last forever.

Tarboro started the season being bullish on its manager as well as a second LaGrange recruit with the build of a Georgia pine. William Vernon Parker answered to the less formal nickname of "Gashouse," a fitting description for a hulk of a first baseman blessed with a honey of a bat and cursed with a case of molasses in his slow-moving legs. Despite hitting 13 home runs by early August, the six-foot-four Parker would end his twelfth season as a pro in virtual exile.

For Parker, an innocent-looking, likeable sort with red cheeks and round shoulders, no season could be complete without escapades. When Hamons lectured his team over a shortage of bats and balls, it was inevitable that an angry Parker would crack his 36-ounce bat over his knee after striking out.

Sometimes, the slip-ups came between the lines. Parker, according to one person close to the team, once fielded a grounder, wheeled, and threw his glove toward second without releasing the ball.

Hamons and Parker had been friends since their childhood days in LaGrange, but the manager's patience evaporated before season's end, and Parker was banished to seventh-place Roanoke Rapids.

"I guess Bull may have thought Gashouse set a bad example for some of the younger guys," pointed out Ray Komanecky, a Tar outfielder in 1947 and 1948. "Gashouse just liked his beer. One night I know he went over to Ralph Caldwell's and wound up face down in a bowl of green peas."

Roy Kennedy was as stable as Parker was volatile. The 31-year-old Canal Zone star, who had played in the league eight years earlier at Kinston, brought his wife and two children to Tarboro in a deal that included a salary of $500 a month, travel expenses, and free lodging. The family's living quarters proved to be a little cloistered, just a single room in the rectory of a Catholic church.

The veteran outfielder had hooked up with Hamons in 1940–41 when the two were teammates at Diablo Heights and Hagerstown (Maryland) of the Class B Inter-State League. He respected Hamons' knowledge of the game, but regarded the manager as a violent man to be avoided at times of temper outbursts.

Kennedy still had not forgotten that season in the Canal Zone when a cousin of his was forced to defend himself after questioning the right of Hamons' date to sit in a reserved section. After bolting into the stands, an enraged Hamons was cold-cocked by a single punch.

Kennedy confined his battles to the basepaths. He stood just over five-foot-seven and weighed only 155 pounds, but he ran with abandon, hit with occasional power, and kept infielders guessing by bunting or faking bunts at least once a game. He came to Tarboro with one condition attached: in late August he would return to his government job in the Canal Zone after his four months of accumulated vacation time ran out.

Kennedy packed a full season and more into those four months, leading the league with a .381 average, the highest since the Coastal Plain had become affiliated with organized baseball. The short season probably cost him two other records. He hit 16 triples, two under the record, and stole 65 bases, five short of the new high of 70 stolen that season by New Bern's Salvatore "Zippy" Zunno.

Kennedy thrived on challenging pitchers and picked up many of his steals in a nontraditional way: moving from second to third. He and Neville always finished in a dead heat in head-on competition in the Canal Zone, Kennedy without a stolen base and Neville without a pickoff. "You never knew it was coming," Kennedy said of Neville's move to first. "He just wouldn't give himself away."

While most Coastal Plainers were Ty Cobb types with fists held high, Neville tucked his first under his chin: the classic thinker who would sit atop the dugout steps and look for the weaknesses in opposing batters. At the receiving end, Russ Hand and backup Art Ferguson benefited from Neville's knowhow and control. When Neville shrugged off signs, the more experienced Hand let him have his way. "I just figured he knew more than I did," admitted Hand.

The sandy-haired Ferguson was more demonstrative, sometimes challenging Neville's stubbornness. "One time, I signaled a fastball, then a curve, then a fastball again, and he shrugged me off every time," recalled Ferguson. "When I went out, he said he wanted to throw a change, but I told him that was about all the guy could hit. I went back, called for a fastball again, and watched a change get hit out of the park."

With Neville's signing, the Tars suddenly had two of the most talked-about southpaws in the league. Pete Clark, who had won nine games in 1946 as a rookie out of North Carolina State College, was being touted as a possible 20-game winner.

Clark saw his opposite in Neville. "I would just lean back and fire, and only the good Lord knew where it was going," he said. "I had two speeds—hard and harder. Neville didn't throw that hard, but unlike the rest of us he could change speeds on every pitch. He also knew what every batter could do, and it came down to just him and them."

Neville also ignored tradition. "If you put Eddie in front of a meat block and told him exactly how to chop the beef, he would figure out a better way to do it," said Clark, who remained in his native Tarboro after retiring from a career in sales. "It was the same way with baseball. What he did just went over the top of everyone else's head."

Some players interpreted Neville's combination of baseball confidence and personal shyness as arrogance. "He knew he was a little bit better than anybody else," said Stan Russelavage, who would become the Tars' third left-handed starter. "We were teammates, though, and all of us listened to Bull and kept any differences we may have had away from the park. Eddie even helped me work on my pickoff move."

After only one appearance, Russelavage discovered that no one could spell or pronounce his Lithuanian name. On Hamons' advice, he switched to Stan Russell. It was not an uncommon practice. Joe Collins, the New York Yankee first baseman, was really Joe Kollonige. Boston Red Sox infielder Johnny Pesky started out as Johnny Paveskovich. And there were others who streamlined their European names to make it easier for writers, broadcasters, fans, and teammates.

Although he would find himself answering to Stan, Stanley, Russell, Russelavage, and his longtime nickname of "Stiney," the new name appeared to have immediate benefits. Before the change, he entered a game with the Tars hopelessly behind Wilson and gave up nine runs in five innings. As Stan Russell, he ranked second behind Neville in wins with a 13–9 record.

In later life, he would enjoy success in baseball with his original name. For nine years before his retirement in 1987, Russelavage was the head groundskeeper at the Pittsburgh Pirates' spring training complex in Bradenton, Florida.

Tarboro's opening-day roster also included a raw, 18-year-old fireballer a year out of high school in Hegins, Pennsylvania. Ray Dietrich, the youngest player on the squad, threw so wildly that he intimidated his own teammates on the first day of practice. When old-timer Ray Skelton went down after an errant Dietrich pitch brushed the button of his cap, Skelton remarked, perhaps only half jokingly, that he would be forced to quit the team if he planned to continue supporting his family.

Dietrich was cut in May but returned the next spring, still carrying memories of his abbreviated rookie season. He had taken one look at players such as outfielder Bill Jeffries, all of them older and experienced, and knew it would end soon.

"Jeffries looked like DiMaggio and could run like DiMaggio," recalled Dietrich. "He could do everything but hit like DiMaggio." Said Jeffries: "People always called me Little Joe. I had his profile ... the same nose, the same chin." Unlike Dietrich, Jeffries survived the roster cut from 18 to 15 a month into the season.

When the squad was trimmed to eight regulars, a backup catcher, and six pitchers, Neville played even more. In strings of games, he would be the starting pitcher, play right field or first base, relieve, and then start again. He relished—even thrived on—the roster limit that meant expanded roles for those who could hit as well as pitch.

Neville hit the ground running, winning his first three starts and taking seven of his first ten decisions, including one game when he picked three runners off first and another when he retired the first 20 Wilson batters before giving up four hits. Wilson broadcaster Clint Farris livened up the radio account by referring to "a fireball that ignited the corner of the plate" and labeling pitches down the middle as "steak and onions."

What really started the folks at the Dixie Cafe talking, though, was Neville's seven-game winning streak that lifted the Tars to the league lead. As the folks at the popular Greek-run eating spot marveled over his pitching and drank second cups of coffee poured by brothers Gus and Chris Pistolis, the lefthander took a track that would lead to tying Bill Kennedy's league record of 28 victories.

Neville rode a hitting streak at the same time, slugging a home run in each of three contests against Roanoke Rapids. His batting average for the year would be a modest .241, but his ability to hit in the clutch and with occasional power produced six home runs, ten doubles, and 31 runs batted in.

A league record crowd of 2,303 turned out at Tarboro to see Neville stop Rocky Mount for his sixth straight win. His confidence level reached such a point that, with only three days rest, he asked to pitch both ends of a home doubleheader against Roanoke Rapids. Hamons refused, watched Neville give up a single run in the opener, then cringed as the visitors scored 13 runs in the nightcap. The Tars responded with 16 of their own, however, and moved into first place by a game and a half.

With just over half a season to play, Tarboro had won six in a row and 17 of 20. Then came the jinx. Just as a cover photograph in *Sports Illustrated* often leads to declining fortunes today, the Tars turned in reverse after the local newspaper, the *Daily Southerner,* published a page one picture of Hamons.

On the eve of the doubleheader sweep, a shot of the successful manager was spread across three columns. Hamons, under the headline "Guiding Red Hot Tars," appeared to be staring into space, as if posing for a serious portrait, his lips tight, his cap cocked back as usual, and his chest ready to pop out of a too-tight uniform. Still, he had the look of a man on top. He would be there only a short time.

The Tars lost six of their next seven, and Neville's winning string ended at seven. Kinston surged into first by winning six of seven, including two over Tarboro, and the Tars trailed by three and one-half games only five days after the publication of Hamons' photograph. They would chase first place the rest of the season.

As the team declined, so did the crowds. Neville interrupted the slide with a 9–1 home victory over Roanoke Rapids, but only a handful of the original 500 remained when he lost his shutout bid in the ninth.

The team boarded a bus the next afternoon for a 45-mile trip to Roanoke Rapids' Simmons Park, confident of running its winning streak over the Jays to nine. Halfway there, a crew from the Scotland Neck Fire Department intercepted the bus and relayed the news that the game had been rained out. The jinx continued.

The bus returned to Tarboro, the team took batting practice, and Hamons reflected on the losing streak. "When your long-ball hitters are in a slump, you just don't score runs and win ballgames," he said. Referring to three doubleheaders in four days, Hamons said the Tars "were playing baseball in their sleep. I might as well have moved their bunks right out to the park."

Hamons, who had been the toast of Tarboro only three days earlier, had been criticized for not removing starting pitcher Stan Russell after he gave up six runs in the first inning against Greenville. "I had no one else to put in, unless it would have been one of the infielders," Hamons responded. "That string of doubleheaders had played havoc with my pitching staff, and I couldn't use Neville again. He had been tossing with two days' rest, and had already tossed three games that week."

Slowed by a back injury and recurring blisters on his pitching hand, Neville dropped five of his next eight decisions as the Tars volleyed between second and fifth place. Even then, he continued to hit with authority as he slugged home runs in two consecutive wins at home against Goldsboro and Roanoke Rapids. After being called out on strikes one night later, he threw his bat and drew a $5 fine and a reprimand from League President Ray Goodmon.

The jinx and a three-game Neville losing string ended simultaneously with his three-hit shutout over Roanoke Rapids in mid-August. That victory launched a nine-game Neville winning streak over 27 days as the Tars headed toward a 76–66 record and a third-place finish in the final standings.

Despite assorted physical problems, including a pitching hand badly bruised by a batted ball, Neville pitched four shutouts during the streak. Shortly before the end of the regular season, Hamons vowed he would not

use his overworked and battered star until the playoffs. He quickly re-
neged. Hoping to break a second-place tie with Kinston, Hamons used
Neville in relief on the final day of the season in a home game against
Goldsboro. The lefthander gave up five hits and five runs in one inning as
the Tars lost and settled for third after a Kinston rainout.

The difference in second and third was costly. For Tarboro players,
the average share came to about $40, some $13 less than second-place
money. And while $13 could pay the rent for nearly two weeks, it
was a paltry sum—even in a 1947 economy—compared to the risk of
damaging the arm of one of minor league baseball's most promising
pitchers.

Neville hardly objected, however, because a victory would have given
him—at least officially—a record-setting 29 for the year. His final record
was listed at 28–9 (matching Bill Kennedy's league record for the most
wins), but two of the victories apparently were credited by mistake. Box
scores for the season listed only 26 wins but credited Neville with the same
number of appearances (43) and the same number of losses as the official
league statistics. Neville's own diary listed his win on September 4, three
days before the end of the season, as his twenty-sixth and last.

Phantom victories or not, Neville established himself as the best
pitcher in the league, perhaps the best in the lower minors. He completed
28 of 32 starts in compiling a 2.31 earned run average.

Neville would continue to see heavy duty in the four-team playoffs,
an idea still considered novel after being originated in the 1930s to sustain
fan interest when pennant races turned into routs. For years, the
postseason games were referred to as the Shaughnessy Playoffs in recognition of Frank Shaughnessy, the minor league executive who suggested the
plan. The Coastal Plain playoffs matched Tarboro against Kinston in a
seven-game semifinal series, with the winner advancing to the championship against either first-place Wilson or fourth-place New Bern.

Hamons, his pitching staff hit by a series of ailments, started Neville
twice in the first five games—each time with only two days' rest. The lefthander split two decisions, winning the second game with a three-hit
shutout and dropping the fifth after giving up eight runs and losing an early
three-run lead.

A second shutout by Hamons himself, who was making only his tenth
appearance, gave the Tars two wins in the first five games. The sixth game,
however, found the homestanding Tars so short of infielders that Kinston
was asked to waive a league rule prohibiting roster additions after an
August deadline.

One Tar infielder, Chuck Riddle, was on the sidelines with 13 stitches
in his right hand. Riddle had been spiked by Steve Collins when the
Kinston manager stole second base in the second playoff game, but Collins

refused to allow last-minute replacements. The injury situation, he told the Tars, was "just a good break for me and a bad one for you."

Neville, shifted to right field in a shuffled lineup, tripled, singled, and drove in a run off the league's top righthander, Sam McLawhorn, but the night belonged to Kinston and Collins. A solo home run by the Eagle manager, a former Atlanta Cracker infielder, contributed to a 5–3 series-clinching victory and assured his continuing unpopularity among Tar fans. Although the five-foot-six Collins would continue to answer to "Shorty" in Kinston, he became "Spike" in a town whose team would gain revenge a year later.

In the meantime, the Tars could be consoled by the $294.34 that fans had contributed at a playoff "Appreciation Night" game. The per capita contribution from the crowd of 2,407 amounted to slightly over 12 cents each.

Neville was named to Coastal Plain All-Star teams sponsored by the Sports Writers Association and *The Evening Telegram* in Rocky Mount. He was second in the balloting by the newspaper, third among the writers.

Word of his talent reached far beyond the boundaries of eastern North Carolina. At midseason, Chattanooga's Lookouts of the Class AA Southern Association expressed interest after he was recommended by Max Wilson, manager of the Wilson Tobs and a former Lookout pitcher who had brief trials with the Philadelphia Phillies and Washington Senators.

Wilson, whose team would lose seven of eight decisions to Neville, may have been looking for a way to get him out of the Coastal Plain League, but Tarboro owner Charles Allen refused Chattanooga's reported offer of $2,500 and waited out the season. Cincinnati later assigned Neal Millard to scout Neville. Four other clubs made inquiries: the Boston Red Sox, New York Yankees, Philadelphia Phillies, and the Southern Association's Atlanta Crackers.

At the end of September, Allen struck a deal with the independently owned Beaumont Exporters of the Class AA Texas League. Neville's contract was assigned to Beaumont on a 30-day option basis. If he succeeded, Allen would cash in, and the lefthander would jump four classifications in a single season.

But Neville never made it to Beaumont. He was sidetracked by a desire for more money and a second season in the Canal Zone, where his overworked left arm would spend much of the winter warming up under a heat lamp.

# The Boys of Winter

*Four of us watched a movie full of bare-breasted natives. It turned out to be a documentary so boring that we demanded our money back for false advertising. For all I knew, they dressed the same way in the Canal Zone. I mean, why else would someone go there every winter when they could stay in places as nice as Durham and Baltimore?*

---

For eight years, few if any pitchers in professional baseball threw as often as Eddie Neville. He led two pitching lives, one on U.S. soil from Tarboro to Toledo, the other in winter baseball near the beaches of the Canal Zone and Panama.

The Boston Braves had two rubber arms in that era, winning a pennant in 1948 with "Spahn and Sain and two days of rain." Johnny Sain pitched 315 innings that season, Warren Spahn 257. Neville's figures were even more numbing: 397 innings in his first full year in the Canal Zone and Tarboro, 392 in the Canal Zone and Durham two years later. Before his final abbreviated season in the Class A Eastern League in 1955, he threw an average of just over 301 innings a year in starting 247 games and appearing 141 times in relief.

Neville's spectacular run in winter baseball rests in the record books of leagues that no longer exist, one vaporized by financial headaches, the other by organizational problems and continuing political turmoil. There are no longer any records to be chased, no players to pursue fading statistics in worn-out books and find themselves whipped by grit and perseverance.

Consider these accomplishments: a member of seven championship teams in seven seasons; an overall record of 50 wins and 17 losses, with an earned run average of 2.74; holder of the Canal Zone League record for the most consecutive wins in a single season (ten); twice named the Most Valuable Player in the Canal Zone League; and a batting average of .304 when an injury to Al Kubski forced his return to first base in the 1952 Caribbean Series.

What he accomplished in winter baseball takes on even more significance when combined with his minor league record. In the period running from December 1946 to March 1950, he won 105 games and lost only 33, at .761 one of the best winning percentages by any pitcher over an extended time period.

If Neville destroyed his own pitching arm, as some observers claim he did, the act of self-destruction at least took place on land that became as familar and alluring as the sandlots of Baltimore. In following the trail to the Canal Zone and Panama seven times, he was exceeded only by Kubski, whose unbroken line of championships as a manager lured him back for 11 seasons. Catcher Ray Dabek, who married the daughter of a Panama Canal tugboat engineer, made the trip six times.

For most players, however, the trip was a once or twice-in-a-lifetime experience. Some had families; others didn't want to play every winter; others found one or two Christmases away from home to be enough. But Neville, a bachelor until 1953, broke his string of trips only once after his first excursion in 1946. In the winter of 1952–53, he stayed home hoping to land a job as manager of the Carolina League's Durham Bulls.

The Baltimore connection was at least part of the attraction. In addition to Neville and Kubski, three other players from Baltimore made the trip more than once. Pitcher Bill Sweiger was a Motta for three seasons; second baseman Bob Young and outfielder Don "Tex" Warfield each played two winters.

Sweiger shared Neville's passion for winter baseball, and likely would have run up a long string of his own had it not been for his tragic death in the Korean War at the age of 27. A blond, rosy-cheeked righthander who stood six-foot-four, Sweiger had signed with the Pittsburgh Pirates in 1943 after leading City College to high school baseball and basketball championships his senior year.

He served in World War II, earned his stripes at Officer Candidate School, and saw his baseball career interrupted a second time by a call to Korea. In a letter dated October 4, 1951, First Lieutenant Sweiger told his parents he planned to listen to the opening game of the Yankees-Giants World Series on the armed forces radio hookup. He was killed in action the same day after setting himself up as a target to cover for his retreating troops.

Another pitcher from Baltimore, lefthander Lou Sleater, believed that one season in the sun was enough if he wanted to preserve his pitching arm. He won five of six decisions in 1947–48, then turned down future trips as well as an opportunity to play in Cuba. "They were paying just about everybody a thousand a month plus expenses to play in Cuba, but

I was told the St. Louis Browns probably would call me up the next spring so I stayed home," Sleater recalled.

The Browns first called Sleater up for a short stay in 1950. He had enough of an arm to pitch for six American League clubs over seven seasons.

Neville actually recruited Sleater, although the two had never met. Sleater's record at Mount St. Joseph was enough of an endorsement; he had finished his high school career by winning Baltimore's championship game at Oriole Park less than two months before it burned down.

As other players came and went, Neville discovered a second home. He would spend seven Christmases, seven New Year's Eves, and even one Thanksgiving in either the Canal Zone or Panama. The hospitality, friends from Baltimore, and all the privileges aside, what really made it seem like home was the smell of a game. At one season opener, the First Infantry Battalion Band played two songs that summed up his winters abroad: "Jingle Bells" and "Take Me Out to the Ballgame."

Once the minor league season ended in September, Neville would become restless as soon as he hit the streets of Baltimore. He would join pickup games at the Bloomingdale Oval or appear in Sunday All-Star games that matched top white pros against players from the Negro leagues. He would drop by Mount St. Joseph or visit Spring Grove Hospital, the sponsor of the 1946 national amateur champions. He would listen to college football games on the radio or catch a late-season Washington Senators game at Griffith Stadium. Twice he would go to the World Series, at Cleveland in 1948 and New York in 1951.

For the most part, however, the period between mid-September and the first week in December represented lag time between starts. When December arrived, he would pack his loud sport shirts with his glove and spikes and board the *S. S. Mossdale* at New Orleans or the *S. S. Panama* at New York for a trip made more bearable by card games and meals in the captain's quarters.

Off the field, Neville became hooked on tarpon fishing in later seasons, although he rarely landed one that weighed more than 30 pounds. He also enjoyed golf, bingo, boxing matches, poker, pinochle, days at the beach or by the pool, and a steady diet of movies. He would shoot pool, play the lottery, take in the horse races, go to a cockfight, and do all the other things that winter league players did to fill in the leisure hours.

Like other players, he was a frequent visitor to the home of Cristobol Motta President Gilbert Morland and his Brooklyn-born wife, Virginia. "Our house was open to all those kids," said Virginia Morland, who turned her British husband's mind from cricket to baseball when she took him to his first Canal Zone League game in 1934. "Eddie always impressed me with his quick mind. I was stuck with a puzzle one time, and he figured it out algebraically. I always thought he should look beyond baseball, but he just seemed to love it so much."

Neville usually favored puzzles over parties. He was a teetotaler who would turn down a drink at team gatherings, but he couldn't resist a favorite player pastime of swimming in the nude after beach picnics. He preferred one steady date at a time and relaxing in the comfort of a house where he could sit down for a meal with his date's family or engage "the old man," as he called them, in a game of cribbage. For two winters, he had a sometimes stormy romance that shared equal billing with baseball. Even when it ended, he remained close to the family and would continue to join them for meals and special gatherings.

But winter baseball was idyllic and destructive at the same time. Had Neville resisted returning more than once or twice, he surely would have been better prepared to meet the challenge of baseball at higher levels. In the months before he was to report to Beaumont in March of 1948 for a shot at Class AA competition after his outstanding year in Class D, he demonstrated incredibly bad judgment by pitching in the Canal Zone with a pitching arm that ached from the moment of his arrival. He slept under a heat lamp every night, "baking (his) sore flipper" as he liked to say. He became concerned about a broken bone, but X-rays proved negative. Doctors told him that heat, massage, and rest would be the only cure. In January, a physician said the likely cause of soreness was pressure on a nerve.

Even then, Neville continued to throw. He pitched 91 innings, only two fewer than the winter before. His motion was so smooth that it appeared to be effortless, but every assignment amounted to a physical gamble in a faraway league that was blacklisted by most major league clubs.

Neville, however, did play with the blessing of the Detroit organization. In the winter of 1950–51, the lefthander submitted a written request to Robert B. Evans, general manager of the Tigers' Toledo Mud Hen farm club in the Class AAA American Association.

Evans gave his clearance, expressing more concern that Neville might play with or compete against players on baseball's ineligible list. "You could jeopardize your entire baseball career if you inadvertently should become associated with such a player," Evans wrote. As for playing time, Evans told Neville to "use good judgment in deciding how much pitching you should do. There's no sense leaving your victories in Panama."

Neville pitched very little that winter, but not by choice. In January, he injured his left knee sliding into second base, the same knee that already had been scarred by three operations. The injury, which required 21 trips to the hospital for treatment, may not have been the deciding factor in his decline, but by mid-May he was out of Triple A baseball for good.

For Neville, however, a game was a game, and a victory in the Canal

Zone counted the same as a win in the states. As he saw it, his one hundredth win in professional baseball was not a game he pitched at Durham in 1952, but the eight-hitter he threw in defeating Diablo Heights on Sunday afternoon, January 15, 1951.

Neville also took pride in being aligned with Kubski and Dabek as the core of two dynasties, first at Cristobol and later as a member of the Carta Vieja club in the Panama Professional League. As other players left after a season or two, only the three of them could understand and appreciate the tradition of winning a championship year after year, including the memorable 1948–49 season when Cristobol assembled a team that is conceded to be the best by far in the history of the Canal Zone League.

In addition to Neville, Dabek, and Sweiger, Kubski had recruited three infielders from Houston in the Class AA Texas League: first baseman Don Bollweg, shortstop Bud Hardin, and third baseman Claude "Pappy" Wright. Bollweg would play with four major league teams over five seasons, including 1953 when he batted .297 in 70 games with the New York Yankees. Hardin would play briefly for the Chicago Cubs in 1952. Another Motta newcomer, pitcher Fred Baczewski, would head for the Texas League after the season and would have a lifetime record of 17–10 with the Chicago Cubs and Cincinnati Reds.

The Mottas took 12 of their first 14 games, never lost two in a row, and finished nine games ahead of second-place Diablo Heights with a 35–7 record. Neville won more and worked more than any pitcher in the league. His record over 118 innings was 11–3.

Neville had been named Most Valuable Player two years earlier, but this time the honor went to Dabek, an outstanding defensive receiver whose promotion past Triple A with the Brooklyn Dodger organization was blocked at least partially by the success of Roy Campanella.

When he later joined the New York Giant farm system at Minneapolis, Dabek caught the most famous knuckleballer of all, Hoyt Wilhelm, at spring training. Dabek respected Neville's knuckler, but he was awed by the future Hall of Famer's. "Hoyt's was more active; it was never the same," he said. "Eddie's was a little more consistent. But both of them were able to get the thing over the plate."

Dabek stayed in the minors 19 years before settling in Houston, where he had played on two teams that won the Dixie Series. He continued to stay in touch with baseball by serving as a crowd supervisor at the Astrodome for 25 years.

Dabek's MVP season ended with an Isthmian championship thanks to three straight wins over Spur Cola, champions of the Panama Professional League. The most suspenseful moment of an otherwise dull Isthmian series came before the first pitch when the three umpires staged a sitdown strike for more pay. They asked for—and received—the grand sum of $35 each for all three games.

The spotlight would switch from Dabek to Neville the next season. Before reporting to Toledo in 1950, the lefthander broke the record of nine consecutive wins he shared with Mickey Harris. With the financially troubled league reduced to three teams with the folding of Colon, Neville had a devil of a good time dominating a Diablo Heights lineup full of left-handed swingers.

While Neville won so easily that a record seemed inevitable, another southpaw created an aura of unpredictability. Joining the staff that season was Tommy Lasorda, slim, trim, and 22 years old. Lasorda, a member of the Dodger organization and destined to become the parent club's manager, had ranked second in strikeouts pitching for Greenville (South Carolina) in the Class A South Atlantic League. With a fastball and sweeping curve that were often as out of control as his flamboyant personality, Lasorda also walked more than his share of batters. He had issued just under seven walks a game at Greenville, and this extra winter of pitching would not increase his effectiveness.

In his first start for Cristobol, Lasorda walked ten in seven innings. He would continue to be erratic for the next 11 years. In brief stops at Brooklyn and Kansas City, he struck out 37 and walked 56, posting a career record of no wins and four losses.

Lasorda had been recruited by Dabek, who had been his catcher at Greenville. "We always had a fight when Tommy pitched," Dabek said. "He was always knocking somebody down. He was one mean son of a gun."

"Tommy really didn't throw very hard, but he did have that big, breaking curve and a lot of guts," added Kubski. "He was a determined, tough kind of guy."

There were early signs that Lasorda one day would assume a leadership role. Youngsters in the Canal Zone, fascinated by his charm, often followed Lasorda when they spotted him heading for the commissary. He would line them up like soldiers, equip them with broomsticks, and march them off to a game of stickball.

Lasorda demonstrated a desire to win even when he wasn't pitching. Sitting on the bench in a game against Balboa, he raced to home plate when umpire Willie Williams ruled a bunt had rolled foul. Williams ejected both Lasorda and Kubski, but Canal Zone fans had seen for the first time how Lasorda would defend his troops as a manager.

Lasorda had a miserable year in winning only two of five decisions and leading the league with 58 walks. His true contribution to the team was measured by an enthusiasm that carried over from the playing field to a postseason celebration that he warmed up with some of the loudest hillbilly singing ever heard in the tropics.

**Future Los Angeles Dodgers' Manager Tommy Lasorda as a Cristobol pitcher during the 1949–50 season. (Courtesy Janet Neville.)**

"He was a terrific character," said Virginia Morland. "There was a time when Tommy was having arm problems, and Gil [Motta president Gilbert Morland] thought he would have to cut him because the funds were getting kind of slim. Al [Kubski] went to Gil and asked if there was any possible way the team could keep Tommy. Al said he kept the boys happy, that they liked to have him around. So Gil kept him."

As a west coast scout for the Kansas City Royals, Kubski continued to enjoy Lasorda's company. "Tommy [by then manager of the Dodgers] would put his arm around me and tell everybody I taught him everything he knows," said Kubski. But Kubski forced in the final word. "I just said, 'Yeah, Tommy, but you don't know anything.'"

Neville's most memorable moment with Lasorda came between seasons. They had been joined in a Baltimore restaurant by two other players who were Lasorda's teammates at Montreal in 1950: Chuck Connors, who would become famous as television's *Rifleman,* and former Brooklyn

Dodger Al Gionfriddo, who was back in the minors after his catch of Joe DiMaggio's long drive to left field in the 1947 World Series.

Neville recalled in a 1980 interview that Connors lit a match and tossed it on Gionfriddo's expensive new suit. "Tommy and I were laughing so hard we couldn't stop," he said.

Lasorda never returned to the Canal Zone after the 1949–50 season, but he did become a winter baseball fixture as a player in Cuba and Venezuela. He later managed five winters in the Dominican Republic and one in Venezuela.

At Cristobol, Lasorda left the winning to Neville, who defeated Diablo Heights eight straight times, paused for a win over Balboa, then stopped Diablo again to break the record for most consecutive victories and run his two-season Canal Zone streak to 15. He would lose his next start against Diablo, drop an exhibition game in an All-Star series against the Panama Professional League, and defeat Diablo two times out of three to finish the regular season at 12–2.

Cristobol, slumping badly in the final weeks of the season, moved into the best-of-three playoffs against a Balboa club that had won 16 of its last 24 games to capture the second-half title and tie for first for the full season. Neville wasted a shutout when rain forced the cancellation of a scoreless game after seven innings, then won the final game 5–4 despite giving up 11 hits.

Neville earned Most Valuable Player honors for the second time in four seasons. He won the most games, had the most complete games with 12, and the highest winning percentage at .857. His earned run average was a closer call; at 2.009 it bettered the second-place figure by .002.

For Al Kubski and the Mottas, the season marked a fifth straight league championship. Three other managers had won four league crowns, but none could claim five. Kubski would capture his sixth straight title in 1950–51, but that would be his last. Faced with declining attendance after operating with three teams two years in a row, the league went out of business and ended a dynasty at the same time.

Neville's knee injury in late January kept him on the bench most of that final season. From that vantage point, he witnessed the development of a skinny 20-year-old righthander whose previous pitching experience was limited to high school. Humberto Robinson, a native Panamanian spotted by Kubski at a tryout camp for local players, was one of seven blacks on league rosters that season, the color line being broken a year earlier with Balboa's signing of catcher Yancey Miller.

Kubski sized up Robinson as a pro prospect despite his wildness. He recommended the hard-throwing young star to the St. Louis Cardinal organization after an 8–4 season, but no offer was made. Another black native who played in the Panama Professional League, infielder Hector

Lopez, also was turned down after a Kubski endorsement. The initial rejection of black athletes such as Lopez and Robinson was hardly surprising. In 1951, four years after Jackie Robinson played his first game for Brooklyn, only six of the 16 major league clubs had integrated rosters.

Both players eventually signed with other clubs, and their performances confirmed Kubski's early evaluation. Lopez hit .269 over 12 seasons with the New York Yankees and Kansas City Athletics; Robinson showed promise in the bullpen for the Milwaukee Brewers, Cleveland Indians, and Philadelphia Phillies. Robinson's real baseball legacy would not be his eight wins over five seasons; he would be remembered more for reporting a bribe attempt in 1959 by the co-owner of a Philadelphia bar.

Robinson told a Municipal Court judge that he was offered $1,500 to deliberately lose the second game of a doubleheader with Cincinnati. The charge resulted in a two-and-one-half to five-year jail sentence for Harold Friedman, who was found guilty after a one-day trial.

"This is my profession," Robinson testified that he told Friedman. "I take this money and I never pitch again. I like to play baseball."

Primarily a relief pitcher, Robinson had started for the Phillies against Cincinnati and pitched one of the best games of his career, giving up only three hits in seven innings. It would be the last major league victory the hero from Panama ever recorded.

Two other future major leaguers were on that last Cristobol club. Clem "Scooter" Koshorek, a five-foot-six shortstop who would play three different infield positions for Pittsburgh in 1952, was named the Most Valuable Player after leading the league with a .362 average and setting a record with 29 stolen bases. A newcomer in the outfield, Walt "Moose" Moryn, batted .319 and drove in 25 runs in demonstrating the power that would earn him a spot as a regular with the Chicago Cubs for four seasons.

In Cristobol's final game, a pitcher who never escaped the minors turned the team's disbanding into a memorable occasion. Facing a team of Service All-Stars in an exhibition contest to raise funds for the American Red Cross, righthander Dave Thomas pitched a perfect game as the Mottas won 7–0. Thomas struck out 16 batters and allowed only three balls out of the infield—a fly ball to each outfielder.

Cristobol players were more fascinated by another Thomas streak of perfect. "He was," laughed Kubski, "the world's oldest virgin."

"They were always trying to line me up," said the Canadian-born Thomas, who also resisted temptation when a teammate occasionally wandered into one of Panama's notorious "blue houses."

Thomas and the rest of the Mottas were out of winter jobs after the league closed down, but that was only a technicality for the top players. They always had the option of swapping the comfortable familiarity, political stability, and side benefits of Cristobol for the higher-paying, more competitive Panama Professional League.

When the Mottas' Gilbert Morland took over as general manager of the Panama League's Carta Vieja club, he signed Kubski as the manager and brought back Neville, Dabek, Koshorek, and Thomas. The Yankees (sponsored by a rum distiller) had won the pennant two years earlier and would be installed as favorites in 1951–52.

In the six seasons since its founding, the Panama League had earned enough of a reputation to prompt a warning from the president of minor league baseball. "You will see some days when a highly effective Triple A pitcher will get his ears pinned back," George Trautman advised in a letter that included an agreement requiring players to pledge high standards in their performance and conduct. "Don't go down there expecting to find a lot of baseball yokels who don't know what the game is all about. A player who 'jakes it' will hear from the crowd even more quickly than in our own country."

Neville signed for $300 a month that first season in Panama, but he was far from happy because of his demotion the summer before from Toledo to Williamsport (Pennsylvania) of the Class A Eastern League. Still, the contract offered an opportunity to play before considerably larger crowds and a chance to compete in the Caribbean Series against leading teams from Cuba, Venezuela, and Puerto Rico.

Neville, who would have a forgettable 5–3 record, would reach the series in a role that was forced by a bizarre off-the-field injury to Kubski, who suffered temporary paralysis on the left side of his face after being punched in a postgame parking lot fight with Spur Cola pitcher Vibert Clarke. Kubski, who tried to break up a dispute between Clarke and Koshorek, became the first Carta Vieja regular not to start a game when Neville replaced him at first.

After returning to his old high school position, Neville quickly ended his season-long batting slump of four hits in 33 tries. In the final four regular season games, he went seven for 17, drove in five runs, and stole a base. He started a double play that protected Carta Vieja's lead as the Yankees clinched the pennant and headed for the fourth annual Caribbean Series.

The most heralded player at the start of the series was Chico Carrasquel, the star shortstop for the Chicago White Sox who was permitted to play winter baseball as a native Venezuelan. Other than natives, the majors barred active players who had at least 45 days of big league experience.

Future stars and former major leaguers such as Lou Klein and Bert Haas (who would manage Neville at Albany, New York, in 1955) dressed up other rosters. Puerto Rico's starting first baseman was Victor Pellot, who later would play for the New York Yankees and Kansas City Athletics as Vic Power. Cuba countered with right fielder Edmundo Amoros, whose resemblance to boxer Sandy Saddler would lead to his nickname of "Sandy" when he became a Brooklyn Dodger. And Carta Vieja boasted major-leaguers-to-be in Koshorek and two future Philadelphia A's: right-handed pitcher Marion Fricano and second baseman Forrest Vandergrift "Spook" Jacobs.

With Panama hosting the series for the first time, fan interest was high. Advance ticket sales and radio broadcasting rights pushed series income past the reported breakeven point of $50,000 before the first pitch. A morning workout by Carrasquel and his Caracas team attracted a crowd estimated at 2,000.

More than 17,000 spectators packed Panama City's Olympic Stadium 30 minutes before the opening game. They cheered as the injured Kubski, out of uniform after turning over managing duties to outfielder Dale Lynch, marched onto the field with his team in opening ceremonies.

Neville went hitless in an opening loss to Venezuela, but seven hits in his final 19 trips helped Carta Vieja split six games and finish in a second-place tie behind undefeated champion Cuba. His .304 average placed him seventh among all players with ten or more times at bat.

Amoros earned Most Valuable Player honors with a series-leading .450 average, but Neville had outperformed Carrasquel, who had a disappointing series with only three hits and missed the final game after being spiked on the left forearm in a play at second base.

Neville sat out the next winter, then made his final trip to Panama for the 1953–54 season. A second honeymoon with his bride of less than a year overshadowed a five-win season and a seventh league championship. Postseason play was less productive; the winter league career that started with a run on a record ended in the anonymity of six innings of mop-up duty in a Caribbean Series that saw Carta Vieja and Cuba finish in a second-place tie behind Puerto Rico.

Kubski's championship string reached nine in Neville's final season, a close call that took a playoff victory over Chesterfield to break a regular season tie. A year later, he claimed his tenth straight championship in a season interrupted for a week by the assassination of President Jose Remon at a race track.

In 1956, Carta Vieja finished a distant third in a three-team league. Kubski never went back after that. "I was fired for not winning another pennant," he joked. Married, travel weary, and rattled over the political unrest, he cut his baseball life in half and continued his managing career in the lower minors.

For 14 seasons, he was the guy in the background grooming future stars such as Pittsburgh's Willie Stargell. "That donkey has a future,"

Kubski said of Stargell when he managed the future Hall of Famer in 1959 in the Class D Sophomore League. When his name was spelled incorrectly in Stargell's biography, all he could do was wince.

After his managing career ended, Kubski served as a Baltimore Oriole scout for ten years before switching to California and later to Kansas City. As Kubski tracked talent for the Royals from his home base in Carlsbad, California, his son Gil, became a west coast scout for the Chicago Cubs. Gil Kubski, the namesake of the later Gilbert Morland, lived out his father's dreams for a brief time in 1980 when the California Angels called him up to play the outfield. And the Kubski name, famous for years in Panama and the Canal Zone, finally showed up 22 times in big league box scores that traveled coast to coast.

# Striking Gold

*This would be the summer I learned to talk like baseball players. My teachers were two brothers whose father was a bricklayer. They said the word so many times and it sounded so good that I tried it out on my mother as soon as I arrived home. I was uncertain of both the meaning and spelling. All I knew was that it sounded like "futt."*

---

As his second winter season in the Canal Zone neared an end in 1948, Neville refused to sign a contract that would put him within two steps of the major leagues in only his second year as a professional pitcher. Beaumont President Guy Airey offered him $350 a month to sign a Texas League contract, but Neville asked for more in a letter written in late February.

Airey responded quickly, stressing that his offer was considered above average for first-year players with a Class AA club. Emphasizing that his contract had been assigned to Beaumont on a 30-day conditional basis, Airey urged Neville to report to the Muti Hotel in Cuero, Texas, for the opening of spring training on March 8. "It is . . . necessary to have just as long as possible to look at you in order for you to get a fair chance," wrote Airey.

On the day other pitchers and catchers reported to Cuero, Neville remained in the Canal Zone. He spent his day going to the movies, shooting pool, and playing poker. Airey wired Neville on March 26, upping his offer to $375 after watching his pitchers give up 19 walks and 29 runs in an exhibition game.

Neville continued to hold out. He told Al Kubski that he could make more in Tarboro, where his first contract in 1947 only called for a salary of $175 a month. Kubski knew that highly competitive Class D leagues such as the Coastal Plain would pay top performers under the table despite signing an affidavit with the National Association of Professional Baseball Leagues to abide by the terms of the player contracts.

50

Any team found paying additional compensation faced the threat of a $500 fine; the club official signing the contract would be banned from organized baseball for two years. But independent teams such as Tarboro, without any major league ties, skirted the rules to attract star players.

Neville's motivation was more than money; he simply used dollars as a scoreboard to determine his pitching value. Kubski urged him to accept the Beaumont offer, reminding him that he could make considerably more the following year with a promotion to Triple A.

Neville was not one to express his feelings openly, but more than a contract was at stake. The pitcher knew he had a sore arm that really wasn't ready for the Texas League. If he had any doubts about the continuing problems apparently caused by pressure on a nerve, they were confirmed on April 2 when he gave up 18 hits in seven innings in a meaningless Canal Zone exhibition game.

He left the Canal Zone six days later, arriving in Baltimore early the next morning with his knees still wobbly after he became airsick during a turbulent flight from Miami. After resting three days at home, he boarded a train bound for North Carolina and what he expected would be the beginning of a second season in the Coastal Plain League.

But Charles Allen told Neville otherwise when the owner arrived in Tarboro April 16 to watch his two clubs—the Tars and the Durham Bulls—play an exhibition game. Neville learned that he had been suspended by Beaumont President Airey for refusing to report for the opening of the Texas League season. Under terms of the 30-day option, Airey had the right to keep Neville on the suspended list and out of organized baseball until May 14.

Allen watched Neville take the field that night, but not as a player. Instead, the lefthander served as the base umpire—a skill he had sharpened in the Canal Zone when he occasionally called nonleague games.

Neville, through George Earnhart, business manager of the Tars, asked Airey to lift the suspension but received no response. He hounded Hamons to put him on the roster, and wrote that he was "fed up with Bull" when the manager refused to let him play.

Returning to Baltimore, he pitched two scoreless innings in a semi-pro game and gained credit for a win after scoring the tiebreaking run. He arrived in Tarboro the day before the suspension was lifted, worked out at his own expense for a week, then signed a contract, presumably for a hefty raise. Ironically, after losing one month's salary, his pay for the season likely came up short of Beaumont's final contract offer.

Sore arm or not, it was something of a surprise that he returned to Tarboro instead of moving up to Durham and the Class C Carolina League. Durham Manager Willie Duke wanted Neville, and two pre-season newspaper reports said he was expected to sign with the Bulls.

Duke recalled, however, that Neville was "Bull Hamons' boy." It was the Tarboro manager, Duke said, who originally "corralled Neville. If Bull wanted him back, I wasn't going to intercede."

Allen apparently saw no reason to convince Hamons otherwise. By mid-May, it was obvious that even Neville would be unable to lift a weak Durham club out of the second division.

By assigning him to Tarboro, Allen also could be assured of retaining the star pitcher's contract and selling it to the highest bidder just as he had attempted to do with Beaumont. Under a working agreement with Detroit, the Tigers could sign two Allen-owned players in Durham at no cost at the end of each season. Allen knew Neville would be one of the targeted players, and realized he could make a profit only if the lefthander remained in Tarboro. As it turned out, no team showed interest in Neville after the 1948 season. In 1949, after his sensational year at Durham, the Tigers exercised their option and landed him for free.

Once Neville signed with Tarboro in 1948, he quickly dismissed the Beaumont debacle. He was back in organized baseball in a town that loved the game as much as he did. If he had been angry with Bull Hamons before the season, all was forgiven when the manager—along with his wife and the Ralph Caldwells—greeted him when he arrived at the train station in Rocky Mount.

Hamons already had rounded up the firepower required to win a pennant; the train delivered the missing arm that would lift his team from a sputtering second place to a comfortable lead in less than 30 days.

His newest hired gun, 36-year-old first baseman Jake Daniel, was—like Hamons—a product of the LaGrange mill leagues. Daniel was a reformed baseball outlaw who once jumped so many clubs that he was banned from organized baseball for nearly six seasons.

"My mother-in-law used to go on the road with my wife Ruby and me early in the season," Daniel recalled. "They'd go back home after about three weeks. I'd start missing Ruby after a while so I would just take off and not go back."

Daniel, at six-foot-two and 200 pounds, hit the ball with such power and consistency that teams bid for his services despite his unpredictability. He reached the majors long enough to appear in 12 games with the Brooklyn Dodgers in 1937, then hit the backwaters of baseball the next season after being banned when he jumped his contract at Elmira (New York) in the Class A New York-Penn League. "The fields were so rough there that it was like sliding through coal," Daniel said. "I had this big strawberry on my leg and couldn't get out of the lineup. They offered to let me play in North Carolina at Winston-Salem. I told them I would, but once I got there I kept right on going."

He signed with a semipro team in the Tar Heel town of Kannapolis, played under the name of Dan Jacobs, and became the terror of the outlaw circuits before he was reinstated in 1944.

Daniel always would be filled with wanderlust, but his loyalty to Hamons kept him anchored in Tarboro for an entire season. "I would help Bull do his thinking," said Daniel. "He would always be three or four innings behind. There were times when he wouldn't even be watching the game and he would just jump up and go argue with the umpire."

As tough as he was, Hamons was smart enough to avoid a confrontation with Daniel. "He would jump on the players all the time, then he would tell me not to get mad if he ever jumped on me," said Daniel. "He wanted the players to think that he treated everybody the same."

Daniel was the same rascal in Tarboro that he had been at every level of baseball. In the International League, he learned how to order liquor and bill it to the club as a meal expense. "We would order a round of Tom Collins and have the waiter write it up as lemonade," he confessed. "A glass of lemonade only cost a nickel so we knew we'd be caught. Pretty soon the manager asked how we could drink so many 35-cent lemonades."

Since Tarboro and the rest of North Carolina banned liquor by the drink, Daniel specialized in girls. "I've never been to a town where there weren't girls who went after ballplayers," he said. "And I knew only one ballplayer who only went with one girl in his life and never took a drink."

Daniel's style was to hit the streets, find the first pretty face, and make some outrageous comment. One teammate insists Daniel once offered to weigh his own date's breasts. "I never was bashful," he said. "Most people would get slapped for the things I said. I went over pretty good." Daniel went over so well in Tarboro that he once arranged with a banker to supply him with a key to a cabin on the Tar River. "One night the key just wouldn't fit," he recalled. "It turned out to be the key to the bank."

Daniel raised hell on the field as well. He quickly made fans forget Roy Kennedy's flirtation with a .400 average and teamed up with returning outfielder Ray Komanecky to give the Tars the top run-producing duo in the league.

Even with Neville back in the same town that Daniel was painting, more was expected from two Tar wives: Trecia Hamons and Annie Bruce Caldwell. Trecia Hamons was a knockout blonde who was a nightclub singer when she met her future husband near the end of the 1941 season at Hagerstown, Maryland. Hamons' Owl teammates called for a song to recognize the pitcher's pending wartime Army duty, and 18-year-old Trecia—with Piccolo Pete and His Band behind her—belted out "I'll Be Back in a Year, Little Darling." Trecia married Hamons two weeks later.

Their son, Frankie, or "Little Bull," was five years old when the baseball family grew to four with the birth of Betty Jo in Tarboro on June 1, 1948. Trecia, admittedly her husband's biggest fan, was out of the hospital in three days and back at the park in four. "I never ran across anyone I admired more than Lowell," said Trecia, whose respect extended to addressing her husband by his middle name—just as his parents did. "He was the kind of tough man that appealed to me, something like my father, I guess."

Hamons was at his toughest near the end of his managing career at Wytheville (Virginia) in the Class D Appalachian League when he was charged with assaulting the business manager of the Welch (West Virginia) club in a dressing room brawl. Hamons countered by charging Jack Paris with brandishing a deadly weapon, described in the police report as a bucket of money and a broom. Both charges were dropped.

Uproarious incidents like that, Trecia said, actually livened up a marriage that continued for nearly 38 years. On July 10, 1979, Hamons, who was running a used car lot in Cumberland, Maryland, died of a heart attack and went to his grave with a baseball in his casket.

Annie Bruce Caldwell kept the team's pregnancy streak intact after the birth of the first of two Hamons' daughters. The petite telephone company clerk had become a baseball player's bride in the middle of the 1945 season.

Her husband's career had started to blossom at the same time. Ralph Caldwell had been a 23-year-old rookie catcher at Durham in 1946, but finished the season at Tarboro after making seven errors the first three weeks. He was really a man without a true position that summer and the next, playing second most of the time but also filling in as a first baseman and outfielder. It wasn't until 1948 that Hamons rediscovered the obvious; Caldwell belonged behind the plate.

As a catcher, Caldwell took command of his pitchers in a manner expected of an ex-Marine who had earned a Purple Heart after being wounded by shrapnel at Iwo Jima. He was a six-foot, 190-pound package of toughness who earned the right to chew on a pitcher's ear by his understanding of the game and his willingness to endure the pain that came with it. He was all business on the field, his dour expression masking a dry sense of humor that could be traced back to growing up in the textile mill town of Lowell, North Carolina.

Caldwell improved his catching skills during his third Tarboro summer and welcomed the first of two sons on January 22, 1949. The Caldwells kept Ralph as the first name, but switched from Franklin to Michael in the middle. They called their son Mike. No one realized it then, but Mike Caldwell eventually would rate two roadside markers in his native town. George Washington, who once spent a night in Tarboro, earned only one.

Brent Braswell, Mike Caldwell's high school baseball coach for two seasons, joked about his former star's advantage over other young athletes.

"His mother sat behind home plate when she was pregnant with Mike," Braswell recalled. "We always said that gave him a head start."

Mike Caldwell threw three no-hitters at Tarboro High School, two of them back to back. In what remains a national high school pitching record for a single game, he struck out 31 batters in a 2–2 tie that went 18 innings. He was a star quarterback at Tarboro High as well, performing in both sports on the same field where his father played for the Tarboro Tars. It would be years later, however, before he realized he was living out the dreams of a catcher whose baseball career leveled off at Class B.

At North Carolina State, he pitched a one-hit shutout against Wake Forest in an Atlantic Coast Conference title game, facing only 27 batters and throwing only 76 times after giving up that one hit on his very first offering. He seldom noticed umpires in those days, but one of the ACC's men in blue was a former pitcher who would make the calls for 19 years. Umpire Eddie Neville never gave Caldwell a break, but he knew even then that his old friend's son—a lefthander like himself—was something special.

Taking time off after victories over Florida State and Alabama in the 1968 NCAA Regionals, Caldwell returned to Tarboro and discovered he would be the guest of honor in a surprise parade. He joined his old football coach in the back of a Lincoln convertible and moved through the middle of town behind the high school marching band.

His major league career that started at San Diego in 1971 was marked by inconsistency until 1978 when he was named the American League Comeback Player of the Year by *The Sporting News*. His 22–9 record and 2.37 earned run average for the Milwaukee Brewers, compared to a 5–8 record the year before, prompted a headline in New York's *Daily News* that asked, "Does He Or Doesn't He?"

Caldwell admitted that he had compared notes with spitballer Gaylord Perry, a North Carolinian like himself, but said he threw spitters only on the sidelines. Still, he teased New York reporters at Yankee Stadium, pushing his hair back and licking the index and middle fingers of his left hand. Caldwell believed his reputation as a spitballer increased his effectiveness. His wife, Lynda, joined in by ordering a Wisconsin license plate spelling out "SPITTER."

"It was just a palmball that broke down and away from right-handed hitters," he insisted. "I was never accused of throwing a spitter in a game by an umpire."

Caldwell retired after the 1984 season, but he returned to the Brewer organization in 1992 as a minor league pitching instructor after five years as the baseball coach at Campbell University in Buies Creek, North Carolina. He finished with a lifetime major league record of 137–130 and picked up two World Series wins against the St. Louis Cardinals in 1982, including a shutout in the opening game.

Ralph Caldwell never saw his son in the World Series. He was divorced and working in a North Carolina textile plant in 1979 when he suffered a heart attack after the car he was driving struck a telephone pole near his home in Lowell. "He was only driving around 20 miles an hour, but he had been suffering from an irregular heartbeat for three years," Mike Caldwell said. His father died the next day.

The union that produced Mike Caldwell was followed by another Tarboro Tar ceremony at the end of the 1948 season. The second marriage matched Ray Komanecky and Ann Assad, his attending nurse when the 30-year-old outfielder received hospital treatment for a sprained ankle. Komanecky's marriage also ended in divorce, but the midwesterner's long love affair with the fiddle, nurtured over two seasons at Tarboro, never stopped.

"My dad had me take violin lessons for a while, and I also played a little in the Navy," recalled Komanecky. But it was in Tarboro, at radio station WCPS, that Komanecky hit full stride with the fiddle as a member of the Carolina Serenaders. "I heard them playing one day, and after a while I asked to join in," he said. Komanecky demonstrated so much talent that he appeared with the group on live radio every Saturday morning.

He also carried his fiddle to the clubhouse. During the race for the 1948 pennant, he reeled off the "Spanish Two-Step," made popular by Bob Wills and the Texas Playboys. Tarboro won that night, and Hamons called on Komanecky to play the same song before every game for the rest of the season. "It became known around the league as our national anthem," related Komanecky, who would relieve the monotony of road trips with string music from the back of the bus.

Komanecky also gave a solo performance for a Tarboro fan who never saw him play a game. "There was a blind man, an older guy, who listened to our games on the radio," said teammate Stan Russell. "He said he wanted to meet me, so Ray and I went to his house. I guess that was my favorite time in baseball. We talked and he touched my face. Ray kept playing the fiddle for him."

Late in the 1948 season, Komanecky retrieved a drive off the center field fence, wheeled, and threw toward second. He heard a pop in his right shoulder, and his throwing ability was never the same after that. After attempting a comeback in 1949 at Goldsboro, he retired from baseball and restricted his playing to the fiddle and country-and-western music.

As a Tarboro Tar, the barrelchested Komanecky was a masterful hitter. As a member of Peg and the Rural Rhythm Boys, the retired resident of Livingston, Illinois, achieved even greater recognition by being named the championship fiddler six years in a row at the Illinois State Fair.

Backed up by the Komanecky-Caldwell-Daniel attack, Neville

moved through the first half of the 1948 season with the same form he demonstrated in the final weeks of 1947. He simply didn't lose.

They fell like dominoes: Roanoke Rapids three times; Goldsboro, New Bern, and Rocky Mount twice; Greenville and Wilson once. His 11 straight wins over 38 days pushed his overall streak over two seasons to 20. He completed 11 of his first 12 starts.

Tarboro's bats were on fire as well, staking Neville to an average of ten and a half runs per game. His fifth win saw the Tars pour across a record 29 runs in a single game against Goldsboro, a cushion that enabled the lefthander to give up eight runs himself and still win by the widest margin in league history.

The Goldsboro runaway hung a punishing defeat on Nelson Suitt, who pitched the entire game, picked up two of his team's eight hits, and suffered a final humiliation when he was replaced by a pinch hitter in the top of the ninth. The Tars drilled Suitt for 22 hits and stole ten bases on the way to a season total of 133.

In late July, Helen Neville proudly occupied one of the concrete seats at the Tarboro park as her son went to the mound against Kinston seeking his twelfth straight victory. Instead, she witnessed a one-run loss, declared herself a jinx, and headed back to Baltimore. She vowed not to return for the rest of the season.

One night after Neville's first loss, Hamons summoned him in the ninth to preserve a lead at Kinston's Grainger Park. When the Eagles scored three runs to hand Neville his second defeat in as many games, no one could blame his mother.

The losing streak reached three in one of the worst performances of Neville's career. After being slapped around for ten runs and 22 hits by Goldsboro, he gave in to recurring back problems and rested four days before going on the disabled list another ten. He stayed away from the park most of the time, but listened to the games and talked baseball with George Rimmer, a telephone company employee who liked to recall his three years as a Coastal Plain outfielder before retiring from the Tars in 1939.

Despite Neville's personal misery, the Tars salted away nine of their next 14 contests and maintained a lead of five games or more. A lineup that would average nearly seven runs per game provided plenty of cushion as another pitcher picked up the slack: Bill See, a skinny but hard-throwing rookie of 26 whose only previous pitching experience had been in the Navy and for a West Virginia paper mill team.

As a seaman third class stationed at a submarine base in Pearl Harbor, See had absorbed pitching advice from teammates Lynwood "Schoolboy" Rowe of the Detroit Tigers and Walt Masterson of the Washington Senators. Stateside, the jug-eared righthander won 18 of 19 in weekend

semipro outings over two years before becoming the Coastal Plain's domi-
nant pitcher in his first and only full season of organized baseball.

As See headed toward a 25–6 season, Neville returned to the mound
against Kinston the second week in August. Back pains forced him out in
the third inning, leading to speculation that he was finished for the season.
Some even said his career was in jeopardy.

The turnaround came four days later in a home game against New
Bern. With both Daniel and Hamons ejected after disputing an umpire's
call that Daniel's fence-clearing drive to right went foul, Hamons inserted
his ailing pitcher at first. Neville drove in the winning run in the bottom
of the ninth with a two-out single.

The next night, a supposedly exhausted Neville received a starting
assignment on the road against the same Goldsboro team that had hammered him 19 days earlier. This time, Neville limited the Goldsbugs to five
hits in ten innings, at one point retiring 16 in a row as he broke his three-
game losing streak. Goldsboro radio announcer Jack Lee was so surprised
that he tacked on more adjectives than usual. The wake was over; Neville
would win four of his last five decisions in the regular season.

Hamons, with only 19 games left and holding a lead of eight and a half
games, took time after a rainout to examine the rest of the schedule. "I may
sound cocky saying this," he began, "but I do feel confident that we won't
end up any lower than second place. I won't say we'll cop the flag." With
a huge lead and no sign of a letdown, the publicly cautious manager had
pulled off a classic understatement.

With one exception, the final week of the season was a light-hearted
time for the Tars. The pennant was theirs, being clinched on the same
night that a successful protest wiped out a victory at home over archrival
Rocky Mount. Second-place Goldsboro also lost to remain nine games
back with eight to go.

The protest came after Rocky Mount Manager Cecil "Turkey"
Tyson spotted a man out of uniform warming up a Tarboro pitcher.
Although the incident had no effect on the outcome of the game, League
President Ray Goodmon agreed with Tyson's interpretation of a little-
known rule and awarded a victory to the Leafs.

Hamons had protested the game as well, claiming that Tyson had run
his team from the grandstand after being thrown out. When the deadline

*Opposite:* **The 1948 Tarboro Tars, winners of the Coastal Plain League
pennant as well as the playoffs. Front row, left to right: Bill See, Eddie
Neville, Eddie Luszcynski, Jimmy Townes, Ray Komanecky, Steve Mar-
kos, Ray Dietrich, and Bob Stapenhorst. Back row: Manager Bull
Hamons, Ralph Caldwell, Jake Richards, Tommy Pritchard, Jake Daniel,
Ray Urban, Ken Andrewsh, Stan Russell, and Ed Smith. The batboy is
Bobby Frye. (Courtesy Janet Neville.)**

Cecil "Turkey" Tyson, Rocky Mount's colorful manager in 1948, hitches up his pants as a member of the 1947 Durham Bulls. (Courtesy Cecil Tyson.)

arrived for paying a fee of $100 for the grievance to be heard, the Tars backed off. The club saved another $25 by voting not to appeal Goodmon's decision calling for a forfeit.

The euphoria of a pennant was interrupted two nights after the protested game when Hamons and Kinston Manager Steve Collins swapped insults and came close to a fist fight. The feud that started in the 1947 playoffs—when Collins spiked a Tarboro player and refused to waive a rule banning late roster additions—was erupting once again. It would reach a climax in the coming weeks.

That one temper flareup aside, Hamons eased up in the closing days of the regular season and made sure his club would be loose at playoff time. To please his fellow Georgian and to rest his staff, he allowed Jake Daniel to pitch an entire game at Guy Smith Stadium in Greenville. Greenie batting averages benefited from 15 hits as the big first baseman gave up seven runs in a losing effort.

Catcher Ralph Caldwell started on the mound at home the next night, retired the Greenies in order, then rotated to a different position every inning. It would be a night to remember for Caldwell, who also picked up two hits and drove in a run.

Neville was equally effective, pitching seven innings of three-hit relief and scoring the winning run after doubling in the last of the eighth. His final record of 15–4 resulted in an even higher winning percentage than 1947 (.789 to .738) despite an earned run average that jumped from 2.31 to 3.22.

The final game of the regular season saw Hamons at his softest. A Tarboro barber, Carl Weaver, had promised infielder Ken Andrewsh a beagle puppy for batting .300. When Andrewsh failed to hit in his first two times at bat against visiting Goldsboro, Hamons benched him and preserved his average at .303. Hamons was more of a motivator than a mathematician; Andrewsh actually could have gone hitless in seven trips and still have been eligible for his prize hound.

It was a surprising about-face for the Tarboro manager, who only nine days earlier had suspended the adventurous Andrewsh for breaking a clause in his contract that required all players to "conform . . . to standards of good citizenship and good sportsmanship." The Pennsylvanian missed the pennant-clinching Rocky Mount series and one game against Kinston, but returned to the starting lineup with a full week to go in the regular season.

After finishing first with an 87–53 record, Tarboro took dead aim on fourth-place Rocky Mount in a best-of-seven series to determine the opponent for the winner of the playoff between second-place Kinston and third-place Goldsboro.

Along the Coastal Plain, the Tarboro–Rocky Mount rivalry had become as explosive as Harry Truman's strategy to end the war. The 17 miles between the communities was a suitable spitting distance. And neither was pleased that part of Rocky Mount spilled beyond a boundary that Tarboro ruled as the county seat.

The very honor of two towns was at stake every time little Tarboro was matched against a larger and more prosperous neighbor that touted itself as the site of Jim Thorpe's professional baseball debut. Thorpe played for the Rocky Mount Railroaders for part of the 1909 and 1910 seasons, just long enough to lose his amateur status and be forced to give up the gold medals he won at the 1912 Olympics. His contribution to baseball suffered in comparison to that of Rocky Mount resident Walter "Buck" Leonard, a future Hall of Famer who would retire that same summer of 1948 after a 15-year career as a first baseman with the Homestead Grays of the Negro National League.

But neither Thorpe nor Leonard counted in the Coastal Plain playoffs. The spotlight fell on two field generals whose hard-nosed approach to baseball had been drilled into their very souls. Hamons and the Leafs' Cecil "Turkey" Tyson had met when they played on the same club in Hagerstown, Maryland, striking up a friendship that would have watered down the Tarboro–Rocky Mount rivalry had fans realized the closeness of the two off the field.

Jake Daniel recalled the time he and Hamons visited the Tyson family's Elm City farmhouse to sample an ample supply of white lightning stored in the cool of the basement. "The stuff came in all sorts of flavors," Daniel said. "Some of it even tasted like peppermint candy."

After emptying several glass jars, the three left the basement, stood momentarily in the sun, then staggered around the farmyard in a brotherhood that would be forgotten at game time.

Tyson, forever branded with a nickname that described his turkeylike running and what some players perceived as his gobbling way of talking, was far more serious on the field despite antics that included swiveling his hips at the plate to force a slight drop of the pants.

The lanky, left-handed first baseman had followed a baseball trail that carried him from the tobacco fields of Elm City to the playing fields of Oak Ridge Military Academy, to England (where he was one of six Americans selected to instruct young Brits on the finer points of the game), from Class D to Triple A, and then—for a short time in 1944—a stop in the majors with the Philadelphia Phillies. When he returned to Class D as a 34-year-old player-manager, his reputation as an ex–big leaguer made him even taller than his six-foot-five frame.

A tough bird like his nickname and one of the most colorful characters ever to play minor league baseball, Tyson actually feared going to

Tarboro. "Those people would ride the devil out of you," he said. "Our fans, when they went over there, could get locked up in a damn minute."

Tyson himself avoided the jailhouse, but found himself flanked by police after arguing too long and too strenuously in one game at Tarboro. Tyson baited the plate umpire throughout the game, finally growing so enraged over ball and strike calls that he protested in nose-to-nose fashion. Refusing to leave the field after being ejected, the feisty manager was escorted to the dugout by Tarboro police.

Tyson's cousin, Jasper Tyson, was even less fortunate when he came to Tarboro with two friends from Elm City. One of the visitors caught a foul ball in the stands and refused to return it to the field. To aggravate the situation, the threesome played keepaway and a near-riot ensued.

Cousin Jasper and his pals ended up in jail. Tyson and others from Rocky Mount appealed for their release, but they remained in the lockup until a call was placed to Congressman L. H. Fountain, a Tarboro resident. It took that much power to rescue Rocky Mount fans from enemy turf.

Tyson perceived baseball as a game of being knocked down by pitches, standing up, dusting yourself off, and preparing to go down again. "There was no law then," he said, "about knocking 'em down."

He was prepared for the physical challenges, not by sophisticated training programs, but by managers who, as he put it, would "take you out there and run your tail to death." And Tyson was such a manager, running his charges up and down fields across North Carolina until retiring after the 1952 season.

Baseball, Tyson admitted, had been the biggest part of his life, "more important than anything else. That's what I mainly was, a ballplayer. It was a way to get off the farm."

After leaving baseball, Tyson returned to his home town to live on the same family farm where his father once traded mules for extra cash. He leased the land to others and retired to the life of a gentleman farmer as he rode his pickup truck around town with his favorite dog at his side and stopped off for a cup of coffee with the boys. Even as the years passed, he continued to sign autographs as requests came from across the country.

Tyson would square off with Neville over two seasons, at Rocky Mount in 1948 and at Raleigh in 1949 when Neville won 25 games at Durham. As a lefty facing a lefty, Tyson was always at a disadvantage. So he was not disappointed in 1950 when the two went in opposite directions, Neville to Toledo and Tyson to Lumberton, North Carolina.

In the playoff showdown with Hamons, he knew he was in for a genuine street fight against a manager and friend that he described as "just as mean a man as ever walked." For Hamons, that was a compliment. "All of them boys from LaGrange were tough," said Tyson. "You had to be tough to play."

His toughness aside, Hamons had been outmaneuvered by Tyson on at least two occasions. In addition to his successful late-season protest that led to the awarding of a Rocky Mount victory over Tarboro, Tyson had managed to one-up his former teammate in a 1947 exhibition game matching the Tars and Durham.

With Tyson playing first base for Durham, Hamons called for a "reverse shift" in an attempt to take advantage of his old rival's tendency to hit to the opposite field. Positioning his entire infield and outfield to the left, Hamons saw his strategy backfire when Tyson—in his first time at bat—tripled to deep center field.

Even in the case of a promotional stunt, when Tyson and Hamons were matched in a foot race around the bases, their competitive instincts took over. Tyson, trotting like a turkey, and Hamons, charging and plodding like a bull, squared off as laughter replaced the usual jeers and heckling.

Who won? "I did," swore Tyson. "Bull couldn't run a lick." Hamons actually tried to cut across the field from second to home, but Tyson tripped him and victory was assured.

The playoffs represented a far more serious confrontation than the foot race. "They'll be hanging from the light poles out at the Tarboro ballpark tonight," wrote Lewis Heilbroner in the *Daily Southerner.* "In Tarboro and Rocky Mount, suppers will be gobbled up hastily, the dishes left undone, and the families will pile in the jalopy and head for the Tarboro park."

Not only was the series the social event of the season, it also matched a Tarboro club with a combined batting average of .303 against a pair of workhorse Rocky Mount pitchers—Harry Helmer and future Wilson mayor Horace "Red" Benton—who between them had won 54 games. But even those two, backed by a team that led the league with 114 home runs, could do little to stop a batting attack headed by Jake Daniel at .367 and Ray Komanecky at .366.

Hamons entered the series with only two healthy pitchers who had been with the team since the start of the season—himself and Bill See, who would follow up his selection as the league's Most Valuable Player with three playoff victories.

Stan Russell was among the missing pitchers; he had been promoted to Durham in mid-August. When the Tars team picture was taken, Russell was off the roster but stayed around long enough to pose in his street pants and a borrowed jersey.

Neville continued to have back problems. He performed poorly in two relief appearances, losing one and pitching ineffectively in an opening game setback that saw Hamons remove himself after walking four and giving up four hits in the first inning.

The Tars lost two of the first three before finishing in a dead heat in the most suspenseful game of all—a fogbound 8–8 tie at Tarboro that was called by the umpires shortly after Hamons threatened to pull his team off the field.

Tarboro bats took over after that with 20 hits and 16 runs in one game and 16 hits and ten runs in another. Tyson knew the series was over in the sixth game when the first five Tar batters reached base in the bottom of the first. He went to the mound, told starter Bob Jones he was through, and watched as the frustrated pitcher wheeled and threw the ball over the left field fence.

Hamons, his life enriched by the $225 that fans had collected before the game, turned his attention to a Kinston team that had reached the playoff finals after eliminating Goldsboro. He hardly expected the bizarre developments that followed.

The series started like a Rocky Mount rerun. The same Ray Dietrich whose wildness had frightened one of his own teammates a year earlier walked the first five Eagle batters and Tarboro never caught up.

Kinston players, however, were steaming over the team's failure to pay a bonus that they claimed had been promised for reaching the playoffs. "We had a clubhouse meeting just after I joined the team in July," said outfielder Bill Jeffries, the Joe DiMaggio lookalike who started the season at Tarboro. "We were in fifth place at the time, and the owners said we'd get a bonus for making the playoffs."

The bonus never came. "They told us it was illegal to pay bonuses, but that was kind of ridiculous," said Jeffries. "Some of us were getting paid under the table anyway."

After the first Tarboro game, the Kinston players met the next morning at a pool hall. Eleven agreed to a wildcat strike. Manager Steve Collins scrambled around town for enough warm bodies to fill a lineup card and showed up in Tarboro that night with only five regulars and an assortment of semi-pros. A year earlier, Collins had refused to let Tarboro replace injured players in the playoffs. This time, he tried to forfeit the rest of the series but was ordered onto the field.

Tarboro had 22 hits that night and won by 13 runs. League President Ray Goodmon threatened the players with a lifetime ban if the strike continued. The Tarboro club complained to the national minor league headquarters.

The wildcatters returned but continued to fume over a bonus they never saw. Several complained about the club's tight-fisted policy that led to the sale of star first baseman Fred "Pap" Williams—a one-time Cleveland Indian—to Rocky Mount late in the season. Goodmon sided with the owners. He denied the existence of a bonus arrangement, fined each player $50, and took away a day's pay.

One of those hit by the fine was outfielder Frank Fabianich. Fabianich, who first played for the Eagles in 1946, had given up his job at a
Weirton, West Virginia, steel mill and rejoined the team in August. "My
father was out of work, and I sent part of my pay to him," recalled Fabianich. "I left Kinston with almost nothing."

The series wasn't the same after the second game as the Tars turned
40 hits and 36 runs into three straight wins. Kinston's Jeffries knew it was
over when he stepped to the plate and saw a newspaper story on the strike
taped to one of Ralph Caldwell's shin guards.

Neville wasn't exactly laughing. His back problems had been replaced
by a swollen knee, but he preserved a win in the series-clinching sixth game
with eight shaky relief innings. The playoffs marked the end of Neville's
double-duty seasons except in winter baseball. He picked up ten playoff
hits, most of them as a right fielder. His .265 average for the season was
up 24 points over 1947.

His latest pitching numbers came up short only against the backdrop
of the season before. His shutouts dropped from six to none; his earned
run average jumped from 2.31 to 3.22. He finished with a 15–4 record,
completing 17 of 19 starts. But this time there would be no offers from the
Beaumonts or Chattanoogas. He would remain under contract with
Charles Allen and pitch the next season for the Tarboro owner's other
North Carolina team, the Durham Bulls.

In the meantime, he settled for all the accolades that accompanied a
championship season. Two fans, Clara Ruth Mashburn and Dot Howard,
were inspired to write poems for the newspaper in honor of Neville and the
rest of the Tars. Mayor H. I. Johnson was more ecstatic than poetic, issuing
a statement that praised the players as "hard-playing athletes" and "clean-
living men." Caught up in the excitement of victory, Mayor Johnson could
be forgiven for an overly generous tribute that was only half right.

Many of the Tars would move "up baseball's ladder" as the good
mayor predicted, but none would reach the very top. Of the more than 200
players who appeared on league rosters during Neville's two seasons, only
one would make it to the major leagues.

In 1948, a 21-year-old rookie lefthander from Puerto Rico struck out
Coastal Plain batters at a rate of more than one an inning and demonstrated potential far beyond his 9–13 record and 4.34 earned run average
for last-place Greenville. Screwballer Luis Arroyo won another five of
eight decisions that season after his contract was sold to Greensboro of the
Carolina League, and his 21–10 record for the same club in 1949 included
a victory over Neville in their only pitching matchup over two seasons. Arroyo's most memorable season came in 1961 when he made a league-high
65 relief appearances for the New York Yankees, posted a 15–5 record, and
picked up a World Series victory over the St. Louis Cardinals.

An inability to develop a larger number of young stars was not the only sign of the league's imminent decline. Teams tottered atop a house of cards consisting of shaky finances and increasingly shoddy operations. Most Coastal Plain clubs operated in the red in 1948, several reportedly losing $10,000 or more as costs were driven up by competition for veteran players.

Coastal Plain rosters had been expanded that season from 15 to 16, with the number of veteran players increasing from three to four. Splattered by red ink, the league reduced the number of veterans back to three in 1949, trimmed the number of limited service players from eight to four, and doubled the rookie allotment from four to eight.

The days of powerhouse clubs full of characters, charisma, and even a little chaos began winding down after that. In Tarboro, the joy of a championship season that would lift an entire town's spirit in September would be nothing more than a pleasant memory by April.

When the 1949 season opened, Tarboro players took the field as farm hands of the Philadelphia Athletics. The team's Carolina-flavored nickname had been replaced by the parent club's. Not one player from the championship team returned to the friendly park on Panola Street, the characters and old pros replaced by youngsters willing to accept lower wages.

Bull Hamons became manager at New Bern, taking Jake Daniel and Bill See with him and recruiting Roy Kennedy from the Canal Zone once again. Hamons would settle for a third-place finish, two notches above Tarboro, then fall in the first round of the playoffs to his old rival Collins, who privately admitted that even he had a fondness for the portly hothead from Georgia.

Hamons resurfaced as manager of last-place Rocky Mount in the middle of the 1951 season. Roanoke Rapids' fans welcomed him back with a special night, but no one cheered or booed in Tarboro; their own team had run out of money and quit the league 19 days before Hamons' return.

Tarboro tried again in 1952, but finished seventh and drew next-to-nothing crowds. The league went out of business shortly before the scheduled start of the 1953 season, a victim of changing times.

Most of the players from the Neville era went on to ordinary jobs like many of the fans who once had cheered them. Steve Collins wore a different uniform when he left his house in Browns Summit, North Carolina; he was a brakeman and conductor for the Southern Railway Company. Gashouse Parker remained in Edenton, North Carolina, after managing there at the end of the 1952 Coastal Plain League season; he later worked for a fish market and became a popular storyteller at the town fire station. Both Collins and Parker are deceased, and it is not difficult for an imaginative baseball mind to visualize the two squabbling somewhere with Bull Hamons.

In their retirement years, Pete Clark, Ray Komanecky, Stan Russelavage, and Cecil "Turkey" Tyson could savor some of the same moments
recalled by Jake Daniel in LaGrange, Georgia; Ray Dietrich in Seven
Valleys, Pennsylvania; Art Ferguson in Zanesville, Ohio; Russ Hand in
Pottsville, Pennsylvania; Bill Jeffries in Glenn Dale, Maryland; Roy Kennedy in Englewood, Colorado; and Bill See in Keyser, West Virginia.

They played so long ago and in such provincial places that most of
them will be remembered more for their lives after baseball instead of the
magical time when all those things happened that made the bush leagues
a blend of the outstanding and outrageous. When Neville received a free
train ticket and $2.50 in meal money to move on to the loftier heights of
Class B the next season, he left behind a vanishing piece of America.

# The House of Outs

*The general manager of WDNC always gave me a quarter when he arrived at our house for a poker game and found the dial on our console radio turned to his station. When he visited on summer nights in 1949, I gratefully accepted the quarter and went upstairs to listen to the Bulls' game on rival station WSSB.*

The first piece of real estate owned by Eddie Neville occupied most of a city block in Durham, a baseball arena known as Durham Athletic Park. Not that he had title to the property, but he did become the master of a place that tortured batters from the right side, then teased left-handed swingers when they faced Neville and other southpaws.

It was a park of eclectic dimensions dictated by the boundaries of streets and business buildings. Fence distances started at a healthy 360 feet in left, swept out to an imposing 460 feet in center, and tightened to a snug 301 feet in right.

Home run shots had to soar rather than merely fly, the elevation pushed up by a bank that bordered the outfield. A ten-foot tin fence sat atop the bank and stretched from the left field foul line to dead center. The barrier, including the bank, reached 25 feet starting in far right center field and running to the right field foul line, first with a brick building housing an automobile dealership and then with a kingsize scoreboard that backed up to a tobacco warehouse.

The wooden scoreboard extended some 50 feet inside the foul line and was fronted by a porch that enabled a youngster to mount a ladder to post tin signs with numbers painted on each side. Green lights operated from the press box signaled balls. Strikes were flashed in red, outs in orange. A white light signaled an error on questionable scoring plays.

The deepest point in center field was uncharted territory for even the best in the game. Ted Williams and Jimmie Foxx played at the park in exhibition games in 1939 and 1940, but their best shot was a home run over the right field wall by Foxx. Joe DiMaggio couldn't clear center in 1941, nor could Stan Musial in his lone plate appearance in 1942.

Musial's St. Louis Cardinal teammate, second baseman Frank "Creepy" Crespi, hit an inside-the-park home run in that same game when he connected on a pitch by Detroit's Paul "Dizzy" Trout and drove the ball atop the bank in left center. A handful of inside-the-park homers by Carolina League sluggers would follow Crespi's feat, but fans who watched the Bulls and Bees and Leafs and Luckies were more likely to see extra base hits assisted by one of four light poles that stood in the field of play and threatened to flatten fly-chasing outfielders.

Although there is no record as to the number of Carolina Leaguers clearing the fence in deep center, long-time Durham fans do agree on one name: Greg "The Bull" Luzinski, whose blast came in 1969 when the future Phillie and White Sox star played first base for the Raleigh-Durham Phillies, a team that split its home games between the two cities.

The left field fence was more reachable but hardly friendly. The record for individual Durham batters clearing the barrier and sending baseballs bouncing toward West Geer Street stood at a mere three per season. Visiting clubs, in town for only 20 games, seldom collected that many as a team.

Neville quickly converted the park into his personal house of outs, a gracious and properly spacious place that might have earned him a spot in Cooperstown if he could have carried it on the road for the rest of his career. He was troubled by the close confines of the scoreboard only in his first Durham season; after that, he was more likely to reach it with his own bat rather than serve one up to the opposition.

Closing out its first decade of play in Neville's first season, Durham Athletic Park was a thoroughly modern arena compared to its ancestors. The first game in Durham under the banner of organized baseball was played in 1902 at the George Lyon Ball Park, a modest facility with a cemetery for a neighbor. Doherty Park, owned by the electric light and power company that operated the city's streetcars, had been used by city league teams for three years before the Bulls occupied it in 1913. When female fans started staying away from Doherty because of its rundown condition and the vulgarity of some of the spectators, a group of investors—including team owner Dr. L. E. Booker—purchased an eight-acre site just before the start of the 1926 season and in less than three months built a wooden park they named El Toro.

Hoping to broaden the team's fan base, the Bulls' management provided a maid in the women's rest room and waited just one game to offer free passes on "Ladies' Day." After that, general admission tickets for women cost a quarter—still a bargain at half price.

With a Pathe cameraman shooting newsreel footage that would be

**El Toro Park, the predecessor of Durham Athletic Park. (Courtesy Special Collections Library, Duke University.)**

seen in movie houses across the country, El Toro was dedicated on July 26, 1926, in ceremonies presided over by North Carolina Governor Angus W. McLean and Judge Kenesaw Mountain Landis, the powerful baseball commissioner. Six years earlier, in one of his first declarations after taking office, Landis had insisted that Shoeless Joe Jackson and six other members of the Chicago White Sox accused of throwing the 1919 World Series had "absolutely no chance . . . to creep back into organized baseball." At El Toro, the white-haired authoritarian stepped out of his courtly character just long enough to ride the live but tranquil bull that had been introduced as the official mascot at the park's opening game 19 days earlier.

After the 1933 season, El Toro became the property of the City of Durham. Philanthropist John Sprunt Hill and his wife presented a check for $20,000 to the city to buy the park and land from Homeland Investment Co., a Hill-related firm that had assumed ownership after the original investors had run into debt during the Depression.

Hill, chairman of the board of Durham Loan and Trust Co. and president of Home Savings Bank, attached three conditions to his gift. He specified in the deed that the park be sold for cash at public auction if it ceased to be used for athletic, recreational, and park purposes. Funds from the sale, he stipulated, should be reinvested in other property for the same use. Hill expressed hope that the park would not be used on Sundays for "commercialized athletics" charging admission. He also asked that it be renamed Durham Athletic Park.

The city met Hill halfway. When the Bulls resumed play in 1936 after a two-year absence because of the Depression, the schedule included Sabbath games in a park that no longer had a Spanish name.

Although it was just an infield throw from the five-story brick tower where city firemen conducted drills, the original Durham Athletic Park was destined to go down in flames like its wooden counterparts in Baltimore and Tarboro. On June 17, 1939, less than two hours after the Bulls had lost to the Winston-Salem Twins, the park fell victim to a fire that originated in the adjacent Big Bull tobacco warehouse.

A passerby noticed the fire and called police headquarters at 11:20 P.M. Groundskeeper Walter Williams, who slept under the stands, had stored his equipment and retired for the night when he heard the crackling of flames. He ran to safety through the center field gate.

Hundreds of people, many of them dressed only in pajamas or robes, watched as the park was reduced to ruins in less than two hours. As firemen struggled to keep the blaze from spreading to nearby houses, the proprietor of a nearby lunch room started selling sandwiches and soft drinks.

Damage estimates ran as high as $125,000. The Bulls lost everything but their road uniforms, which were salvaged only because they had been taken to the dry cleaners. Without a park, the city had to move quickly for the Bulls to retain their Piedmont League franchise. Bleachers were borrowed from Duke University. Temporary wooden stands running 126 feet down the third-base line were ready for play in 15 days. Since some of the wood was salvaged from the old grandstand, the net cost to the city—including a new fence—was only $1,010.61.

After playing a doubleheader at Duke's home field, the Bulls hit the road before returning home July 2 to meet the Charlotte Hornets. Although an estimated 1,000 fans turned out for that Sunday afternoon contest, the Bulls were forced to switch seven home dates in late July to Norfolk and Portsmouth when attendance declined after newly ordered lights failed to arrive on time.

A permanent lighting system costing $6,300 was in place when the Bulls met the Rocky Mount Red Sox on August 3. The contest was illuminated by 160 bulbs, 40 more than the pre-fire figure.

Less than two months after the season ended, bids totaling $48,467 were approved for the construction of a new Durham Athletic Park. The original plans had to be trimmed back after initial low bids of $85,747 far exceeded the city budget of $50,000, but architect George Watts Carr still managed to create a cozy and personable facility whose 1,909 grandstand and box seats offered an up-close look at dramas being played out on a field with the strangest of dimensions.

Except for the replacement of wood with concrete and steel in the construction of the grandstand, the new and old parks were similar in design. The seating arrangement was exactly the same. The "colored bleachers" at the new park were on the right field side of the 14-row grandstand; bleachers for white fans were on the left field side originally and later

**A record crowd of 6,492 overflows Durham Athletic Park at the Durham Bulls' final home game of 1992. (Courtesy *The Herald-Sun*.)**

were expanded to include a separate section in right. (When Durham High School and North Carolina College football games were played at the park, the left field bleachers became the home side. The football playing field ran parallel to the bleachers.)

The park made its debut on April 7, 1940, when Cincinnati defeated the Boston Red Sox in a Sunday afternoon exhibition game. The announced crowd of 5,574 was said to have been surpassed only by a game several years earlier when fans were admitted for a dime. Ten days later, only 1,587 fans were on hand when the Bulls lost their home opener to Winston-Salem.

By the time Neville arrived nine years later, the city had enjoyed some of its grandest years in baseball, with attendance climbing to record numbers after the formation of the Class C Carolina League and the subsequent end of the war. The man behind the formation of the league was none other than Herb Brett, Neville's manager at Wilmington for that trial run in 1942.

Brett had trooped through city after city in 1944, convinced that baseball could gain enough support from war workers and others who remained behind. "We are going to win the war soon," he said, "and the sooner we start making plans to form a league the sooner we will have baseball again."

Brett lined up a league so geographically compact that rain usually forced the postponement of all four games. Two cities—Danville and

Martinsville—were just over the state line in Virginia, a fact that prompted a proposal at an early directors' meeting to name the league Caro-ginia. North Carolina entries included Burlington, Durham, Greensboro, Leaksville (replaced by Reidsville in 1948), Raleigh, and Winston-Salem.

With Brett continuing to play a key role as a league director and as president and manager of the Danville club, an estimated 536,000 people paid to see a combination of teenagers, older players, and 4-Fers in the inaugural season of 1945. The figure topped a million two years later, but settled back to 789,539 in 1949 despite the league's new Class B status.

The league was so young that only one major leaguer had been produced before Neville's arrival. Tom Wright, a Durham outfielder who hit a league-leading .381 in 1946, became the first graduate when he reached the Boston Red Sox for a brief period in 1948.

In 1949, alumni ranks increased by three with the promotion of first baseman Steve Bilko to the St. Louis Cardinals, outfielder Gus Zernial to the Chicago White Sox, and outfielder Tom Saffell to the Pittsburgh Pirates. In the early fifties, the list would expand to include such familiar names as third baseman Ray Jablonski, outfielder Eldon "Rip" Repulski, and pitchers Luis Arroyo, Hal "Skinny" Brown, Harry Byrd, Art Fowler, Harvey Haddix, Johnny Klippstein, Stu Miller, Wilmer "Vinegar Bend" Mizell, and Tom Poholsky (who was only 15 years old when he pitched at Durham in 1945).

Arroyo, a Greensboro Patriot, and Repulski, a Winston-Salem Cardinal, became the only big leaguers of note to emerge from the 1949 season as most clubs took advantage of the jump in classifications and loaded up with veteran players whose glory years were no longer in front of them.

Although Durham ranked as North Carolina's third largest city that year with a population more than 70,000, it really was just a grown-up tobacco town that proudly produced 19 percent of the nation's cigarette supply. Country clubbers ruled the "Bull City," but blue collars in tobacco factories and textile plants kept it running.

The city and its baseball team derived their nicknames from a famous smoking mixture known as Bull Durham, as did, according to most accounts, the baseball term bullpen.

In the early 1900s, large bull-shaped signs advertising the roll-your-own tobacco towered above the outfield fence at almost every minor and major league park, including Doherty in Durham. The bullpen designation, most baseball historians say, originated from relief pitchers warming up in the shade of the 40-foot by 25-foot signs in the days before night baseball.

The signs enjoyed other uses as well. When a record crowd overflowed the Huntington Avenue Baseball Grounds in Boston in 1911, men in

**The 1913 Durham Bulls in front of one of the famous Bull Durham signs that most baseball historians say led to the baseball term bullpen. (Courtesy Miles Wolff.)**

derbies, skimmers, and touring caps scrambled for space between the sign's horns and along the back all the way to a looping tail.

Blackwell's Durham Tobacco Company, one of the predecessors to American Tobacco Company, once offered $50 to any player hitting the sign. A carton containing 72 packs of tobacco was awarded for a home run in a park with a sign. In 1910, with some 150 signs in place, the company coughed up $4,250 in cash and more than 10,000 pounds of tobacco. No extra incentive was offered for striking the bull's increasingly controversial testicles, which in later advertising disappeared behind conveniently placed shrubs and fence posts.

Neville, a pack-a-day Pall Mall man, had the same bulge in his shirt pocket as most Durham adult males—their habits confirming equal portions of civic pride and nicotine addiction. And long before the "You've Come a Long Way, Baby" advertising campaign, multitudes of raspy-voiced Durham women puffed and emptied ash trays at the same time.

The city's cigarette smokers could choose from among 44 locally made brands. Liggett & Myers featured Chesterfield, which owed much of its popularity to its billing as "The Baseball Man's Cigarette" that somehow was "Always Milder, Better Tasting, [and] Cooler Smoking." As rival American Tobacco punched back with Lucky Strike and Herbert Tareyton, the city's economy was fueled by a stream of tobacco smoke that could have formed a cloud resembling an atomic bomb blast if every puffer had stood outside and exhaled at the same time.

In September, farmers hauled millions of pounds of cured tobacco into Durham warehouses and listened attentively as the golden leaves were sold off amid the chants of auctioneers. The sharp and curiously appealing aroma of aging tobacco drifted toward Durham Athletic Park from factory-owned storage areas both to the east and west, including the sprawling Bullington warehouse just two blocks away and the smaller R. J. Reynolds building behind the scoreboard.

For the most part, Durham remained an unspoiled, unsophisticated place whose working-class people fit the description in the theme song of a hillbilly disc jockey who called himself "Country Boy" and complained about the "humi-didity." Just like their radio host, they were plain, cornbread-lovin' folks who raised Cain on Saturday but went to church on Sunday. Sabbath afternoons often started with lunch at modest eating places like Durham Dairy, where white-haired folks decked out in aprons and little paper hats served milk shakes and toasted sandwiches that came complete with pickle chips.

Signs that Durham had an unstuffed shirt were all around. At Gates' Cash Grocery, Erskine Gates presided from his perch atop a kingsize stool as the boys swizzled beer and shared laughs when youngsters would buy the soiled but still colorful balls of gum from a machine that had a removable top. Most of the time, the gum would be recycled as customers put in pennies and gambled on matching up colors in a crude form of five-card stud.

At a hot dog emporium named Amos & Andy (after the radio show starring the two-man team that first met in Durham), customers in suits sat alongside tieless types at school desks that lined the wall across from the counter. After they deposited one hot dog on the desktop in a chili-stained wrapper, they washed another one down with a six-ounce bottle of Coke or a 12-ounce Pepsi.

Norris Eubanks, sweat dripping from his brow, dressed the wieners in Olympian fashion after slapping them into soft rolls lined up along the length of one arm to meet rush hour demands. The dogs were considered such a delicacy that latecomers were satisfied to slip to the back and down a hurried lunch in the company of garbage cans and flies.

Down the street at the Cosmopolitan Barber Shop, a paradoxical form of segregation was practiced as black barbers catered to white-only clientele, dutifully dusting them off with talcum powder amid a symphony of chatter. The snipping would be interrupted by an occasional sideshow when one of the barbers would spin in a circle as he rotated the customer's chair.

Walking the streets of downtown Durham could be equally entertaining—as well as enlightening. The usual street sounds often were interrupted by chanting female members of a religious group called the "Heavenly Light." Dressed in white robes and white headpieces, their message was always the same: "The Lord done told me to tell the world that Jesus is soon to come." And since their performances were always solo, most citizens assumed it was the same woman every time.

When the fast-walking evangelists looked the other way, the fun-seeking citizenry could duck into movie houses that screened just about every B-grade film to make it out of Hollywood. The Rialto, Criterion, and Uptown offered the Dead End Kids, Monte Hale, and Lash LaRue, while the more upscale Center booked Martin and Lewis. The Astor, a girlie-show spot said to be a haven for rats that ran up customers' legs, salvaged its reputation in later years when the building was turned into a tabernacle. At the Carolina, they gave out free Donald Duck twin popsicles at Saturday morning cartoon shows.

Radio listeners could enjoy a local program called "Scavenger Hunt." The weekday show offered a prize of $25 to the first person to bring in six specific items, including such unusual requests as a picture of ventriloquist Edgar Bergen's dummy, Charlie McCarthy. When two competing neighborhood groups started winning almost every day, station officials cancelled the show after realizing the rest of the audience had disappeared.

For literary types, downtown Durham offered the Drive-In News Stand, perhaps the first and last business of its kind. Long before drive-in windows at fast food places, the Drive-In News Stand was just that—a garagelike place where you could drive your car alongside an assortment of magazines and comic books, take your pick, and drive out. It lasted only a few years, presumably a victim of poor business and carbon monoxide fumes.

The more fashionable set could spend their time decorating their homes with Venetian blinds custom-made right in the city. The latest in aluminum blinds offered a plastic finish touted as "fireproof, rustproof, and warp-proof." They showed up in windows all over town, a symbol of both beauty and danger to housewives who hung the sharp-edged blinds on clotheslines and suffered nicked fingers soaping them down.

When it came to sports, however, Durham was as sophisticated as the sidewalks of New York on an Easter Sunday. Games rotated from baseball summers at Durham Athletic Park to football falls at horseshoe-shaped Duke Stadium, where on January 1, 1942, Oregon State's Beavers defeated Duke University's Blue Devils 20–16 in a Rose Bowl that had been transplanted because of the threat of bombing attacks on the Pacific coast. The stadium for years boasted an on-site barbecue pit where the Carolina delicacy was prepared for sandwiches on game day after butchered hogs had been cooked over hickory coals the night before.

In the winter, fans had followed basketball ever since North Carolina's first intercollegiate game had been played in Durham in 1906. Durham High School had run up a winning streak of 72 games that ended in 1941. A year earlier, Duke had dedicated its 8,800-seat Indoor Stadium, which at the time was the largest arena south of the Palestra in Philadelphia. The gymnasium was later renamed Cameron Indoor Stadium in honor of longtime Duke Athletic Director Eddie Cameron.

Called "Cameron Crazies" today, the Duke students were almost as vocal then, but their lunacy was limited to the tossing of fresh apples to one another after buying them at the concession stands at halftime. The gym also housed two game clocks whose faces turned red, not with embarrassment but only to signal the final minute of each half.

Durham was full of fans who pulled against Duke as well, saving their cheers for North Carolina's Tar Heels at nearby Chapel Hill or two other institutions only a half hour away: North Carolina State at Raleigh and Wake Forest in the town of the same name. The schools made up the notorious Big Four, a name still used today even though Wake Forest pulled up stakes in 1956 after being lured to Winston-Salem by financial guarantees from the Z. Smith Reynolds Foundation.

Durham was more than a mere site of games. For 15 years, it served as the headquarters for the National Association of Professional Baseball Leagues during the presidency of Judge William G. Bramham. Given the judge's title since he was older and more stern-looking than other students at the University of North Carolina Law School, Bramham had organized and served as president of both the North Carolina and Piedmont leagues. He also had served as president of the Bulls from 1913–15.

For most of his tenure, Bramham ruled the minors from twelfth-floor offices in Durham's tallest building, where he developed a file of over 100,000 index cards that tracked the move of every player. He was a stern sort who railed against gambling and insisted that league presidents hand out suspensions of 90 days or more for attacks on umpires. In 1942, he slapped a one-year suspension on Ben Chapman, a former major league outfielder and player-manager at Richmond in the Piedmont League, for slugging umpire I. H. Case.

During a reign that ended with his retirement shortly before his death in 1947 at the age of 72, Bramham demonstrated his love for the purity of the game and shunned stunts to boost attendance. "Damn the monkeyshines," he would say. His outspokenness was never more apparent than when he implied that Branch Rickey considered himself a "Moses" for signing Jackie Robinson.

Bramham was not the only baseball power broker with Durham ties.

Two general managers presided over the Bulls on their way to front offices at the top: Frank "Trader" Lane and E. J. "Buzzy" Bavasi.

Lane was a former college football and basketball official whose first assignment when he entered baseball at the age of 38 was to run the Bulls for the Cincinnati Reds. Lane later would wheel and deal in making over 500 trades for four major league clubs. His assignment in 1936 was to sit and watch as two future Reds' stars led the Bulls to a second-place finish behind Norfolk.

Johnny Vander Meer, a 20-year-old lefthander from Prospect Park, New Jersey, set a league record with 295 strikeouts and was named Minor League Player of the Year by *The Sporting News* after compiling a 19–6 record. Two seasons later, Vander Meer joined the Reds and became the only pitcher in major league history to pitch two consecutive no-hit, no-run games.

Vander Meer was supported at the plate by Frank McCormick, a six-foot-four first baseman who would bat .299 in 13 National League seasons with Cincinnati, Philadelphia, and Boston. He tuned up in Durham with a .381 average, 15 home runs, and 138 runs batted in.

Bavasi inherited far less talent. Running the club for Brooklyn in 1943, he was blessed with a healthy pair of Genes for a short time (future major leaguers Mauch and Hermanski), but watched helplessly as the Bulls stumbled to a last-place finish 46 games behind pennant-winning Portsmouth.

Fortunately, the Dodgers remembered Bavasi more for times such as the 1939 season in Americus, Georgia, when he left the front office to fill in for his injured second baseman. By 1950, he was general manager of the Dodgers and bled blue until 1968 when he became general manager of the newly awarded San Diego franchise.

Durham also had been the birthplace of four major leaguers and in six years would claim a fifth. Roger Craig, nicknamed "Rock" in his days at Durham High School, was a senior when Neville arrived and had started to discover that he was a better pitcher than infielder. The future manager of the San Diego Padres and San Francisco Giants would have his moderately successful seasons as a Brooklyn and Los Angeles Dodger pitcher upstaged by 46 losses in two seasons with the infant New York Mets.

The first Durham native to reach the majors was George "Possum" Whitted, a versatile performer who played the outfield and all four infield positions with five clubs. Whitted, who started his career in 1912 with the St. Louis Cardinals, played in back-to-back World Series with two teams that had finished sixth the season before: the "miracle" Boston Braves of 1914 and the Philadelphia Phillies of 1915.

Whitted became a Bull five years after his National League career ended in 1922. He took over as player-manager late in the 1927 season, starred and called the shots for five successful years, and for a time even owned the team along with his brother, Hugh.

Whitted was followed to the majors by pitcher Leo "Blackie" Mangum, who had a lifetime record of 11–10 with three clubs and was Babe Ruth's teammate on the 1935 Boston Braves; catcher Rick Ferrell, who grew up in Greensboro and was named to the Hall of Fame in 1984 despite spending the majority of his career from 1929–47 in the second division with the St. Louis Browns and Washington Senators; and catcher Dewey Williams, who batted .233 as a part-time performer for the Chicago Cubs and Cincinnati Reds from 1944–48.

Whitted and Mangum were youngsters when the Bulls were born in 1902, but it is unlikely their careers were inspired by the six-team North Carolina League, which folded after two months and two days.

One of the league's most action-filled moments came when Wilmington Manager E. J. Bear forced his way into Umpire George D. Proud's hotel room in Durham and attempted to assault him. Bear was absent when his team lost to the Bulls earlier in the day, but became enraged when he learned that Proud had levied fines totaling $11 against two Wilmington players for protesting calls.

Freed from custody after paying a $25 fine and another $3.40 in court costs, Bear continued his rampage that same afternoon by pulling his team off the field in protest of a Proud call at first base. What had been a scoreless tie in the seventh inning turned out to be a 9–0 forfeit victory for Durham when the Sea Gulls refused to return.

Joining a revived North Carolina League in 1913, the Bulls made a run for the pennant thanks to the pitching of Lee Meadows, a 19-year-old country boy from nearby Oxford who was summoned to the majors two seasons later and went on to win 188 games in the National League with St. Louis, Pittsburgh, and Philadelphia.

On the next to the last day of the season, Meadows won his twentieth and twenty-first games by pitching shutouts in both ends of a doubleheader against Raleigh. When all league games were rained out on the final day, Durham had to settle for a second-place finish one-half game behind Winston-Salem.

The season had started in an equally unfortunate fashion. In the home opener, a 13–0 no-hit game pitched by Winston-Salem's Carl Ray was interrupted by the collapse of the so-called "Negro bleachers" at Doherty Park. According to a newspaper account, the packed bleachers "broke down and precipitated about two hundred Negroes to the ground with a great crash. The accident came very near [to] breaking up the game, and hundreds of people rushed across the field to look at the remains, expecting to see some of the Negroes mashed under the debris. Only a few bruises and slight sprains were sustained in the fall of the stand."

The Bulls survived that near disaster and remained in the Class D circuit until World War I forced its closing on May 30, 1917. That short season ended the 29-game Bull career of Charlie Grimm, who had switched to the outfield after losing the first base job. Fifteen years later, Grimm—a .290 lifetime hitter in the majors—took over the Chicago Cubs in the first of his 19 seasons as a successful manager.

In 1920, the Bulls resumed play as a member of the Class D Piedmont League, a circuit that moved up to Class C the next season and Class B in 1931. The association with the Piedmont would continue through the 1943 season, interrupted only by the suspension of play because of financial problems in the Depression years of 1934 and 1935. When the Piedmont became an all-Virginia league in 1944 because of wartime travel restrictions, Durham sat out of baseball a year before becoming a charter member of the Carolina League.

The Bulls had finished a distant sixth in 1948, 21 games back of first-place Raleigh. And despite the return of star pitcher John "Mickey" McPadden, the addition of Neville, and the appointment of a legendary athlete as manager, writers around the league forecast a decline to the bottom of the 1949 standings.

Durham's finest team—the 1941 club that captured the Piedmont League pennant by ten and one-half games—was now a mere memory, as were stars of the past such as Meadows, Grimm, Vander Meer, and McCormick.

Would this latest team produce a Wright, Mauch, or Hermanski? And could anyone match the talent of other Bulls who had advanced to the big leagues? The list seemed endless: Ed Albosta, Chuck Aleno, Ferrell Anderson, Rex Barney, Hank Behrman, Mace Brown, Dusty Cooke, Gil English, Ernie Koy, Jack Kraus, Vic Lombardi, Merrill May, Glenn Moulder, Tom Oliver, Vance Page, Marvin Rackley, Bob Ramazotti, Stan Rojek, and Monte Weaver.

McPadden, a Brooklyn native and a graduate of St. John's College, would never join the list, but his career had taken a storybook turn when he arrived in Durham two years earlier sporting a beard and a sharp-breaking curveball.

McPadden originally came to Durham Athletic Park as a member of the touring House of David team, an outfit whose members wore beards and entertained the crowd before the game with a pantomime of an infield drill minus a baseball. Minor league clubs scheduled exhibition games with the House of David as a form of preseason batting practice, usually drilling the "impotent bearded team," as one writer called them, for a dozen or more runs while raking in extra cash from fans foolish enough to buy a ticket to see the whiskered wayfarers excel in clowning rather than real baseball.

The original House of David team was the offspring of a religious colony founded in Benton Harbor, Michigan, in 1903 by an eccentric who claimed a white dove had landed on his shoulder and proclaimed him the sixth son of the House of David. The founder also had a passion for baseball. He started a touring team that remained competitive through the 1930s, disappeared during World War II, and then reappeared in several revival attempts through the early 1960s.

McPadden started the Durham game in right field, but was summoned as a reliever in the first inning after the first seven Bulls reached base in a Saturday night contest in April of 1947. Durham scored nine runs in the first, two of them charged to McPadden, but the righthander limited the Bulls to two runs the rest of the way as his teammates rallied for a 12–11 victory.

"I had already told my players to try to start making outs when McPadden came in," recalled Willie Duke, who managed the Bulls and ranked as one of the league's top hitters despite a squat physique that had earned him the nickname of "Wee Willie." McPadden, who struck out Duke the first time he faced him, received a contract offer immediately after the game.

At 23, McPadden had hopes of landing a pro contract when he joined the barnstormers after leaving the service earlier in the year. He thought about Duke's offer for two days before leaving the House of David team behind on the North Carolina coast and boarding the first bus to Durham.

McPadden went straight to the Bulls' spring training headquarters at the somewhat seedy Malbourne Hotel, checked in, then headed for the hotel barber shop and ordered the removal of his neatly trimmed brown beard. He won eight games that season, 18 the next, and 61 over five seasons to become Durham's second-winningest pitcher of all time behind Neville.

One of his wins that first season came in a memorable May affair as the Bulls set a league record by scoring 17 runs in one inning to defeat Leaksville 35–8. A parade of 21 batters poured across all those runs in the seventh without the benefit of a Leaksville error. Five bases on balls supplemented thirteen hits, including five doubles and a triple. Three players came to bat three times, including Jim Coleman, a pinch hitter who singled twice before grounding into a force play his third time at bat. If Coleman was not the first pinch hitter in history to go two for three in the same inning, he certainly was the first to perform the feat and then be released by his team immediately after the game.

On an equally bizarre note, Durham first baseman Cecil "Turkey" Tyson, in the season before his Rocky Mount managerial debut, found himself in jeopardy of making three outs in the same inning—a feat his teammates believed would be a baseball first. Tyson had opened the seventh by flying to left, then was nailed on an infield grounder the second time around. Durham scored eight more runs after that second out, bringing Tyson to the plate again for a shot at infamy. Duke, standing in the on-deck circle, actually encouraged his first baseman to make an out, but Tyson resisted and worked the pitcher for a walk.

Leaksville dropped out of the Carolina League after a seventh-place season, and the town eventually disappeared from the map. Once part of a series of three towns along with Draper and Spray, Leaksville—the birthplace of the infamous baseball Triplets—merged with its two neighbors into a newly incorporated city named Eden.

Willie Duke, who set a Durham club record in 1947 when he hit .385, stayed another season with the Bulls before taking the manager's job at Winston-Salem. His successor in Durham for the 1949 season was Clarence McKay "Ace" Parker, a former Duke University football great who immortalized himself as a Blue Devil halfback by returning a North Carolina kickoff 105 yards for a touchdown in 1936.

Parker, a Duke baseball star as well, signed with the Philadelphia Athletics after his senior year, went straight to the majors, and slugged a home run over Fenway Park's "Green Monster" in his first time at bat. He returned to the plate 206 times that season and the next, homered just once more, then continued to play in the minors even as his star rose in professional football. Bull fans would have frequent opportunities to see Parker play when he returned to Durham as a member of his hometown Portsmouth (Virginia) Cubs.

For a man who looked at baseball as fun and football as work, it was ironic that Parker became the "ace of them all" for the Brooklyn Dodgers of the National Football League despite breaking both legs in baseball. He won all-NFL honors twice and was named Most Valuable Player in 1940. In 1972, he was named to the Pro Football Hall of Fame.

After Parker broke one leg sliding into home plate for the Syracuse Chiefs of the International League, the Dodgers and Coach Jock Sutherland kept him running with an aluminum brace. Parker padded the brace with foam to prevent further injury, then took the field in the final exhibition game and picked up 68 yards against the Chicago Bears.

Parker was more than a triple threat. In addition to being an elusive runner, he also threw and caught passes, returned punts and kickoffs, punted, and placekicked. Dodger fans and owner Dan Topping thought so much of him that they staged an "Ace Parker Day" and gave him a green Buick. And in the final season of a career interrupted by World War II, he threw 76 passes for the New York Yankees without an interception.

Parker remained close to his pro football playing weight of 180 pounds when he took the Durham job, but his gait was more lumbering than graceful when he played the outfield and filled infield positions as the need arose.

His fastest running times came when he scurried from the dugout to argue with umpires. His fierce competitiveness almost did him in one night at Winston-Salem when everyone in the park but the plate umpire knew the call had been blown. "The park had a foul pole at the right field fence, but there was another pole seven or eight yards away in foul territory," Parker recalled. "One of the Winston-Salem players hit a foul ball over the fence just inside the second pole."

The plate umpire ruled a home run, and Parker soon found himself in the locker room after being thrown out of the game. He removed everything but his pants, then became outraged all over again as he thought about the call.

Moments later, a shoeless, shirtless Parker returned to the field and resumed the argument. He left after being threatened with a suspension by a league official who attended the game.

Parker never lost a chance to prove a point, baseball or otherwise. He once told his players that a home run to right center in Durham Athletic Park was nothing more than a short golf shot. When no one believed him, he stood at home plate before a game and easily lofted a nine iron out of the park.

Durham players knew their manager was a gamer and respected him for it. He was a teacher as well—and he ran the club in an old-shoe style that centered around common sense instead of strict rules.

Parker, who switched sports every fall as the backfield coach for the Duke football team, would turn 37 in the summer of 1949, an old-timer leading the charge of a reputed light brigade that became a competitive unit built around Neville's arm and the speed-power combination of two young outfielders sent to Durham by the Detroit Tigers.

The speed showed up in the legs of 22-year-old Pat Haggerty, a center fielder from Denver whose near-record total of 61 stolen bases included five in one game against Greensboro.

When Raleigh players insisted that tiny center fielder Tommy Martin could run even faster, the two met in a challenge race up the right field foul line at Durham Athletic Park. Haggerty later recalled that he offered to split the prize of $25 with Martin before the race, was turned down, then pocketed the full amount after winning by two steps.

By 1953, Haggerty was out of baseball and teaching physical education in the Denver public school system. He continued to run as a football and basketball referee, an avocation that took him to the National Football League in 1965. Former teammates and fans proudly pointed to official number 40 on televised NFL games as none other than Patrick Andrew Francis Haggerty, one-time Bull base stealer. And over the years, they would see an official skilled enough to call three Super Bowls and fast enough to keep his job into his sixties.

Haggerty also found time to referee basketball games in the Big Eight and Western Athletic conferences before retiring after 20 years. And in 29 seasons as the baseball coach at Abraham Lincoln High School in Denver, he won five city championships and finished second three times in the Five-A state playoffs.

Haggerty often scored in Durham off drives by 19-year-old Carl Linhart, whose father immigrated from Zborov, Czechoslovakia, became a bricklaying supervisor at a steel mill in Granite City, Illinois, then summoned his wife and 12-year-old son to America.

Few pitchers could stop Linhart's left-handed power in his early years. A catcher in high school, he had been signed by Detroit and converted to the outfield because of his speed. He hit .404 in half a season with Lafayette (Louisiana) in Class C Evangeline League, then launched his Durham career the next spring by driving in a record eight runs in his second game. His 23 homers included a record-tying three in one game.

Linhart's life would come full circle after he played briefly for the Tigers in 1952. When he retired from baseball, he stayed in Granite City, learned his father's trade at the same steel plant, and settled in for a long second career as a bricklayer.

Anchoring the starting lineup along with Haggerty and Linhart were first baseman Earl Richmond, a smooth-fielding, 21-year-old Tiger prospect from Beaumont, Texas, who had been with the Bulls the year before, and former Tarboro Tar Ralph Caldwell, who took over fulltime catching duties in May and would gain recognition as one of the league's best receivers over the next five years.

The most disappointing Bull, at least in the first two months, turned out to be shortstop Jack Graham, the 18-year-old son of a Brooklyn banker. Graham had signed for a bonus of $17,000, and under rules at that time had to remain on a roster no lower than Class B for a full season. Converted by Detroit Manager Red Rolfe from the outfield to the infield during spring training, Graham arrived in Durham with a hole in both his glove and bat, sometimes committing two or three errors a game.

Despite his faults, Graham had tremendous range, a strong arm, and a bat that improved with experience. In early June, he smashed a grand slam home run against Danville and stopped a nine-game error string at the same time. After the game, grateful fans, who had booed Graham for weeks, chipped in cash to go with prizes the shortstop received for his home run. He left the park with $26 and the promise of three steak dinners and four free haircuts. The young infielder was falling in love with a game and a girl at the same time; Durham's Ramona Lucas soon would become Mrs. Jack Graham.

By the end of the season, Graham was being touted as a future Detroit
Tiger and was assigned to the parent club's spring training roster. When
he returned to Durham in 1952 after time out for military service and a
brief spurt upward in the Tiger farm system, Graham no longer showed
the same promise and was released after a short stay.

Graham and the Bulls surprised the experts at the start of the 1949
season by winning five of their first six games and taking over the league
lead. Despite sporadic losing streaks over the first three months, the team
that was by far the youngest in the league seemed to be a certainty to finish
in the first division. August would take care of that.

# Mastering
# the Muscle Men

*Reidsville had a top-notch outfielder by the name of Dick Sipek, who in those days was labeled not just deaf but deaf and dumb. Sipek was smart enough to outwit a lot of pitchers over three seasons before playing his last game for the Luckies in 1951. For two seasons in that same era, Reidsville started an outfielder with the almost-reversible name of Andy Piesik. For four of the six seasons from 1948 to 1953, Luckie fans could cheer for one or the other. And 1950 was the best year ever; all four syllables showed up in the same outfield.*

Ace Parker could find only one fault with Eddie Neville. The left-hander drove him crazy with his obsession over picking runners off first. Parker started pacing every time a batter reached base. He didn't mind one or two pickoff attempts, but he did think 27 was a bit too much. Parker continued to remember that number long after his baseball career ended, although he couldn't recall if Neville got his man.

Neville came close to catching a Raleigh runner off first in the opening game of the 1949 season, but the move backfired when first baseman Earl Richmond's throw to home plate failed to stop the front end of what turned out to be a double steal.

The lefthander was more successful throwing to batters that night as he launched his Durham career with a three-hit, 2–1 victory. One Raleigh veteran admitted doing a double take when Neville hit the strike zone with his knuckler and curve on three–one and three–two counts.

The former Tarboro Tar quickly became a fan favorite, a tenacious type who started out as an underdog and somehow dominated the league for an entire season. He was just a little guy swallowed up by a loose-fitting flannel uniform, a bantam rooster with oversized legs and a torso that appeared abbreviated once he hitched up his pants and headed for the mound.

On the bench, he was both businesslike and brash. He studied batters with the same sharp eye, but he also took verbal swipes at umpires and laughed all the way to the showers one night when the entire Bull bench was ejected for singing "Home on the Range" to the umpires in a game at Greensboro. Neville's fastball was certainly no faster, but his knuckler danced and his curve nicked the corners as he remained a master of control and changing speeds. The soreness that haunted his spring of a year ago had vanished despite another winter in the Canal Zone.

Walter "Teapot" Frye was like most Carolina League batters. He was convinced he could hit one of Neville's slow ones out of the park, but he settled for less. Frye and others would nick Neville for singles before becoming a "left on base" statistic. Many of the lefthander's games were like a movie serial; several innings featured a scene showing the star bailing out of trouble.

"We always thought we could wear him out," said Frye, a talented shortstop who set a league record by playing in 953 games over seven seasons at Reidsville, Winston-Salem, and Leaksville. "We just couldn't wait to get up there even after he got us out the first time. Then he would just get us out again."

"I don't throw my fast one often because that's the one that batters like to tee off on," Neville admitted in a newspaper interview. "I'd rather feed them that deuce [curve]. That'll get them out. I try to throw my fastball when they least expect it."

Frustrating banjo hitters and free-swingers alike, Neville won his first four starts and ultimately would be credited with over one-third of his team's victories. His delivery was smooth and precise, his methods so foxy that he often was compared to the New York Yankees' Eddie Lopat. He kept most of his pitches low and away. He guarded the mound and dared batters to drive the ball by him. He forced runners to hug the bases.

He was cued by the opposition. He figured the fastest base runners only stole when they took short leads. He believed batters who crowded the plate showed a weakness for outside pitches, and he resisted brushing them back. When he expected a suicide squeeze, he would dust off right-handed batters and go to the far outside for lefthanders.

He could play the game both ways. He understood the strike zone so well that at one point he reached base ten straight times with six walks and four hits. He slid into bases and slapped out hits at a .260 rate. He learned to compete with a Durham Athletic Park scoreboard that was close enough to accommodate a home run of his own. He lost two over the right field barrier in his second start, then four the rest of the year.

One of the home runs that cleared the scoreboard was struck by one

**Leo "Muscle" Shoals, who clouted 55 home runs for the Reidsville Luckies in 1949. (Courtesy *The Herald-Sun*.)**

of minor league baseball's all-time great sluggers, Leo "Muscle" Shoals of Reidsville. Shoals would hit 55 homers, drive in 137 runs, and bat .359, all for a seventh-place club.

Shoals had biceps almost as large as the hams in the smokehouse during his childhood days in Parkersburg, West Virginia. He stood only five-foot-eleven, but his arms bulged like the eyes of pitchers who faced him from the time the St. Louis Cardinals discovered him in 1937 until the day he hung it up in 1955 as a player-manager in Class D.

Shoals substituted a crosscut saw for a weight program, helping his partially disabled father cut wood that would be swapped to a farmer for beef and pork. That was back in the days of the Depression, and the Shoals family suffered more than most after his father lost the fingers of his left hand in a rubber plant accident in Akron. Shoals, the oldest of five children, delivered newspapers to supplement his father's income from odd jobs. The family grew corn and beans in the back yard, froze some of the vegetables, and traded the rest to a neighborhood grocer for staples.

After dropping out of high school and concentrating on semipro baseball, Shoals carried his reputation as a left-handed power hitter to a Cardinal-sponsored tryout session at Albany, Georgia. With a number pinned to the back of his home-style uniform, he tore the cover off the ball before being summoned to run a series of sprints. "I would run, then walk a little, then they'd have me running again," Shoals recalled. "I figured they wanted to see if I was fast enough to play the outfield. I was so slow they asked me if I had ever broken a leg or an ankle. They put me at first base after that."

The young West Virginian was plain Leo then, but a year later he returned to Albany after playing in Class D and started hitting shots to the distant bank that stood in the place of an outfield fence. "They put me and Johnny Mize of the Cardinals in one of those hitting contests before the game," Shoals said. "We were the only two to reach the bank. It must have been 600 feet away."

Shoals played three innings that day, picked up a single off Cardinal pitcher Lon Warneke, then ran into Warneke that same night at a bar. "He told me it was the best curveball I would ever hit," Shoals said. "We stayed in the bar until two in the morning."

When Shoals read the newspaper the next day, a game account compared his power to the dam in Muscle Shoals, Alabama. Leo and "Muscle" became one and the same after that.

Shoals also made the news when he fought in the clubhouse with his manager at the start of the 1938 season at New Iberia (Louisiana) in the Class D Evangeline League. One season later, playing at Johnson City (Tennessee) in the Class D Appalachian League, he was shot by the owner of a roadhouse and seriously wounded. He recovered during the winter, but his career in the Cardinal organization was over.

Before coming to Reidsville, Shoals had been the top home run producer in three different leagues, but had never hit more than 32 in a single season. Shoals himself was unable to explain his sudden power surge in 1949. "It seemed like I could hit anybody," he said.

Shoals connected for three straight home runs in Greensboro one night after doubling his first time up. In his last time at bat, he slapped a shot to right. "I knew it was gone," he related. "I gave it that trot, dropped that head, and rounded first." The drive came within two feet of clearing the fence. Shoals settled for a single, but for the first and only time in his career he had a five-for-five night and three home runs.

When August arrived, Shoals was convinced he could hit 60 and become the Babe Ruth of the Carolina League. "I would swing at anything close to the plate," he recalled. "The pitchers started getting careful and threw me all sorts of junk stuff. I even had a couple of pitches bounce off my back end."

Shoals, who shortened his uniform sleeves to give his muscles breathing room, clouted home runs that year at the rate of one for every nine official trips to the plate. And that was reason enough for Carolina

League pitchers to walk him 116 times. The fear of his power extended to his own teammates. "He would hit these low shots hard enough to kill a person," said Alton Denson, a shortstop for the Luckies. "If we had a runner on first and he was up, it was like standing on egg shells. We were afraid to leave the bag."

"That was my happiest year in baseball," added pitcher Mike Forline. "It was like being a little boy watching him hit all those homers. He had a great sense of humor. He would always tell me to keep the ball on the outside to lefthanders so he wouldn't have to field it."

Forline also marveled at Shoals' ability to make musical sounds by covering up one nostril and blowing through the other. "It sounded like a harmonica," he laughed.

Shoals received feelers late in the season from both the St. Louis Browns and Pittsburgh Pirates. With his wife expecting their first child, he turned both teams down. "The major league minimum ($5,000) wasn't that much different from what I was being paid," said Shoals, whose under-the-table pay at Reidsville jacked up his total earnings to $800 a month. "The Browns just wanted me to pinch hit. It would have been nothing but a cup of coffee."

Cincinnati was impressed enough to draft Shoals and send him to Columbia (South Carolina) in the Class A South Atlantic League. He tore up two contracts and threatened not to report after the final offer reached only $400 a month. The Reds then bent the rules and doubled the pay by signing him to a second contract in the name of their Tulsa farm club.

Shoals never enjoyed another season like 1949, but his 33 home runs and .362 average in his final season at Kingsport (Tennessee) in the Class D Appalachian League lifted his career homer total to 362 and his lifetime average to .337.

He returned to the game when he worked for a chemical plant in Saltville, Virginia, managing a semipro team nicknamed the Alkalines. By the time he retired from a casket hardware manufacturer in 1980, Shoals had lost some of the physical characteristics that made him so strong that he "could grab a root on a creek bank and pull up an Army platoon with me." The nickname, however, would endure—and so would the colorful stories that Shoals told in retirement in the tiny Virginia town of Glade Spring.

"He'll fight you," Shoals said of Neville in 1949. "He's got a lot of guts for a little guy. He'll stand out there and throw that knuckler where he wants it to go. It cuts up, too. I've had some trouble hitting it. You never know where it's going."

Neville was just a novice compared to the 33-year-old Shoals and other journeymen who filled rosters on every team with the exception of Durham. But experience made little difference; he drew a line that even the best failed to cross.

He struck out Greensboro's much-feared Emo Showfety, a former Bull who would hit .344 for the season, four times in a single game. Danville's Woody Fair, another former Durham star, would finish his four-season Carolina League career with 123 home runs, but managed only one single in 15 tries against Neville. Dick Sipek, a deaf outfielder for Reidsville, set a league record with eight straight hits, but hit .150 against the man often described by writers as the "little lefthander."

Sipek, who saw action in 82 games for Cincinnati in 1945, wasn't the only Carolina Leaguer with major league experience to join Neville's victim list. Jake Daniel, the one-time Brooklyn Dodger who started the season with former Tarboro Tar Manager Bull Hamons at New Bern, showed up for a brief time at Burlington and managed only a bunt single in five tries against his former teammate.

Neville seldom gave Daniel and others time to dig in. He took little time between pitches, usually produced rapid-fire outs because of his control, and completed most of his games in less than two hours. "I believed, if you were in a groove, that you should get the ball and throw it right back," he once said.

In late August, he defeated Burlington 6–0 in what was believed to be the fastest nine-inning game in Carolina League history: one hour and 22 minutes. In giving up only four hits and no walks, he retired batters so quickly that some wondered if any game in baseball history had been played as fast.

No records were available on Carolina League games, but Jack Horner, sports editor of the *Durham Morning Herald,* thumbed through his record books and discovered a 1910 Southern Association game in Atlanta that had taken 50 minutes less. Mobile and Atlanta players agreed before the contest to show how quickly a game could be played. Racing the clock and swinging at every pitch close to the plate, the two teams finished nine innings in 32 minutes.

Of Neville's 25 complete games that season, 16 were finished in less than two hours and two at an even two hours. He pitched a ten-inning game in one hour, 50 minutes, and followed up a one hour, 22-minute affair with a seven-inning game that took three minutes less.

Neville, described by Horner as a "statistical nut," carefully tracked his game times and other data that helped him evaluate his performance. He often showed up at Horner's office after a night game to await the early morning press run, frequently staying long after the first paper came off the press to swap stories and information.

The sports editor was a willing participant in the lengthy bull sessions, once having had his own dreams of becoming a pro when he traveled to Hot Springs, Arkansas, to attend a baseball camp featuring greats such as Stan Hack and brothers Dizzy and Daffy Dean. Convinced after two weeks that he lacked the talent to play, he returned to his home town of Greensboro, North Carolina, and turned to the writing side of sports when he landed his first job with the *Greensboro Daily News* in 1936.

Horner assumed a new first name when his Greensboro boss insisted that he switch his byline from Tommy Horner to Jack Horner—a nursery rhyme name that would bring instant recognition. After Horner arrived in Durham in 1944, it took him only eight months to change the title of his daily column from "In This Corner" to "Jack Horner's Sports Corner." When he wrote his final column in 1968, Horner estimated that he had written 8,285,342 words. (His new position would be wordy as well; he left the newspaper business to become executive director of the Carolinas Section of the Professional Golfers Association of America.)

Except for Ralph Caldwell, Horner saw Neville pitch more games than anyone else. He watched the games from the same perspective as Caldwell as he sat in a small rectangular press box that stood squarely on the ground some 50 feet behind home plate. Horner became so accustomed to the location that he hardly noticed when balls bounced off the press box screen or slammed against its concrete base. Others, with less experience, would flinch every time and raise both hands to cover their faces. The press box was so small that when a second Durham radio station decided to broadcast Bull games in 1949, listeners to either station could hear the voice of the other announcer in the background. And when visiting teams brought in their own broadcaster, the sound and echoes of three voices became Durham's own version of "Who's on First?"

Wally Ausley, who had broadcast Bull games on an exclusive basis the season before, became so annoyed that he convinced the Durham front office to let him move out of the press box and set up an open air booth in a box-seat area on the third-base side of the grandstand. From that vantage point, the 21-year-old Ausley called the games with a smooth delivery that eventually earned him more cushy seating as the longtime football and basketball voice of the North Carolina State Wolfpack.

Horner, who also served as the public-address announcer, remained in the press box. His influence over the team almost matched that of the manager and front office as he watched every move at every home game, typed out a game story for the next morning's paper, and offered candid observations in his daily columns.

For a time, he and *Durham Sun* sports editor Hugo Germino even served as conduits between Manager Ace Parker and a fan identified only as the "Old Timer" in letters he mailed to the newspaper office. The anonymous adviser appeared to have influenced Parker at least once with his suggestion to switch Pat Haggerty from second in the batting order to the leadoff spot. The change came within a week after the letter was published, but Parker denied the "Old Timer" had any influence over his decision.

The "Old Timer," who actually was Bob Craig, a red-headed fan who pumped gas at a Durham service station, also recommended that Parker play shortstop himself in place of the struggling Jack Graham. Parker would have none of that, nor would Horner. The sports editor knew he could run Graham out of town, but chose to encourage the youngster and praise his perseverance. Although the 1949 club was far from a world-beater, Horner liked the club's hustle and saved more critical columns for seasons when he expected more than he observed.

Horner also served as the official team scorer as well as editor of the league record book. Batting and earned run averages could go up or down as he watched the action and made scoring decisions that would stand forever. As Neville's victories started to dominate Horner's scorebook, the lefthander began to embrace Durham as much as he had Baltimore. It even resembled his home town in a way, much smaller but just as blue at the collar and full of baseball folks who recalled the lore dating back to the days of Doherty Park.

Maude "Ma" Gregory, the matriarch of Durham's baseball fans, rooted for Neville with the same patented cheer she used for more than a generation of Bulls. "Come on, Eddie, you're better than he are," she shouted in a crackling voice.

"Ma" Gregory was an original—a plump, gray-haired woman who made her way through the park entrance with the aid of a walking cane, then squeezed into an aisle seat near the top of the grandstand in order to facilitate an easy exit. When the Bull lineup was announced, she whooped once for the first eight players and twice for the pitcher. She filled her boys with the best chocolate and pineapple upside-down cakes in baseball, a reward for home runs or well-pitched games.

When the Bulls were part of the Brooklyn organization in the early 1940s, the club and a group of fans paid for her trip to Ebbets Field to see her beloved Dodgers. Although grateful for the trip, she said she would never return. "For one thing, I don't understand what they say," she explained.

The language at Durham Athletic Park was more to her liking. On the third-base side of the grandstand, Bush Thompson—whose trademarks were a well-worn hat and a missing finger—bellowed every time an opposing pitcher ran the count to three balls. "He'll walk you," Thompson predicted in a voice that could bring cows home. Worth Whitfield, a first-class umpire baiter, leaned over the wire fence next to the Durham dugout and roared so loud that he was labeled "Leather Lungs."

A. R. Wilson, who ruled on misdemeanors as judge of Recorder's Court, rooted for the Bulls in a more dignified fashion and joined with his wife every season to treat the team to a watermelon slicing.

County Manager Ed Swindell presided over a group that laid claim

Maude "Ma" Gregory, one of Durham's most vocal fans, chats with Bull outfielder Malcolm Stevens before the 1948 home opener. (Courtesy *The Herald-Sun.*)

to the top row of the right field bleachers. A former all-conference basketball player at Duke University, the loquacious Swindell described game strategy with the eloquence of Mel Allen and Red Barber.

Buster Poythress and Willie Wilkerson, both employees of American Tobacco Company, formed a two-man team that followed the Bulls at home and occasionally on the road, once complaining that Danville greased its seats at League Park in order to rent more cushions. One never went to a game without the other: Poythress, a tall fellow with square features and a jutting jaw, accompanied by the squat, globular-shaped Wilkerson.

The most outrageous fan drove over from Oxford, limiting his trips to Sunday afternoons at first but later showing up almost every night. "Bevo" Beavers came complete with Bermuda shorts, wildly colored ties, a Salvation Army-style coat, and a straw hat. An Uncle Sam beard trimmed a reddened face and provided a backdrop for a light bulb of a nose that was nurtured by the bottle Beavers carried in his back pocket. Every time he swigged, he let out a loud sigh of satisfaction with the comic timing of Jack Benny.

**Worth "Leather Lungs" Whitfield, with both arms folded over the fence, was a classic umpire baiter in Neville's era. Whitfield and other fans trade smiles in 1948 with Durham Manager Willie Duke, who—as manager at Winston-Salem—questioned Neville's pitching ability at the start of the 1949 season. The sign behind Whitfield calls attention to segregated seating. (Courtesy *The Herald-Sun*.)**

Beavers faced a tough competitor in the less sartorial but equally annoying Joe Holleman, who often rode his bicycle to the park. Holleman, decked out in a white T-shirt, would utter some nonsense through a wad of tobacco, tilt his head, and glare through his glasses at the nearest bystander before delivering his "Ain't that right?" punch line. A Durham home run lifted Holleman to such a level of excitement that he would run the length of the grandstand with enough speed and enthusiasm to qualify for a contract.

Durham players escaped the insanity of the park by frequenting places such as Aubrey's restaurant, where the front door was locked after home games as the boys moved back to the supply room and chugged beers atop benches and drink crates. The host, Aubrey Veasey, allowed the players to run up a tab payable at the end of the month.

Neville avoided Aubrey's but savored other devilish moments as he freed teammates of pocket change over the poker table and earned a

reputation as a Romeo who could take his pick of the young women attracted to the ballpark by men in uniform. He enjoyed Chinese food at the
Oriental Restaurant, lunch over the counter at Walgreen's drug store,
stage shows at the Carolina Theater, and movies at the Uptown. On one
of those rare Sundays off when rain postponed a game, he spent the afternoon with a favorite date absorbed in watching Dean Stockwell play a war
orphan in *The Boy with Green Hair.*

He roomed with Earl Richmond at widow Annie Pierce's house only
a block from the park. The friendly, low-key Texan found Neville to be
as adept in a pool hall as he was on a baseball field. "He didn't like to lose
at anything," Richmond recalled. "We'd be in our room, and he would
just look at me and say, 'Richmond, I can beat you at anything.'"

Richmond won his own battle in spring training that season when he
competed for the first base job against six-foot-seven Curtis Ballentine.
Ballentine towered over his rival by a good eight inches, but Richmond had
one advantage. He had been voted the Most Popular Player by Durham
fans the season before—and he drove the team bus. "They paid me maybe
$250 a month for playing and another hundred for driving the bus," said
Richmond, who used some of his savings from baseball to pay his way
through Lamar Tech in his native Beaumont and prepare for a long career
with a major oil company.

Richmond tolerated being called "bussie" and ignored the players
when they encouraged him to weave between motorcycles. He even survived the night the motor burned up on a return trip from Danville. As a
bus driver, he stayed within the speed limit. As a player, he never reached
it. Manager Ace Parker, he said, "always accused me of running backwards."

Richmond once struck up an agreement with Ralph Caldwell to share
the proceeds if either of them hit a scoreboard sign and earned a $50 prize.
"I hit one straight at the sign one night and all I could do was shout, 'Fifty
dollars, fifty dollars,' when I ran past our dugout," he said. "The ball fell
short and I barely made it into second base. Ace and Ralph never let me
forget that."

For Neville, it would be a season of few low points. He reached the
bottom over an 11-day period in May. Burlington started the slide by drilling him for eight runs in the first two innings—a loss Neville later blamed
on too many fastballs. "I was trying to throw the ball harder that night than
ever before, and I got knocked out," he said. "I'm not fast, so it's foolish
to try to throw the ball past anybody."

He was sharper in a home loss to Raleigh as all four Capital runs were
unearned. He took a second-inning shower at Martinsville after blowing
a six-run lead in the first game of a Memorial Day doubleheader.

Neville arrived at Durham Athletic Park one night later in street

**Charles Allen, left, owner of the Durham Bulls, and Curtis "Sis" Perry,
the team's business manager. (Courtesy *The Herald-Sun*.)**

clothes, leading to speculation that he was unhappy and planning to quit
the team despite his 6–3 record. He was in uniform the next night, denying
the rumors. "It's all a mistake," he said. "You can say that I plan to stay
with the club. I don't know how all those rumors got started in the first
place." Word never got to the press, but Neville revealed in his diary why
he had a change of heart. There it was, summed up in a single word and
an exclamation point. Wrote Neville on June 1: "Raise!"

Owner Charles Allen and Business Manager Curtis "Sis" Perry would
continue to reward Neville throughout his Durham career. Although his
Bull contracts were not included among Neville's papers, he likely received
more than $500 a month in his final three seasons—perhaps as much as
the $800 offered to stars like Leo Shoals. That was above the Class B maxi-
mum, but other players and a former team official confirmed Durham was
no different from many other clubs when it came to unreported pay.

Allen, who owned several businesses and later became president of a
bank, was a logical candidate to operate the Durham franchise when the
Carolina League started play in 1945. He was recognized as one of the
city's most influential sports fans, and owning a baseball team offered an

outlet that close associates felt could ease at least some of the pain he had suffered in the unexpected death of his wife four years earlier.

Allen may have been the first baseball executive to experiment with a "sky box." His personal box was located atop the R. J. Reynolds tobacco warehouse behind the scoreboard in right field. Allen, according to Jack Horner, arranged with warehouse officials to watch games from the roof, and would invite a few friends to share an afternoon or evening complete with bourbon and chasers.

As Durham attendance declined in the 1950s, fans became convinced every winter that Allen would sell the franchise and the Bulls would leave town. But Allen, a scrappy sort, never gave up; he continued to own the team until his tragic death in 1960 when a former state legislator whose ex-wife Allen had been dating shot the 60-year-old executive twice in his own front yard.

As an owner, Allen turned over the numbers and details to his cigar-smoking sidekick. Friends called Curtis Perry "Sis" because of his high-pitched voice and a wardrobe that included bow ties and hats. A lanky fellow who sported a thin mustache, Perry surely had not been considered a sissy when he played for some outstanding University of North Carolina basketball teams known in those earlier days as the White Phantoms.

A thrifty, industrious type who sold soft drinks at Durham games as a boy, Perry owned a small piece of the team and protected his investment by taking gate receipts to a night deposit box in the company of a police officer. For several years, he combined his baseball duties with a day job as a clerk at the Seaboard Railway office. And on football weekends, he manned ticket booth number six at Duke Stadium.

Neville and Perry would become close off-the-field friends as well as weekend golf partners. And when Perry died years after both men had severed ties with the Bulls, Neville served as one of his pallbearers.

Neville's raise came just before a visit by his mother, her first since she had exited Tarboro in the belief that she brought her son bad luck. Helen Neville witnessed one of her son's finest overall performances against Raleigh in late June.

It was not just win number twelve and a typical Neville night of nine well-spaced hits, one run, four strikeouts, and no walks. He also handled seven fielding chances without an error, picked his usual runner off first, and completed the game in one hour and 35 minutes. What really stirred up the crowd and "Mom" Neville, however, was his hitting performance, a reminder of the old days back in Baltimore. He started with a single and a steal of second, then drilled a home run over the scoreboard. A second drive nearly cleared the barrier, but Neville settled for a double that drove in a runner from first.

"I see where he is going to get five dollars from this place, five dollars from another place, and other gifts for hitting that homer," said Mrs. Neville. "Well, I don't have much money, but I'm going to give him five dollars myself—and a big kiss to boot."

The performance also stirred a mother's memories of a younger Neville. "He had his tonsils removed when he was six years old and just before the operation we told him we would buy him anything he wanted if he would be a good boy for the doctor," she recalled. "Well, he asked for a baseball bat, glove, and ball, and we got just what he wanted. And he has been playing the game ever since."

His father would arrive later to see a lesser—but still impressive— performance. Neville pitched a seven-hit victory over Greensboro, his eighteenth of the season, but his proudest moment before the man he called "Pop" came when he trotted into second base with a double.

Neville even made a believer out of Willie Duke, Ace Parker's predecessor who started the season as Winston-Salem's manager. "He's not so hot, I don't think," Duke said after seeing Neville for the first time. "He'll lose a lot of ballgames this year. They'll get on him after he's been around the league once."

By mid-June, Duke had been replaced as manager and had moved on to Danville to play the outfield. He insisted he wasn't serious when he made his first assessment. "Neville is a good pitcher, a real good pitcher," said Duke, whose .349 average would be the league's third highest. "He's got a lot of stuff on the ball, and I would not want to take anything away from him."

On July 4, readers of the *Durham Morning Herald* woke up to a cartoon showing the arm of a pajama-clad man curving a shoe around the corner of his house and striking a cat atop a fence. Said the caption: "Why didn't you tell me that's where Neville is staying?"

His pitching was so superlative that Neville eventually accepted the fact that he no longer could play virtually every day. He would pinch hit six times over the season, slapping out a single and a triple with the bases loaded. But Parker never asked him to fill in at first base or as an outfielder. Instead, the lefthander waited with the patience of a race horse for his next pitching assignment. He continued to record in his diary when he "didn't play at all," but he came up with a more forward-looking phrase that summed up his new role. "My turn tomorrow" translated into trouble for the opposition.

Neville joined Ralph Caldwell and Carl Linhart on the league's midseason All-Star team. Parker, selected as the All-Star manager, gave his favorite southpaw the starting assignment and watched as league-leading Danville, host team for the game, scored two unearned runs in the first and handed the All-Stars a 2–0 setback. Charged with the defeat after pitching three innings and giving up four hits, Neville was asked how a team as talented as the All-Stars could have lost. "We didn't get any runs," he smiled. "You can't win ballgames unless you score."

Neville, who at least left Danville with an All-Star wrist watch worth $50, was no team comedian, but he did see the lighter side of life when he wasn't deep into baseball or reading the books that he carried on the road. There was little humor to be found, however, when the season that began so magnificently for the young Bulls hit an August free fall that saw the club lose 16 of 27 games and settle for sixth place after being in or near the first division most of the year. A six-game losing streak took the team from fourth place and a five-game lead over Burlington to fifth place and a one-game deficit.

At home, the Bulls were good enough to win nearly two-thirds of the time. A flip-flop on the road led to a 70–72 record, fifteen and one-half games behind pennant-winning Danville but just one game out of fourth place and a half-game out of fifth.

With the exception of Barney Cooke, who finished at 12–10, Neville carried the pitching staff. Mickey McPadden went 7–8 to post what would be his second worst record in five seasons. Veteran lefthander Lacy James struggled to a 7–10 record.

Neville himself never faltered. He captured nine straight victories over a 30-day period, including three shutouts. After Reidsville's Mike Forline set a league record with his fifth shutout, Neville tied him eight days later and then pitched a record sixth shutout two days before the end of the season. His victories stood at 24, one more than the team record set by Joe McManus in 1914 and one less than the league record established by Lewis Hester of Reidsville in 1948.

With two days of rest, he came face to face with Hester on the season's final day, the two tobacco belt teams meeting in a Sunday afternoon doubleheader at Durham Athletic Park. After local merchants demonstrated their hospitality by presenting the visiting Luckies with cartons of cigarettes, the "Appreciation Day" crowd of 2,865 witnessed an opening win and a seven-inning nightcap that was classic Neville: four hits, no walks, and a 3–1 victory in a time of one hour and 19 minutes. He and Hester continue to stand side by side in the Carolina League record book for the most victories in one season.

With the exception of a Labor Day contest against Raleigh, Neville finished every game he won, including four victories in relief. He completed 25 of 31 starts. He was no one-man show, but he was the key to Durham's 24 percent boost in season attendance to 118,356.

His 25–10 record was accompanied by an earned run average of 2.59. He averaged five strikeouts and just over two walks per nine innings, completed 25 of 31 starts, and held the opposition to two runs or less 15 times. Few pitchers in minor league baseball had as many assists as Neville (92) or

Neville with Ace Parker, his manager at Durham for two seasons, before the opening game in 1949. They're shown with Raleigh Manager Glenn Lockamy, right, and Capital pitcher Pat Kelly. (Courtesy *The Herald-Sun*.)

participated in as many double plays (10). And no one in the league matched his 274 innings pitched.

Neville and Linhart were named to the All-League team selected by sports writers. They were joined by Ace Parker, who was named Manager of the Year. Parker contributed in the field as well. Once, after third baseman Claude Swiggett quit the team to return to his former job at an industrial plant, Parker moved to the hot corner himself since two other infielders were out with injuries. He hit safety in 16 straight games, batting .355 and running his overall hitting streak to 20 games. Although he had launched his pro career as an infielder, Parker had become accustomed to a more solitary life in the outfield. After committing seven errors, he finally persuaded Swiggett, a year-round Durham resident, to return to baseball for the balance of the season.

Parker would return to manage in 1950 but without Neville. As expected, Detroit exercised its option to select two locally owned players without reimbursing the Bulls. In addition to Neville, the Tigers selected

Caldwell and assigned both players to Williamsport (Pennsylvania) of the Class A Eastern League. In December, Neville learned he had been reassigned to Toledo of the Class AAA American Association, putting him, as sports writer Elton Casey described it, "only one jump from the big tent." It was a jump he would never make.

# Holy Toledo!

*Not everyone can be a Tar and a Bull before becoming a Mud Hen. Neville would be pitching in a city in far-off Ohio, but somehow the nickname made it seem all right. With Neville gone, we listened even more to Al Helfer on Mutual Radio's "Game of the Day" and Gordon McLendon of the Liberty Network's re-created games. McLendon could make even the worst contests sound exciting by reporting developments on and off the field that never really happened. With the exception of a couple of games that season, Toledo could have used Gordon McLendon.*

---

Before you could say "Boom Boom," Eddie Neville became the talk of Toledo's 1950 spring training camp in Bartow, Florida. Neville was his usual unobtrusive self. Walter "Boom Boom" Beck, Toledo's pitching coach, said it all. "He looks like he gets his teeth into them quick and hangs right on," Beck stated after seeing Neville work for the first time. "He's a little bulldog, that's what he is."

Neville looked and pitched like a man of 25. So when the team brochure cut two years off his age and claimed he really was 25, sports writers had no reason to question the figure.

He made pitching sound easy. He said it was nothing compared to his earlier days as an outfielder. "The outfielders have to play every day and be tense with every pitch," he said. "When you're pitching, you just find the plate and hope somebody behind you catches the ball."

Neville found the plate at Bartow after being sidelined for several days with the flu. In his first two spring appearances, both against Triple A opposition, he gave up five hits and a single run in 11 innings.

By April 4, he was being touted as the opening-day pitcher against Louisville. Manager Eddie Mayo said he would start the lefthander in an exhibition game against Buffalo on April 6 and give him a shot at going the full nine innings. But Neville never threw the first pitch after developing soreness in the arm that had won 37 games over the last year in Durham and the Canal Zone. He would be out for just over a month with what sports writer Larry Marthey of the *Toledo Blade* described as a "cracked left elbow."

Suddenly, a spring that seemed so promising for the Mud Hens triggered memories of the season before when the team finished last in the first year of ownership by the Detroit Tigers. The Tigers had paid $200,000 to buy the franchise from the St. Louis Browns, then pumped in another $300,000 to cover costs that included major improvements to Swayne Field. A losing season and poor attendance ran the deficit up another $100,000.

But that was 1949 and this was 1950. All teams have an equal shot in the spring—at least until they lose a "little bulldog" of a pitcher. Even without Neville, Toledo finished third in the American Association's "Grapefruit League" exhibition standings. Writers around the league were unimpressed; the Mud Hens were picked to finish last for the second straight season.

Mayo, whose nine-year major league career included five seasons as a starting infielder for the Tigers, was so short on talent that he could make only one promise: he would field a hustling team that emerged from training camp in top condition.

When *The Sporting News* named Mayo the American League's Most Valuable Player after a Tiger pennant in 1945, the second baseman from Clifton, New Jersey, was described as "a gent who is affable and polite, a quiet little player who has the temper of a wildcat."

Mayo was temperamental enough to be handed a one-year suspension from baseball after being accused of spitting in umpire Ray Snyder's face when he played for Los Angeles in the Pacific Coast League in 1941. He vigorously denied the charge, appealed the suspension to the minor league executive committee, and was reinstated in less than two months.

"He is the inspiration of our club," Manager Steve O'Neill said of Mayo in Detroit. "He hustles and he makes everyone else hustle. He takes no care of himself. He dives at balls and throws himself around like a rubber ball."

As a manager, the 40-year-old Mayo demanded that his players take care of themselves. He outlined his program in a letter to each player in early January. He encouraged gym workouts at least three or four times a week, along with daily home calisthenics for up to an hour. If the weather prevented road work, he suggested knee-bending exercises for an hour.

"The player in the best shape naturally will look more impressive than the player who is not," he wrote. "And I can truthfully tell you that every position on the club is wide open."

Mayo even threatened two workouts a day in Florida to assure peak conditioning, but that never became necessary. Once the letter arrived, beer bellies began disappearing all over the country.

The svelte Mud Hens could hit and field, but not necessarily at the same time. Outfielders George Lerchen and Don Lund would combine for 49 home runs and 17 errors. Shortstop Johnny Bero balanced his one homer with one error every four games. Veteran outfielder Austin Knickerbocker rediscovered his batting eye in the final month—after being traded to Baltimore in the International League.

"I felt bad for all the players," said Lerchen, who grew up eight blocks from Briggs Stadium under the watchful eye of a father called "Dutch" who had played briefly for the Boston Red Sox in 1910. "We would win one, then lose three. We just didn't win much against the top teams."

Lerchen was battling for a chance to return to the stadium where as a boy he helped shag fly balls for second baseman Charlie Gehringer, who had been inducted into the Hall of Fame in 1949. At 27, Lerchen no longer expected immortality but still held hopes for a season or two before the home folks. He would make it for 14 games in 1952 and would play in another 22 the next season in Cincinnati. That was at least enough to make the name of Lerchen well known when he entered the construction business in Detroit.

After he retired in the Detroit suburb of Garden City, Lerchen had a warning for other former Tigers. With the exception of All-Stars and Hall of Famers, he told them, they would be forgotten 30 years after their final game. "They don't believe me at first," he said, "but then it starts happening a little more each year."

Toledo was an imminently forgettable team in 1950, although the pitching staff, Neville included, was far better than the final records revealed. Tall Dick Marlowe, a North Carolinian who would turn 21 in June, would win only seven of 17 decisions but would be good enough to pitch a perfect game at Buffalo in 1952 and be on the Tiger roster over much of the next five seasons. Marv Grissom, a 32-year-old Californian who would become a reliable relief pitcher for the New York and San Francisco Giants, would finish at 9–10.

Two other pitchers would be called up by the Tigers before the end of the season: Marlin Stuart, who would revitalize his career at 31 by throwing a perfect game for the Mud Hens, and Ray Herbert, a hard-throwing 20-year-old who first attracted attention on Detroit sandlots. Stuart, who had been sent down by the Tigers in the spring, would return on the strength of his 9–3 Toledo record. Herbert would compile a 10–12 record after losing nine of his first 12 decisions.

Herbert, who in later years would serve as president of the Tiger alumni association, believed Neville's lack of speed kept him out of the majors. "If you threw mostly junk, you didn't have a chance," he said.

Herbert would throw hard enough and long enough to win 104 games with the Tigers and three other clubs, but not with enough force to stop Carl Yastrzemski in his first time at bat with the Boston Red Sox in 1961. Pitching for the Kansas City Athletics on opening day at Fenway Park, Herbert surrendered a single to the future Hall of Famer in the second inning of a game that marked the Athletics' debut under controversial owner Charles O. Finley.

Herbert, who would continue to pitch semipro baseball until he was 50, and Lerchen, who would become a slugger in slow-pitch softball, agreed that Neville would have reached the top in the modern era. "He would be just right for short situations in the middle of a game," said Lerchen. "He was a low-ball pitcher who forced a lot of ground balls. Today he could come in for an inning and get out without a run. Eddie almost always kept us in a game."

Mayo, who called on Neville for 20 starts and 15 relief appearances, had another timetable in mind. He believed the lefthander could be ready to pitch in Detroit by the next season. "I thought he could be a great relief pitcher," he said. "That was a long time before relievers had all that prestige, but I could see him coming in under fire and not flinching a bit. I recommended him to the Tigers in my reports."

Neville could have used Mayo's support when he started poorly in 1951, but by that time the former Toledo manager was coaching for the Boston Red Sox under Steve O'Neill. He followed O'Neill to the Philadelphia Phillies for three seasons starting in 1952. After that, he switched to a business career that would take him to high level positions for two manufacturing firms before he retired and began spending his winters in Banning, California, and his summers in Ocean City, Maryland.

"I don't know what happened to Eddie after I left Toledo," said Mayo. "I just know he had the guts to pitch in tough situations."

Bailing the Mud Hens out of trouble was not easy. It was a team with a sorry future and a past that was proud only from a distance. For two seasons, in 1884 and 1890, the city achieved major league status as a member of the original American Association, then a rival of the National League.

The "Toledos" finished eighth in a twelve-team league in 1884, suffered from poor attendance, and dropped out after one season. Even then, long before the days of Jackie Robinson, the team could claim the first black player in major league history, a tall catcher from Steubenville, Ohio, by the name of Moses Fleetwood Walker. Fleet Walker and his younger brother, outfielder Welday Wilberforce Walker, both were members of Oberlin College's first baseball team. Welday joined his brother for five games at Toledo, but no other black would play in the majors until Robinson joined the Dodgers 63 years later.

Fleet Walker, who caught with his bare hands, hit .263 in 42 games for Toledo and moved the next season to Cleveland in the Western League. He teamed with 35-game winner George Stovey in 1887 to form a well-known black battery for the Newark Little Giants of the International League.

In 1990, the John Heisman Club of Oberlin (named after the school's former coach and namesake of college football's top individual trophy), organized a memorial ceremony for Walker at Union Cemetery in Steubenville, Ohio. A marker placed on the grave described Walker as the "gentleman [who] was the first black major league player in the United States."

There was little historical significance to Toledo's return to major league status with the eight-team American Association in 1890. Playing as the Black Pirates, Toledo finished fourth, then dropped out again. The league folded a year later.

Toledo was blessed with nicknames such as the White Stockings and Swamp Angels before becoming the Mud Hens in 1896 as a member of the Inter-State League. The inspiration for the now-famous nickname came from the ducklike birds — known as coots or mud hens — that flocked to the marshland surrounding the team's home park.

The nickname went into hiatus when the franchise was transferred to Cleveland in 1914. When a replacement club was formed that same season in the Southern Michigan League, Toledo fans preferred "Soumichers" even as Mud Hens continued to be used on the Michigan side. After new owner Roger P. Bresnahan brought the club back from Cleveland to Toledo in 1916, he used Iron Men for three seasons before returning to the more popular Mud Hen designation.

One of the team's most memorable seasons came in 1927 as the Mud Hens clinched the American Association pennant on the final day. More than 316,000 fans turned out that season, the first of six under Manager Casey Stengel.

Two years later, with the team headed for a last-place finish, Stengel claimed his players paid more attention to the stock market than baseball. He even suggested that they invest in New York Central Railroad stock. "If they don't start playing better," he said, "that'll be the busiest railroad in the country."

The Toledo that greeted Neville in 1950 was more than five times the size of Durham. Tarboro could be tucked into one of its neighborhoods. Neville had grown up in an even larger city, but he really was more of a small-town guy who remained unimpressed that he was performing in a high-powered industrial city billing itself as the "Glass Capital of the World."

Neville's true home would be confined to the grass and dirt between

**The 1950 Mud Hens were often as comical as their cartoon logo.**

the lines. The real differences, from his viewpoint, would be far more accomplished players, train trips as long as 15 hours, and girls without Southern accents. He could play cards in Milwaukee and Minneapolis and read books in Kansas City and Columbus. And baseball humor was the same in Toledo as it had been everywhere. Some of the Mud Hens referred to Neville as "Sam Spade," comparing him to the radio detective when he wore a trench coat during a spring that was the coldest he had ever experienced. When he wore the coat and went window shopping, teammates accused him of "casing the joint."

Neville wore less before retiring for the night. Emil Restaino, one of his roommates on the road, looked over the first night and saw a nude Neville in the next bed. "Eddie was the first guy I ever saw who slept that way," said Restaino, who was comfortable enough to close both eyes.

Restaino, a former Seton Hall athlete from Newark, N.J., was being rushed by the Tigers even faster than Neville. At 20, he had jumped all the way from the Class D Georgia-Florida League after batting .388 at Thomasville (Georgia) before his season ended in July with a shoulder separation.

Ironically, both player's careers would wind down in similar fashion. Restaino played the final half of the 1954 season with Neville at Durham, demonstrating enough power to clear the distant left field fence three times. He received his release from Albany the next season only a short time before Neville, played semipro baseball in Minnesota the rest of the summer, then settled down in Lakeland, Florida, in a house located just down the street from Detroit's spring training camp.

Neither Restaino nor anyone else could save Toledo from a disastrous start that saw the Mud Hens lose their first seven games. "Boom Boom" Beck compared the first win to an ice jam. "We had been dammed up too long and just finally busted out all over," he said after a 13-run assault of Louisville.

The thaw was brief. The Mud Hens sat in the cellar much of the time, rose like a horror movie corpse to as high as sixth, then finally settled on seventh as the rightful spot for a team capable of winning only 65 games.

Neville had tested his arm the day the team returned to Toledo after an all-night train trip from Florida. He recorded that he "felt pretty good" after a noon workout. By the next day, however, he admitted that his arm was in "sad shape."

He continued to throw on the sidelines. Within two weeks, he was strong enough to warm up for extended periods in the bullpen. Even then, he measured the condition of his arm not by how good it felt, but rather by how bad it didn't feel. He wrote that he "warmed up pretty well." The pain, he said, was "slight . . . but not too bad."

On May 10, he pitched to two batters in closing out a home win over Minneapolis. He retired them both, striking out one. He made his first start four days later in the second game of a doubleheader against Milwaukee. The 2,661 fans at 14,900-seat Swayne Field witnessed what would be Neville's best home performance of the season.

That he won was no accident. He spent an hour before the first game poring through record books for information on Brewer batters. He played solitaire for a short time, then sat in the grandstand behind home plate and took four pages of notes as he studied the habits of future major leaguers such as Johnny Logan, Bob Addis, and Pete Whisenant.

The lefthander faced only 27 batters in the seven-inning game, giving up four hits in a 2–0 victory. He was in trouble only once. In the final inning, an Austin Knickerbocker throw nailed a runner attempting to advance from first to third on a drive down the left field line.

Neville had beaten Chet Nichols, who had grown up in Rhode Island hearing baseball stories from a father who had won but a single game over six seasons with three major league clubs. The son would go far beyond that, compiling an overall record of 34–36 after winning 29 games in his first three seasons with the Boston and Milwaukee Braves.

"Southpaw Shines," declared the newspaper headline. Jack Senn, writing in the *Toledo Times,* said the "stylish southpaw . . . apparently has whipped a sore arm just as he whipped the Brews."

But the sore arm had not been whipped. It simply came with the territory, one tough little pitcher accepting the twinges and stabs of pain as he competed for one of the 160 or so jobs available on big league pitching staffs.

He would win only five more games that season, just one in the final

42 days. Even with a respectable 4.14 earned run average, he would lose 15 on a team that became as laughable as its cartoon logo of a plump Mud Hen called Mortimer. The more Neville would lose, the harder he would try. "He has a lot of moxie, but he's tried to cut the corners too much," said his catcher, Ed Mordarski. "He has better control than he's showed."

Mordarski was on target. After striking out more than twice as many batters as he walked at Durham, Neville would see the ratio reverse itself for the first and only time in his minor league career.

"We kept telling Eddie he was getting too cute," noted George Lerchen. "We even kidded him about walking guys just for the chance to pick them off."

But there always would be THE GAME. On a hot Sunday afternoon in Indianapolis, he turned into one big bulldog, sinking his teeth into a first-place Indian team and yanking his own helpless club out of the basement. His diary entry the day before told it all. It would be the only time that season—and the last time in his career—that he would write, "My turn tomorrow."

The temperature at Victory Field on June 25 was 90, but it was one of those muggy Midwest days when it felt like 110. It was a marathon prize fight of sorts; you pitched until you dropped or somebody scored.

Indianapolis pitcher Fred Strobel became the first to fall out. After giving up only four hits, he left the game in the ninth on the verge of collapsing. Neville stayed. He would change his outer shirt twice and soak four inner shirts and a T-shirt. He would face 62 batters and throw perhaps as many as 200 pitches in a game originally scheduled for seven innings as part of a doubleheader.

For once, the Mud Hens fielded as adeptly as Neville pitched. They even pulled off a triple play in the first inning on a liner to short that trapped runners on first and third in an aborted hit-and-run play. Fans who followed Indianapolis on the radio never heard a word. Luke Walton was at the mike every day except Sunday; WISH (1360 on your dial) had elected not to carry games on the Sabbath.

The game likely would have ended in the ninth had it not been for a strong wind blowing in from right field. Lerchen led off the inning with a drive high off the wall in right center. He settled for a double. Neville, who gave up ten hits and stranded 15 Indian runners, benefited from the wind in the thirteenth when outfielder Dom Dallessandro's drive came within a foot of clearing the wall. In the fourth, the Indians' Frank Kalin had approached home run territory with a drive off the scoreboard.

The game reached the fourteenth inning. Forrest Main, who had given up only one hit since relieving in the ninth, was replaced by left-hander Paul LaPalme. LaPalme survived the fourteenth, then the fifteenth. So did Neville.

**As a Toledo Mud Hen, Neville was one step short of reaching the major leagues. (Courtesy Janet Neville.)**

Plate umpire Joe Serafin went down after that. Jim Duffy looked up from his spot near first and saw his partner keel over. Duffy wasn't surprised; both men had been suffering in their blue serge uniforms complete with tie and suspenders. Serafin also had labored under the weight of a chest protector.

"He was bobbing and weaving and then he went down," recalled

Duffy, the junior umpire of the two-man crew. The 29-year-old Duffy, a Rhode Islander who later would become an American League umpire and a National Basketball Association referee, went behind the plate and called the rest of the game by himself. Neville had one leg up on LaPalme as he led off the top of the sixteenth. Both could pitch; Neville could hit.

Neville had broken two bats during the afternoon. One was an infield fungo bat that created a controversy when he took it to the plate; the other had been borrowed from infielder Bobby Mavis, who in seven years would become manager of the Durham Bulls. This time, he borrowed a heavier bat from first baseman Paul Campbell. It was the right choice. He drove the ball to deep right center for a triple.

An infield grounder, an intentional walk, and a sacrifice that started out as an attempted squeeze play left runners on second and third with two out. Neville scored what would be the winning run after the first pitch to Lerchen got by catcher Ed Fitz Gerald. Lerchen followed with a single, and Toledo moved into the last of the sixteenth with a 2–0 lead.

Neville retired the first two batters before Fitz Gerald singled. Don Gutteridge, an infielder who would manage the Chicago White Sox in 1969–70, was announced as the pinch hitter for LaPalme.

Gutteridge was no power hitter, but Mayo decided to change pitchers since Gutteridge hit from the right side. Neville left the mound reluctantly. The crowd of 7,716 erupted with cheers for a performance that a poet would describe as good enough to make grown men cry.

Righthander Bill Connelly replaced Neville, Indian Manager Al Lopez summoned left-handed batting Del Ballinger to replace Gutteridge, and a game that lasted three hours and 49 minutes ended on an infield grounder. "He [Neville] was a pretty tired boy when it was all over, but he never lost much of his stuff," said Mayo.

Although league record books did not account for consecutive score-less innings in a single game, researchers agreed that Neville's performance had never been matched in the American Association. Robert B. Evans, general manager of the Mud Hens, wired Neville at the Lincoln Hotel in Indianapolis. "Congratulations," he wrote, "on the league's outstanding performance of all time."

A few days later, a fan disputed the record. Vincent L. Thomas wrote the *Toledo Blade* that on August 11, 1912, Milwaukee pitcher Cy Slapnicka had pitched 16 innings in defeating Toledo and Fred Falkenberg, 1–0. "Ed Neville's performance," wrote Thomas, "is that much more remarkable as he pitched in 90 degrees of sweltering heat, while the Toledo-Milwaukee game ... was interrupted by rain ... giving the Milwaukee pitcher that much time to recuperate."

Sports writer Larry Marthey checked newspaper files and discovered Thomas was right. Twenty-three years after setting the record, Slapnicka—who by then was a scout—signed Bob Feller to a Cleveland Indians' contract.

There was more irony to Neville's performance. LaPalme, who lost the game, would win 24 games in the majors, most of them with the Pittsburgh Pirates. Fitz Gerald, who was charged with the passed ball, already had played two seasons with Pittsburgh and would put in ten more with the Pirates and Washington Senators.

A Californian, Fitz Gerald had been drained by the heat and was pleased when Lopez told him he could sit out the second game. When the backup catcher was replaced by a pinch runner in the sixth, the promise was forgotten.

Fitz Gerald would face an even tougher assignment with the Washington Senators. He was asked to room with hard-throwing pitcher Camilo Pascual, a Cuban who knew little English in his rookie season. "I taught him how to order breakfast," Fitz Gerald teased. "It was always bacon and eggs, bacon and eggs."

LaPalme's most vivid memory of the game was of Neville coming to the plate with a long, slender fungo bat. It may have been the first and only time any player dared to use a fungo except in infield drills. "He must have thought he was one hell of a hitter," LaPalme said. "We figured he'd come up with a sword the next time."

"Eddie wasn't hitting with a regular bat so he thought he would try a fungo," explained Mud Hen catcher Mordarski.

Indianapolis protested, but no rule disallowed the fungo. "We knew the bat was going to break," said LaPalme. "The ball comes at you one way and you have to hit it the other way. Fungoes just weren't made to do that."

Lopez, who would take his managing talents to the Cleveland Indians the next season, used 18 players that day. Half of them had played or would play at a level Neville never reached. But on that one afternoon, for nearly four hours, he was better than any of them and—perhaps with the exception of Cy Slapnicka—better than any pitcher in a single American Association game.

"If I never win another one, this one will more than satisfy me," Neville wrote Durham newspaperman Jack Horner.

It would be only two days before another Mud Hen made Toledo fans forget just how incredibly Neville had pitched that day. In the seventh inning of a home contest against Indianapolis, right fielder Don Lund shouted to center fielder George Lerchen that Marlin Stuart was working on a perfect game. "I shook for the rest of the game," recalled Lerchen. "I thought, well, if some guy hits it to me, what am I going to do?"

Stuart became only the second pitcher in the American Association's 49-year history to record a perfect game. The righthander from Arkansas credited his 1–0 victory to his screwball. "Yeah, I couldn't seem to win at all when I was with Toledo a couple of seasons back," Stuart said after the game. "After I had been bounced around a few times, Frank Mancuso, a catcher for the Mud Hens at the time, showed me how to throw a screwball and said, 'You might as well try it; you don't have anything to lose.'"

Stuart, sent down to Little Rock in the Class AA Southern Association later that season, tried the new pitch for the first time when Mobile started eight left-handed batters. "I've been using the screwball ever since," he said.

Neville felt a slight twinge in his arm after the Indianapolis game and rested four days before facing Louisville at home. The Colonels' relief pitcher that night was none other than Gordon Mueller, the victim of Neville's Oriole Park home run in 1940. The six-foot-four Mueller had gained a reputation as the Joe Page of the American Association. He threw with a different arm than the Yankee southpaw, but the two had similar builds and both were outstanding relievers.

Mueller had stopped a Toledo rally in the first game and returned in the bottom of the ninth of the nightcap after two Mud Hens had reached base with one out to threaten Louisville's one-run lead. Neville, on his way to a .240 average for the season, was the first batter scheduled to face Mueller, but Mayo spoiled a replay of the Baltimore championship game by sending in pinch hitter Bobby Mavis. What could have been Mueller's one attempt at revenge turned out to be a save as he retired both Mavis and second baseman Al Federoff to end the game.

Mayo shared Neville's fond memories of Oriole Park. When he played for Baltimore in 1935, he hit only .260 for the season but was a .351 hitter in 20 Sunday home games. Mayo and Neville had something else in common; both shared the given names of Edward Joseph.

The two also had equal admiration for 45-year-old "Boom Boom" Beck, who came out of retirement as a player in August and gave several impressive pitching demonstrations to a tiring staff. Beck had won only 38 of 107 decisions with the Brooklyn Dodgers and five other clubs, but he left the majors in 1945 with one of baseball's most endearing nicknames.

Beck later insisted that he picked up the label after setting up a New York newspaperman in a game of pinochle. The more popular version centers around his objection to being removed from a Dodger game in 1934 by Casey Stengel.

Stengel, in his rookie season as a major league manager, ordered catcher Al Lopez to the mound to remove Beck in the third inning of a game at Philadelphia's Baker Bowl. Beck hesitated, tried to catch Stengel's eye, then became enraged when the 34-year-old manager paced the dugout without looking up.

Before leaving the mound, Beck wheeled and threw the ball toward the right field fence. Hack Wilson, the former Cub great who was winding up his career with the Dodgers, heard a "boom" as the ball caromed off the tin barrier, thought the game had resumed, and fired a perfect throw to second base. "Well, Elmer," Stengel was quoted as saying to a seething Beck, "that's one they didn't hit off you."

Beck, who won more often in billiards than baseball in his second and final Dodger season, was more successful in his Toledo revival. He won his first relief appearance, then lost twice before making his first and only start at home against Minneapolis.

"We had to start Boom," recalled Mayo. "Ray Herbert had just been called up, and we had played several doubleheaders. I wasn't going to tell any of the young guys to pitch so I asked for volunteers. Boom raised his hand. I told him if he got tired to put his glove on top of his cap."

Beck was expected to last no more than five innings, but he was still around in the eighth when the Millers loaded the bases with one out. "I didn't think he was going to make it so I had asked Neville to slip down to the bullpen and get ready," said Mayo.

Neville threw one pitch, retired the side on a double play, and held the Millers scoreless in the ninth. "After I took Boom out, I don't think we had even reached the dugout when we heard the crowd cheering," said Mayo. "Eddie loved to get in those situations. He had a lot of character."

The pitching comeback by the popular coach was one of the few bright spots in a month that included the loss of a game the Mud Hens actually won. After defeating Louisville, Toledo learned that winning pitcher Bill Connelly, who had returned to the Mud Hens after being recalled by Detroit, was ineligible since he had been added to the roster after the August 20 deadline.

Louisville, still in the running for a playoff spot, protested and was awarded a 9–0 forfeit. "That makes me the losing pitcher," said Toledo general manager Evans as he accepted responsibility for the oversight and prepared to share the blame for a seventh-place finish and a 65–87 record.

The bespectacled, heavy-set Evans, who was the son of Detroit general manager Billy Evans, would find contract negotiations with Neville equally frustrating. The lefthander simply never returned a signed first contract.

Evans first experienced that brand of mulishness before spring training in 1950 when Neville rejected an initial offer of $325 a month. Evans also guaranteed an increase to $450 if Neville remained an active player 30 days after the season opened. The matter was settled when the starting salary was increased to $400.

Evans offered $500 a month in 1951, saying in a letter that he had decided on a raise "even though your 1950 record does anything but justify it."

He promised another increase once Neville demonstrated his ability to win at the Triple A level. "I've done this for other deserving players and I want to give you the same opportunity," he wrote.

The general manager ended his letter to the Canal Zone with an attempt at humor. "I just noted that you went down swinging with the bases full last week," he wrote. "Please don't do that any more. It's bad publicity for the Mud Hens."

Neville apparently failed to see the humor. He asked for even more.

"I know everyone would like to make more and more money," responded Evans. "But in your case if I were to start at any higher figure than you have been offered, the home office in Detroit would wonder if I too had been affected by the Cristobol sunshine."

Neville may have had reasons other than money for holding out. He had been asked to report on March 8, but that was two days before he was to serve as best man at Ray Dabek's wedding to Canal Zone resident Joan Reed. He had no intention of missing what he described as "the wake" for his longtime Cristobol receiver. The holdout also would extend the recuperation period for the knee he had injured sliding into second base.

On the day he was due in Florida, he attended a team dinner at the Cristobol Gun Club. After the wedding, he remained in the Canal Zone 13 more days doing little more than fishing, sunning, and playing canasta. He continued to frustrate Evans by claiming he was considering becoming an agent for the Federal Bureau of Investigation. He finally arrived at training camp 16 days late and agreed to Evans' original offer 72 hours later. The raise that Evans promised for a winning record would never come.

In his only exhibition appearance, he walked five batters in three innings of relief against Buffalo. He sat on the bench for the home opener, watching a win over St. Paul as a light snow fell.

It would be a miserable year for one of the latest minor league players to sign an endorsement contract with a Texas glove manufacturer. Neville received two free gloves for the season, one for his right hand and one for his left. The president of the Nocona Leather Goods Company apologized for the error and promptly sent a replacement with the laced-down web that Neville had suggested as a safety measure.

Most of the 158 players who endorsed the Nocona product from the 1930s through the 1950s came out of the Class AA Texas League, including Canal Zone teammate Ray Dabek, who recommended the left-hander to the small manufacturing firm based in Nocona, Texas.

Neville received gloves bearing the signature of Bob Milliken, who pitched for the Texas League's Fort Worth Cats in 1948 and 1949 and who posted a 13–6 record at Brooklyn in his two major league seasons of 1953 and 1954. Unlike Neville, Milliken was a righthander.

Nocona, whose gloves were sold under the Nokona brand since the name of the town could not be trademarked, discontinued its endorsement program when players started demanding fees as well as gloves.

Money, however, was not an objective for pitcher Carl Erskine, who continued to accept two gloves a season as payment in full after he left Fort Worth and became a star at Brooklyn. (Nocona, which started out as a billfold and handbag manufacturer in 1926, concentrates on softball gloves today, although it handmakes a nostalgia collection of gloves that includes the Erskine model.)

With his Milliken glove replacing his Mort Cooper model, Neville made four relief appearances for the Mud Hens. Although he picked up two wins, he failed to make an immediate impression on the team's new field leaders: Manager Jack Tighe and Coach Tommy Bridges, a former Tiger pitching star. The 38-year-old Tighe, who would manage at Detroit in 1957 and part of 1958, had been a journeyman minor league catcher whose toughness was tempered somewhat by his hobby of growing flowers. ("Marigolds and petunias, nothing fancy," he insisted.)

Tighe was more impressed by another Toledo lefthander, an 18-year-old fireballer out of Oshkosh, Wisconsin. The younger lefty, Billy Hoeft, showed he was only a season away from Briggs Stadium when he retired 13 straight Kansas City batters and held the Blues hitless for six innings.

"I remember Neville as a very confident guy," said Tighe, who spent 56 and his 58 baseball years with the Tiger organization before retiring as a part-time scout in 1990. "But we had Hoeft and another lefthander by the name of Dwain Sloat who could throw just a little harder than Neville. He [Neville] was slow rounding into shape so he just became a victim of numbers. We only carried nine pitchers."

Neville's first and last starting assignment in a Mud Hen uniform that season came on May 6 at Nicollett Park in Minneapolis. He pitched five innings, giving up eight hits and four runs to a Miller club whose center fielder, Willie Mays, was celebrating his twentieth birthday. Neville would not be the loser of record, but he had pitched his way out of the American Association.

Word came ten days later; he had been optioned to the Williamsport Tigers in the Eastern League. Neville headed for Pennsylvania the next afternoon. He drove six hours and stopped in Butler to watch a game in the same park where he had played the outfield in 1942. Arriving in Williamsport two days later, he checked in at the YMCA before taking in a movie. A parking ticket served as his official welcome to the city along the Susquehanna River.

Despite being in a fast Class A league that had been around 28 seasons, Neville for the first time found his career in reverse gear. Once acknowledged as a gutsy little competitor who knew how to win, he now had to deal with a new label in a new city as a veteran who was merely "clever."

His summer in front of the green and gray grandstand at Bowman Field would not be one of 28 wins or 25 wins or 16-inning dogfights. Instead, it would be a wasted period when he should have been in top shape and going up against such stars as 19-year-old Kansas City slugger Mickey Mantle.

He would travel in buses again and pitch in the bleakness of Scranton and Wilkes-Barre. He would pass the time by writing poetry during stays at the Arlington Hotel in Binghamton and the Ten Eyck in Albany. It would all be for the glory of another lousy Tiger farm club that would win but 55 games and finish seventh only through the courtesy of an Albany outfit that would win nine fewer.

Neville at least could test his competitiveness by going against guys on the way up, including Dick Gernert, Bob Lillis, Frank Malzone, Faye Throneberry, and Don Zimmer. He would hang tough against six-foot-eight righthander Gene Conley, who was only a year away from the Boston Braves and eventually would double up as a basketball player for the Boston Celtics. And he would have his second reunion of the season with ex–Durham Bull Pat Haggerty, who was one year short of retiring.

Haggerty had led the Class AA Southern Association in batting at Little Rock in 1950, but even a .364 average failed to satisfy a Tiger organization that questioned his throwing arm. After starting the season with Neville at Toledo, Haggerty found himself in Williamsport trying to save his career by switching from the outfield to second base. The transition try failed; Haggerty suffered in the field and his batting average dropped to .209. He was released the next year after a second try at Williamsport, put in one season with his native Denver in the Class A Western League, then started a new life as a teacher, coach, and referee.

Neville and Haggerty played under Manager Lynwood "Schoolboy" Rowe, watching as the six-foot-four former Detroit Tiger star continued to pitch at age 41 with nothing but a knuckleball and a blooper or two. Rowe's season was cursed like the rest of the team; after holding Albany to one run and winning his own game with a home run, he was notified that his mother had suffered a heart attack and was near death in Kilgore, Texas. (Rowe himself would die of a heart attack in 1961.)

Rowe had been a wonder boy at Detroit in 1934, winning 16 straight and 25 overall as the Tigers claimed their first pennant in a quarter of a century. At one point, he was pitching so well that he yelled to his wife in the stands, "How'm I doing, Edna?" The phrase followed him the rest of his career.

He was still the same Arkansas country boy who once stood in the firehouse in his home town of El Dorado and watched as a Tiger scout wrote out his contract on the back end of a hook-and-ladder truck. The arm that had won 151 major league games was long gone, but Rowe remained an imposing figure with a pitching hand large enough to hold seven baseballs at the same time.

Rowe's baseball odyssey had taken him to the same Texas League club that Neville had bypassed in 1948. After developing a sore arm at the start of his fifth year in Detroit, the big righthander was sent to Beaumont for two seasons and returned to win another 88 games before winding up his career with the Philadelphia Phillies at the age of 39.

He was still "Schoolie" or "Schoolboy" to his Williamsport players, carrying the same nickname he picked up as a teenager pitching for a church team. And losing season or not, fans thought enough of the easygoing manager to present him with a pair of hunting dogs.

The club's followers also had high regard for center fielder John "Bubba" Phillips, who finished second in the voting for Most Popular Player. Phillips, after leading the league with a .335 average, wasn't around when the ballots were counted, however. He and pitcher Paul Foytack, both future Detroit Tigers, had been promoted to Toledo in a move that assured Williamsport's second-worst record in history.

Neville failed to measure up to Foytack, but he was impressive enough to earn Rowe's recommendation for another shot at a higher classification. He pitched two shutouts (one of them backed up by Pat Haggerty's four-for-four night), completed half of his 18 starts, and finished with a 3.39 earned run average that some might call fancy.

But his record read 7–11 on a bum team that did nothing to shore up his growing disrespect for a Detroit organization that reportedly considered adding him to the Tiger roster as a late-season relief pitcher. The Tigers did think enough of Neville's performance to recall him to Toledo for the 1952 season, but Neville thought less of the Mud Hens and started to explore other options. One of them was a return to Durham.

# Back in "Bull City"

*A Greensboro television station went on the air in the same September of 1949 that saw Neville win his twenty-fifth game for the Bulls. "The Lone Ranger" was great, but watching Neville in person became a more enjoyable pursuit when he returned in 1952. From a Neville-booster's point of view, it was understandable why the backers of Durham's first station waited until September of 1954 to send out a signal. That was the same month as the left-hander's last Durham game.*

For the first time, the substantial self-confidence that had helped lift Neville beyond his physical limits started to slip away as spring training approached in 1952. He was upset with his own performance and frustrated with the Detroit Tiger organization.

Late in the 1951 season at Williamsport, Neville learned he was close to being called to the majors after the Tigers found themselves short of left-handed relief pitchers. Instead, Detroit acquired 32-year-old veteran Earl Johnson, a little-used Boston Red Sox reliever who was in his final major league season.

Neville was forced to settle for the recalling of his contract to Toledo after the season. But less than two months later, the Tigers sold their American Association franchise and shifted Triple A operations to Buffalo of the International League.

The Tigers' financial loss in Toledo had reached $1 million before the sale. With 1951 attendance in Detroit down by 818,833 as the team nose-dived from second to fifth, the organization found itself in a financial trap complicated by a need for even more improvements to the home of the Mud Hens, 43-year-old Swayne Field. Under the terms of what turned out to be a disastrous business deal, the St. Louis Browns continued to own the park after selling the franchise, but the Tigers remained responsible for rent as well as repairs.

The Mud Hens were bought by a four-man syndicate for a fire-sale price reported to be "in excess of $100,000." Most of the top Tiger prospects headed for Buffalo, but Neville remained assigned to Toledo. His frustrations mounted when he learned Detroit apparently had turned down an earlier offer that would have sent him to the San Francisco Seals of the Pacific Coast League, an ambitious open-classification circuit that was pushing for major league status.

Neville wanted out of Toledo—and he said as much in a letter to Danny Menendez, the Mud Hens' new president and general manager. But instead of voicing his discontent when he hinted at plans to retire, Neville wrote only of his inability to develop another pitch in order to compete at the game's highest level. He never mentioned that Toledo's Marlin Stuart had helped him master a screwball to increase his effectiveness against right-handed batters.

Menendez pointed to Carl Hubbell, Jim Turner, and Lou Fette as three major leaguers who added a pitch late in their careers. "The fallacy of your thinking," Menendez wrote, "is that you need another pitch. From all indications you could win with what you have."

Menendez urged Neville not to "think negatively" and to "hang in there" for what could be an outstanding year. "You have had a couple of nonproductive years and you're a little skeptical of your ability," he continued. "I am not, so why should you be? Give yourself a good thorough chance before quitting. You'll regret it if you don't."

Although only 33, Menendez was an experienced negotiator who had served as general manager of four minor league clubs, including the two previous seasons with the Hollywood Stars in the Pacific Coast League. Still, he probably never had encountered a player as rigid as Neville. After the lefthander repeatedly turned down an offer of $500 a month and refused to report to spring training, Menendez placed him on the Mud Hens' inactive list.

For the third time in six seasons, Neville was in limbo. First came his refusal to report to Beaumont in 1948. That was followed by the delay in reporting to Toledo in 1951.

Predictably, Neville grew restless in Baltimore and headed for Tarboro after learning the manager's job there remained open with the season only a month away. Menendez, however, blocked his shot at the job by refusing to remove him from the inactive list.

Neville suddenly faced a season without baseball—at least in the United States. In late March, he contacted two semipro teams in Canada and learned he could play if he received a release from Toledo or was granted a transfer to the voluntary retired list.

The National Association of Professional Baseball Leagues approved his voluntary retirement April 10, and Neville received a contract offer from Canada within two weeks. James Kendrick, secretary-treasurer of the Guelph Maple Leafs, offered him $400 a month and agreed to pay travel expenses for his trip to Ontario. Another Ontario club, Oshawa, asked for his salary requirements to pitch after Neville originally inquired about a manager's opening.

Jim Kornegay, head of a Durham Studebaker dealership, soon offered another alternative—a job as a car salesman. A puzzle whose pieces seemed so hopelessly scattered in March suddenly came together. He would make one final effort to break his ties with Toledo, sign with Durham, and sell cars in the off-season as he looked at future career choices. Besides, word was out that Ace Parker would resign as Durham's manager after the season to succeed Jack Coombs as baseball coach at Duke University. Neville envisioned himself as Parker's successor, and Bull owner Charles Allen apparently said nothing to discourage him.

This time, since both clubs had ties to Detroit, Menendez relented and assigned Neville's contract outright to the Bulls after the lefthander had his name removed from the voluntarily retired list. He would be on Durham's payroll, rather than Detroit's, for the balance of his Bull career.

Neville's confidence returned as soon as the transaction was completed on May 24. Instead of pitching for a Toledo team that would lose 107 games and move in midseason to Charleston, West Virginia, he would be joining a club seeking its second straight pennant.

When he signed with Durham three days later, Neville's spring training had consisted of a handful of workouts and nine innings of pitching for a semipro team from the town of Ramseur. But even if his arm remained untuned, his long absence at least made him mentally ready for his return to Carolina League competition.

He signed in the morning and pitched that night. It was 1949 all over again as Neville spaced eight singles and a double, picked two runners off first, and beat out a bunt to sustain a five-run, seventh inning rally that carried the Bulls to a 5–1 victory over the Burlington-Graham Pirates. A crowd of 1,584 witnessed his return—one of the largest turnouts of the year and 50 percent more than had attended a doubleheader the night before.

It was neither Detroit nor Toledo nor Williamsport. And it surely was not Guelph, Ontario. For Neville, it was the best place of all. He was back in the "Bull City," back where they stitched blue Bulls on uniform sleeves, back where "Ma" Gregory and everybody else acknowledged him as the pitcher who really was "better than he are."

"I'm pooped," Neville admitted after that first start. "I didn't think I could go nine innings. I told Ace [Parker] I'd go as far as I could but to have somebody ready."

The old pro with the still-curly hair was relaxed and open, laughing about the "pressure" of extending a nine-game home winning streak. "I

**Neville returned to Durham in 1952 after refusing to report to Toledo. Business Manager Curtis "Sis" Perry looks on as the lefthander signs a contract. (Courtesy *The Herald-Sun*.)**

guess they had a nerve risking the streak by starting me," he said. "I didn't want to see it broken."

He promised even more. "I'm not in shape yet," he said. "Give me a couple of weeks and I'll be in better condition to help these boys."

Parker saw a pitcher who had lost something off his fastball since 1949. "You could tell he had lost a little of the zip," he recalled. "But, if anything, he had gotten better with his other pitches."

Durham had discovered another hero after Neville had thrown what was presumably his final pitch as a Bull in September of 1949. Dick Groat, a six-foot guard out of Swissvale, Pennsylvania, launched his varsity basketball career at Duke University less than three months after Neville left. Groat, who would become a two-time All-America in both basketball and baseball, was a handsome college kid who would lose much of his full head of hair during his major league playing career.

Neville's return to Durham came just before Groat completed his baseball career at Duke by leading the Blue Devils to the College World Series at Omaha, Nebraska. Duke would be eliminated after losing two of three games, but fans in Durham would continue to follow Groat's career when he went straight from the campus to become the starting shortstop for the Pittsburgh Pirates.

Ace Parker visited the Duke campus often during Groat's senior season. Sitting in the stands with scouts, Parker sensed that "Dandy Dick's" greatness went beyond stopwatches and sheer athletic ability. "Some of the scouts," Parker recalled in a 1961 article in *Sport* magazine, "would sit there and say: 'How's he gonna hit in the big leagues? He can't pull the ball.' Pulling the ball seemed to mean everything to them, but I can remember lots of big leaguers who couldn't pull the ball.

"Those scouts would look at Groat and say, 'Too slow. Can't run,'" he continued. "But heck, very few right-handed hitters have speed to first base. Groat lacked speed, yes, but I didn't think it really mattered. In the field that boy somehow was always in front of the ball."

Parker was asked why Branch Rickey would spend $25,000 in bonus money to sign Groat for the Pirates. "Well, some scouts were able to see he had something special," Parker said. "They could see he was determined, that all he wanted to do in life was play big league baseball and play it well. He was fierce. He was full of fire inside." (Rickey actually was not that generous. He also signed Groat to a five-year contract at the minimum major league salary of $5,000 a year.)

Making his debut as a pinch hitter on June 18, Groat tapped the ball back to pitcher Jim Hearn of the New York Giants. He moved into the starting lineup the next night at the Polo Grounds and drove in two runs with a third-inning, bases-loaded single off Larry Jansen. His rookie season batting average of .284 on a team that lost 112 games demonstrated that Groat indeed was "full of fire."

Groat had missed nearly half of his sophomore year at Duke after leaving school rather than accept academic probation after he admitted gaining advance access to an economics exam. After his rookie season with the Pirates, he returned to Duke in the fall to finish work on his degree. For a short while, he played part-time for Fort Wayne in the National

Basketball Association before making Fort Belvoir, Virginia, famous in the sports world after he entered the service in January.

Groat continued to play both sports in the service, once returning to Duke with the Fort Belvoir team that won the All-Army Basketball title. When he led the Engineers to the baseball title as well, Fort Belvoir became the first base to win All-Army championships in major sports in the same year.

Yielding to the Pirates' wishes, Groat dropped basketball after his two Army years. He became a big league oddity—a singles hitter respected enough to be named team captain and a slow-footed shortstop who somehow broke a Pittsburgh fielding average record set in 1923 by Walter "Rabbitt" Maranville.

"He kills us," said Manager Fred Hutchinson of the Cincinnati Reds in 1960. "I wish to hell he'd go away." Groat finally went away seven years later after 14 National League seasons with the Pirates, St. Louis, and Philadelphia. He finished with a lifetime batting average of .286.

As Groat's career at Duke neared an end in 1952, Neville found himself in the middle of a pennant race. His first victory kept the Bulls a half game behind first-place Reidsville and three percentage points ahead of Greensboro. And unlike the team of 1949, this was a talented, more experienced squad capable of making a run for the rest of the year.

There was diversity as well. James "Buster" Maynard, a 39-year-old former major leaguer from nearby Henderson, patrolled the outfield with Emil Karlik, a 20-year-old power hitter from Newark, New Jersey. Karlik's statistics would be more impressive, but it would be Maynard who would bring the team a touch of class with his experience as a wartime player with the New York Giants.

In center field, Charles "Chick" King, a highly regarded 21-year-old prospect from Paris, Tennessee, appeared to be Pat Haggerty reincarnated with equal speed and even more power.

Second baseman Howie Henkle was back for a third season, armed with a glove and a pair of scissors that he learned to use at a Winston-Salem barber school. A rookie barber in his first year as a Bull, the 25-year-old Henkle now trimmed hair as smoothly as he fielded.

In the off-season, Henkle practiced barbering fulltime in his home town of Cherryville, North Carolina. He charged a dollar a head back then, but Bulls could get theirs for free.

A Henkle haircut would continue to be a bargain at Cherryville's two-chair Sanitary Barber Shop. Although inflation pushed the price up to $6 after he had been on the job for more than 40 years, stories about his nine seasons as a minor league player were available free of charge.

Henkle and fellow North Carolinian Bob Warren, a veteran third baseman from Goldsboro, brought stability to an infield that had a hole

Durham's 1952 club finished second in regular season Carolina League play before losing out to Reidsville in the final round of the playoffs. Front row, left to right: Jack Miller, Dave Baxter, Ralph Caldwell, Howie Henkle, and batboy Billy Perry. Middle row: Luke Dawson, Delbert Gay, Bob Warren, Eddie Neville, Emil Karlik, and Buster Maynard. Back row: Walter Wilson, Chick King, Marcus Davis, Dick Barr, Andy Frazier, Jim Martin, and Manager Ace Parker. (Courtesy Miles Wolff.)

every Monday night when shortstop Andy "Red" Frazier reported for National Guard duty in Greensboro.

First baseman Don "Tex" Warfield, the Baltimorean who had been Neville's teammate at Cristobol, had no military obligations but would hit the road in August after rejecting a demotion. Warfield's season was starcrossed from the start; early on he missed out on a $3 prize given by a sandwich company when he failed to touch second after hitting what would have been a triple.

At catcher, Ralph Caldwell, who had been assigned to Williamsport after the 1949 season but returned to the Bulls shortly after spring training, was now the senior Durham player since Parker no longer played and pitcher Mickey McPadden had been called up by the Air Force during the Korean War. (McPadden stayed in the service until he retired as a lieutenant colonel in 1967, then settled in the Durham area as a resident of nearby Hillsborough.)

Neville bolstered an already-strong pitching staff that included Jim Martin, a righthander from Detroit who had won 14 games for the Bulls in 1951; Luke Dawson, a talented but unpredictable lefthander from Portia, Arkansas; and tall righthander Marcus "High Pockets" Davis, a Dothan, Alabama, product returning for his third Durham season.

Neville's return, however, was overshadowed by the Carolina League debut of "Rocket" Ron Necciai, a 19-year-old righthander who had been promoted to Burlington-Graham after becoming the first pitcher in the history of organized baseball to strike out 27 batters in nine innings.

Necciai (pronounced Netch-eye) had started out as a first baseman in the Pittsburgh organization after being recommended by a barber in the hotel across the street from Forbes Field. He had been a first baseman in high school at Monongahela, Pennsylvania, but switched to pitching after his manager at Salisbury in the Class D North Carolina State League observed his rifle throws in infield practice. He was tested for three innings his rookie season, then returned to Salisbury and struck out 111 batters in 106 innings before a late-season promotion to New Orleans in the Class AA Southern Association.

Necciai was so wild at New Orleans that he walked nearly four times as many batters as he struck out. After the season, he requested that he be reunited with his Salisbury manager, George Detore, who had been assigned to Bristol (Virginia-Tennessee) of the Class D Appalachian League for 1952. "I still have a lot of kinks in my delivery, and I want Detore to help me straighten them out," Necciai said.

Detore did. Necciai struck out 20 batters in his first game, 19 in his second, and 11 of the 12 batters he faced in four innings of relief.

Only four batters reached base the night of Necciai's record-setting, no-hit performance against the Welch (West Virginia) Miners. Only two managed to hit the ball, one grounding out to first and the other benefiting from a shortstop error. Necciai hit one batter, walked another, and had fanned 25 with two outs in the ninth.

Necciai was credited with his twenty-sixth strikeout after the batter reached first when a third strike hit the dirt and bounced away from catcher Harry Dunlop. The next batter became the tenth to watch a third called strike, and Necciai had his 27.

A crowd of 1,853 turned out for the Welch game, but 5,235 were on hand for his next start against Kingsport. Between starts, Necciai had struck out eight batters in two and two-thirds innings against Johnson City—fanning five in one inning when two batters reached base on two passed balls.

After accepting a shower of gifts from fans and merchants, Necciai struck out 24 Kingsport batters and headed for the Carolina League.

Neville and "Rocket" Ron Necciai, who had recorded 27 strikeouts in one game after starting the season in the Class D Appalachian League, relax in the dugout before their first and only pitching confrontation in 1952. (Courtesy *The Herald-Sun.*)

Detore was left with a pitching staff headed by 18-year-old Bill Bell, who the very next night pitched the first of two consecutive no-hitters and added a third in August.

Physically, Necciai was everything that Neville was not, a good eight inches taller and blessed with a whipsaw body and a powerhouse arm. But he was also a self-described worrier who suffered from stomach ulcers, and he couldn't eat or sleep in spring training until the Pirate team physician prescribed some pills and put him on a diet that eliminated fried foods and dry cereals and required that vegetables be strained.

Necciai also gave ulcers to Carolina League hitters, striking out 21 in his first twelve and one-third innings to post a 2–0 record before running into the Bulls on his home turf on June 9. A turnout of 2,414, unusually high for the weak Pirate farm club, saw both Neville and Necciai that night but not in the same game.

Neville, who had picked up his fourth victory in five decisions the night before at Greensboro, relieved in the opener and suffered his second loss. Necciai, his every move watched by Pittsburgh Pirate executive

Harold Roettger, lost the nightcap despite striking out the side three times. Seven Durham hits, including a double and triple by Buster Maynard, offset a dozen Necciai strikeouts as the Bulls scored a 2–1 victory behind righthander Jim Martin's four-hitter.

The pitching matchup that spelled magic would come four days later in Durham: Neville vs. Necciai, the old hero versus the young gunslinger, a timeworn knuckler against fireballs and fancy curves. There was a sense of history at Durham Athletic Park that Friday night as 4,435 fans turned out for a one-time-only confrontation that would be one of the last golden moments of Carolina League baseball in the decade that followed World War II.

Necciai struck out two Bulls in the first two innings and fanned the side in the fourth. He lost his bid for a no-hitter in the fifth when Ralph Caldwell sliced a one-out single to right for one of five Durham hits.

Burlington-Graham bunched seven of its nine hits against Neville into two innings. The Pirates pushed across two runs in the second after Necciai's leadoff double and added another in the seventh to score a 3–2 victory. Neville struck out five and walked only three, but the night belonged to Necciai as he fanned the last two batters to reach the dozen mark a second time against the Bulls.

Before being called up by last-place Pittsburgh in August, Necciai averaged over 12 strikeouts a game and tamed his walks to just over four. His longest strikeout string was 13 over two games, and his 1.57 earned run average would have set a new league record if he had pitched enough innings to qualify. He finished with a 7–9 record on a last-place team that would win only 45 games. In Pittsburgh, he would join a Pirate team that would win only 42.

Necciai, who had grown up only 15 miles from Pittsburgh, was such a hot item that the Associated Press dispatched a picture of his airport arrival to newspapers across the country. With Dick Groat behind him at shortstop, he made his debut on August 10 in the first game of a doubleheader against the Chicago Cubs. The turnout of 17,773 fans was said to include enough extra customers to pay his salary through the 1953 season.

Necciai's performance was as soft as the recorded sound of Pirate part-owner Bing Crosby singing the national anthem. He gave up five runs in the first inning and left after six—a disappointment to Bristol fans who had given Necciai an oil portrait of himself before the game.

Although Necciai was impressive the next day when he threw eight straight strikes and fanned five in three hitless innings of relief against Cincinnati, he would fail to complete any of his eight starts as he posted a 7.08 earned run average in winning one of seven decisions.

He didn't suffer alone. His Bristol pitching mate, Bill Bell, was called up in September. In four tries, the tall righthander from Goldsboro, North

Carolina, lost his only decision and gave up hits at the rate of one per inning. Except for a single inning at Pittsburgh three seasons later, that was the last National League batters would see of Bell, who would lose his life in a 1962 automobile accident.

Necciai entered the service after the season, but was discharged two months later after losing 35 pounds and dropping to 130 when his ulcers rejected Army food. He had regained half that weight by the time he started working out at Forbes Field.

In the end, it was a bad arm that stopped Necciai instead of ulcers. "One day my arm went bang and it was over," he said.

Necciai had been warming up when he felt a shoulder pain with the intensity of an icepick wound. "Every time I pitched it would hurt 30 or 40 seconds. It would bring tears to my eyes."

Necciai returned to Burlington-Graham in late May, but he would never be the same pitcher again. The Pirates tried cortisone and Novocain and asked the advice of specialists. "Today it probably would be called a torn rotator cuff, but back then they just didn't know," Necciai said.

He sat out the 1954 season after a comeback attempt in spring training, then pitched briefly the next year for the Hollywood Stars in the Pacific Coast League before retiring.

"If I had stopped pitching the first time it twinged maybe nothing would have happened," Necciai said. Without the benefit of hindsight, he headed back to Monongahela and turned to a career in sales that was unaffected by the pain that never left.

But on that one June night in Durham, when he was but five days short of his twentieth birthday, he threw so hard and so masterfully that Neville became a forgotten man for the ever-so-brief two hours that the game lasted. "One of these days," said Necciai, "I may go back and see where it all happened. It seems a lot more special now than it did then. I thought striking out 27 was the kind of thing baseball pitchers did. I didn't know until the next morning that I was the first." (Necciai remains the only pitcher in the history of both the minor and major leagues to strike out 27 batters in a nine-inning game.)

Neville won seven of his next eight decisions after the Necciai encounter, running up a string of 12 complete games before being removed in the seventh in a home loss to Greensboro.

After Reidsville and Greensboro fell back in a four-team pennant scramble, the final two months turned into a showdown between the Bulls and an old neighborhood rival, the much-despised Raleigh Capitals.

Raleigh always seemed to have more of everything than Durham — more people, more money, even a better baseball team most of the time. It was white collar against blue collar, the bluebloods from the state capital against the boys from the "Bull City." Only Duke University, Raleigh fans believed, stood between Durham and total ignorance. Durham fans, in turn, pinned a "cow college" label on North Carolina State at Raleigh.

The rivalry was real, the players actual warriors who represented not just teams but the very heart and soul of two cities thrown together by geography but polarized by clear cultural differences. Even the name of Raleigh's park—Devereaux Meadow—had the ring of aristocracy.

As early as 1887, Durham teams had one mission in mind: "Beat Raleigh at any cost." One citizen who witnessed the games of that era claimed that Durham fans who went to Raleigh by train sometimes returned with "broken heads and black eyes."

The hostility continued after Durham beat Raleigh in the Piedmont League opener in 1913. Jerry Markham, a Durham fan who went to the games dressed in tails and a top hat, was egged during a return match at Raleigh, but, according to newspaper accounts, "blurted out that every man in Raleigh would be unable to keep him away from the games played in Durham."

When Durham dedicated El Toro Park in 1926, Raleigh spoiled an otherwise pleasant afternoon with a 3–2 victory. And in the first five seasons of Carolina League play, Raleigh won one pennant and finished ahead of Durham every time except 1946, when the teams tied for second. Even then, Raleigh won a playoff game with the Bulls to determine second-place money and went on to capture the league playoffs. The 1946 pennant race was so hot that 15,232 fans turned out for a three-game September series (two in Raleigh and one in Durham) as the rivals chased first place along with eventual winner Greensboro.

Raleigh beat itself in 1950, finishing seventh to Durham's sixth. One season later, the suddenly snooty Bulls finished first to Raleigh's third, then lost some of the luster by falling to Winston-Salem in the playoffs.

As an independent club, Raleigh once spent $15,000 in a single season buying up some of the best talent in the lower minors. Durham, with most players supplied by Detroit in Neville's era, was more tight-fisted but sometimes loosened up when it came to outbidding the Caps.

At times, the rivals even raided each other's rosters. Cecil "Turkey" Tyson performed as both a Bull and Cap, as did center fielder Tommy Martin. Even in 1952, a former Capital, left-handed hitting first baseman Dave Baxter, would turn up on the Durham roster in late June and take dead aim at the right field scoreboard. And the heart of the Raleigh infield that season was ex-Bull Lawrence "Crash" Davis, a 33-year-old Georgian who had been a utility infielder for the Philadelphia A's from 1940–42. (Davis authorized the use of his name for the character of "Crash" Davis, the journeyman catcher played by Kevin Costner in the movie, *Bull*

**Lawrence "Crash" Davis, left, a Durham infielder in 1948, agreed to the use of his name for the fictional hero of the 1989 movie, *Bull Durham*. Davis is joined by Earl Richmond, center, a first baseman who was Neville's roommate in 1949, and pitcher John "Mickey" McPadden, a former House of David barnstormer whose 61 career victories for the Bulls rank him second behind Neville. (Courtesy Earl Richmond.)**

*Durham.* When the film came out in 1989, the real "Crash" Davis, living in Greensboro, became something of a celebrity himself.)

Raleigh had amassed the second best overall record in the Carolina League with deep, experienced pitching staffs. The 1952 staff would be anchored by slender righthander Ben Rossman, who would set a league record by running up a string of thirty-eight and one-third consecutive scoreless innings.

After leading the league for much of the first half of the season, the Caps qualified to serve as the host team against an All-Star club composed of top players from the rest of the league. At times, the contest took on the flavor of a Durham-Raleigh matchup as five Bull players and Manager Ace Parker trotted out in All-Star uniforms. Neville was there, along with Ralph Caldwell, Howie Henkle, Emil Karlik, and Chick King. All except Henkle would be named to the postseason All-League team along with pitcher Luke Dawson.

Herb Brett was on hand as well, this time in the Raleigh dugout. Neville's manager of a decade ago was now the field boss of his third Carolina League club after previous stops at Danville and Reidsville. The heavy-set Virginia native had been all business when he spearheaded the league's founding, but he now had a reputation as a colorful sort who stirred up fans by waving a red bandanna.

In the fifth inning of a scoreless All-Star game, King reached first on a force play, stole second, and scored on a two-out single by shortstop Jimmy Edwards of Fayetteville. In the ninth, Neville faced four batters and preserved a 1–0 victory.

Durham continued its pennant bid in spite of the sun, a mock funeral, and military duty—all of which resulted in the absence of three key players.

Dawson was a victim of the sun, his fair Arkansas skin being baked during a visit to a Durham lake in late June. "Here we were, right in the middle of a pennant race, and this guy comes back and he's so burned he could barely stand up," Parker related.

The players laughed at Dawson; Parker didn't. The team docked his pay for the ten days he missed. Dawson returned to the lineup on the fourth of July, but there was hardly reason to celebrate. The peeling pitcher took an 18–9 basting and went the distance without relief. Dawson recovered in time to win his next five games. His record reached 13–4 before he passed an Army physical and left the team in August.

Outfielder Emil Karlik attempted to burn Parker with a phony story about a funeral. Parker agreed to give him time off to grieve for his grandmother, but became suspicious when Karlik failed to return. Talk among the players indicated Karlik had pulled a hoax.

Parker enlisted the aid of his wife, Thelma, who called the Karlik home in Newark, New Jersey, to offer her condolences. "Karlik's mother told Thelma the grandmother was alive and sitting on the front porch," Parker said. "Emil was at home, too."

Karlik had led the league with a .363 average before taking off in mid-July. He muscled his hits with massive arms and shoulders built up in the off-season by working as a longshoreman on the docks of Newark. He stood five-foot-ten and was cursed with a ducklike running style, but he hit with power and had a throwing arm that had cut down six runners by mid-season.

Parker, however, remained unimpressed. His instincts told him early in the year that Karlik's cavalier attitude toward the game would keep the outfielder out of the major leagues. Karlik drew a fine and lost his pay for the six games he missed. After the season, he went to Parker and asked for his lost wages. Parker stared and said just enough for Karlik to give up the argument.

His final average of .347 was the league's best by nine percentage points. He was fourth in runs batted in with 93 and third in home runs with

17. But Parker was right. Karlik, hurt by a two-year service stay as well as what his manager perceived as indifference, never reached Detroit.

The Bulls' chief contribution to the majors that season would be a player off the campus of Auburn University rather than the docks of Newark. Inman "Coot" Veal, a "bonus baby" shortstop, played just 17 games as a replacement for Durham's third "missing" player. Andy "Red" Frazier was no culprit, however; he had departed for two weeks of National Guard duty at Fort McClellan, Alabama.

Frazier, who had played with Neville at Williamsport, had been ticketed for a promotion to Little Rock in the Class AA Southern Association until the Korean War put his guard unit at nearby Greensboro on 24-hour notice and forced the Tigers to assign him to Durham.

One of those happiest to see him head for summer duty was Lindy Brown, a Reidsville pitcher who had grown up with Frazier in Greensboro. Brown, whose brother, former Durham pitcher Hal "Skinny" Brown, would have a 14-year major league career, had lost a no-hitter at Reidsville when Frazier connected for a two-run homer with one out in the seventh. "Andy still apologizes for doing that," laughed Brown, who picked up a two-hit victory.

Frazier's replacement was less potent. The 20-year-old Veal met his match in curveballs and batted only .215 as Frazier's fill-in. Even with his weak bat, the slender Georgian reached Detroit in 1958 and used his glove to stick around six seasons with three teams.

Chick King was Durham's only other contribution to Detroit that season. King would reach the majors faster than Veal but play far less. The Tennessee speedster, who would lead the Carolina League in hits with 186, bat .315, and steal 33 bases, was recalled by the Tigers three times starting in 1954 and also played briefly with the Chicago Cubs.

But it was neither Veal nor King nor Karlik nor a lobsterlike Dawson who drew spectators to Durham Athletic Park that summer. The real attraction was Neville. When the lefthander pitched, the Bulls could count on a crowd 40 percent above the average. Neville responded with equal admiration for Durham Athletic Park; he would not serve up a single home run there the entire season.

His games still came in capsule form, and the fast times became contagious. In a doubleheader against Danville, Durham's Jim Martin pitched a one-hit shutout in a seven-inning opener played in 59 minutes. Neville followed up with a two-hit, nine-inning shutout that took one hour and 38 minutes.

The smallest crowd to turn out for a Neville home performance came three days before the end of the regular season. Raleigh had clinched the pennant the night before. Durham was assured of second place. The game with Greensboro meant nothing except to those hardcore fans who realized that any Neville appearance would be worth the price of admission.

For nine innings, neither team scored, the Bulls blowing opportunity after opportunity and leaving 12 runners on base. In the last of the ninth, the Bulls loaded the bases with one out against starter Ray Simmons but failed to score. In the bottom of the tenth, Simmons gave up a leadoff triple to Karlik, then walked Frazier and Dave Baxter intentionally to set up force plays.

Greensboro Manager Kemp Wicker summoned knuckleballer Gene Pereyra to relieve Simmons. Pereyra threw a called third strike past Buster Maynard, retired Ralph Caldwell on a foul pop to the catcher, and closed out the inning on a Neville grounder.

Pereyra, who would not walk a batter, survived two more Durham threats. Howie Henkle and Bob Warren singled with one out in the eleventh before Pereyra retired Karlik and Baxter. Maynard never advanced past second after doubling with one out in the fifteenth.

Neville was the same bulldog that he had been in the marathon at Toledo, only this time he kept runners off the bases. Greensboro, stranding only six runners through 17 innings, never threatened seriously until connecting on two straight one-out singles in the eighteenth. Neville, who would strike out eight, walk three, and give up only eight hits in what amounted to two complete games, then retired shortstop Dick Rigazio on a fly to right and forced Pereyra to ground out.

With one out in the bottom of the eighteenth, Neville came to bat for the eighth time. As had been typical of a season that he would see him finish with a .147 average, he had been retired seven straight times, twice when he had an opportunity to win the game.

It was nearly 11:15 P.M. when Neville smashed a drive that came within two feet of clearing the right field wall near the scoreboard. He pulled into second with a double, then watched as King flied to center for the second out.

Henkle then slapped one of Pereyra's slow, taunting pitches past second base into short center. Add Penfield, broadcasting the game back to Greensboro fans, knew the play would be close. "Eddie wound up tumbling across the plate because he didn't know whether to slide or dive," Penfield said years later.

Neville scored and a contest that matched the most number of innings in Carolina League history came to an end. The game itself required only three hours and 15 minutes. Years later, a *Raleigh Times* staffer misread a feature on the game, thought it ended at 3:15 in the morning, and wrote the headline, "When Eddie Neville Pitched All Night."

"Only 666 people were there that night to see history made," Penfield recalled. "But it was like that Duke-Pitt football game in the snow [in

1938]. I've probably run into a half million people who say they were there, and Eddie tells me at least 10,000 people have told him they were in Durham Athletic Park that night."

Thomas "Tinker" Parnell, a 15-year-old junior high school catcher, was one of those 10,000 who told the truth. Generally regarded as the number one fan of the modern-day Bulls, Parnell attended the game with his father, John, a truck driver, and still regards the contest as the best he has ever seen.

The only other Carolina League game that had lasted 18 innings ended without a decision. In 1945, Durham righthander Wallace Mitchell went the distance against Martinsville in a contest that was stopped by the midnight curfew with the teams tied at 4–4.

Neville and Mitchell remain in the league record book for pitching the most consecutive innings in a single game. Ironically, Mitchell's game would have ended in regulation had it not been for a four-run Martinsville ninth.

Neville admitted he lost his pitching edge in the final inning. "I was pooped in that eighteenth," he said. "I didn't have anything on the ball. I lost all my stuff."

Exhausted but wired up after the game, Neville tried to calm down by walking to the nearby Five Points section of downtown Durham before returning to the park. "Then I went home and I couldn't sleep," he said the next day. "I plopped on the bed, rolled, squirmed, twisted, perspired, got up, and smoked several cigarettes. It was terrible. I guess I got three or four hours sleep. And to top it off, I lost eight pounds."

Neville continued to view his 1950 performance against first-place Indianapolis as his biggest thrill. "It also got us out of eighth place," he grinned.

Durham finished two and one-half games behind Raleigh after sweeping a Labor Day doubleheader before a home crowd of 2,267 that longed for a second shot at the Caps in the playoffs. Had the Bulls performed on the road even reasonably close to the home record, the pennant would have been run up the Durham Athletic Park flagpole instead of Devereaux Meadow. Neville and crew finished with a 49–21 record at home, including a 7–3 margin over Raleigh, but fell on the road to 27–38 against all opponents and 2–7 against Raleigh.

The Durham-Raleigh rivalry ended with the regular season after the Caps fell in three straight playoff games to fourth-place Reidsville. When the Bulls won three straight over Winston-Salem, including a Neville shutout, the stage was set for two games matching two of the league's most productive pitchers.

Neville had surpassed Reidsville's Mike Forline in 1949 when the two first pitched in the league, winning 25 versus 18 for the husky New

England righthander. But Forline remained after Neville left in 1949, and those two extra seasons had given him a 74–42 margin as the 1952 regular season ended. They had faced each other only once, with Forline winning an 8–3 decision in 1949.

Forline would go through a self-imposed ritual before every start. Five hours before game time, he would isolate himself and play mind games. Mentally, no batter ever reached first as he repeatedly reviewed his pitching pattern. "I knew every pitch I was going to throw," he said.

Physically, Forline bordered on being a 30-year-old wreck who had ignored constant arm pains and pitched an average of 257 innings in his first four Reidsville seasons. He had overcome the back problems that led to earlier releases from the New York Giant and Boston Brave organizations, but he remained a question mark every spring. "It would take me longer to get in shape," he said. "It was like my arm was dead. Sometimes, success for pitchers just comes with a lot of pain. When you're too strong, you're wild."

Forline survived on savvy and—some say—a spitball. "It looked like a spitball, but it wasn't," he said. "It was a trick pitch I learned in high school; I would get a spin on the ball by twisting it at the last second. It was a natural pitch for me, but people would just laugh at me when I tried to show them how. No one else could do it."

His manager for two seasons, former Chicago White Sox outfielder Ralph Hodgin, backed up Forline on the spitter charges. "It was something like a split-fingered fastball," he said.

Hodgin also recalled Forline's effectiveness with a ball that had been doctored by the game itself. "We were playing in Danville, and I brought Mike in to relieve in the ninth," Hodgin said. "The ball had become kind of egg-shaped from the dampness, and his eyes were wide open when I gave it to him. He knew how to use scuff marks and things like that. He took that lopsided ball and made it dance."

Forline's spitter-like pitch was so effective that he became known around the league as "Magic Mike." If he could survive the first inning, a time he often became jittery, rival teams realized they were in trouble.

"Pitching is a very simple thing," he explained. "A fastball inside, a curveball outside, a little off here, a little faster there. And I would challenge fastball hitters. They thought I was crazy."

Forline saw Neville as a pitcher who "would have the players talking to themselves. He'd just set them up and get them out."

The championship series opener was one time that didn't happen. Neville was routed in the third inning, and Forline recorded a 7–0 shutout at Durham. After reaching the playoff finals for the first time in five years, the Bulls made a quick, embarrassing exit after four games. In the final meeting at Reidsville's Kiker Stadium, Forline gave up two runs in his usual shaky first but bested Neville 4–3 after the Luckies scored single runs in the eighth and ninth.

Forline would go on to become the Carolina League's all-time winning pitcher. His 89 wins in six seasons placed him 14 ahead of Neville, who is fifth on the all-time list. After baseball and several business ventures, the man they called "Magic" retired and turned his skills toward piloting a 37-foot sailboat in waters near his home in Durham, Connecticut.

For Neville, the series marked a disappointing end to an abbreviated but outstanding season that saw him win 17 of 26 decisions. Although he completed 17 of 19 starts and set a new league record with a 1.72 earned run average, he welcomed the end of a season for perhaps the first time in his career. "It's all over!!" he wrote in his diary.

Three days later, the Carolina League mailed out shares of the playoff money to the Durham and Reidsville players. As a member of the winning team, Forline received $27.44. Neville settled for $20.58.

Neville was so worn out that he spent one of his first days at home in bed. By the next afternoon, he was back on the Baltimore sandlots pitching in a local All-Star game that would mark his final game until spring training. He lost once again, then waited out the fall and part of the winter fully expecting to become the next manager of the Durham Bulls.

Duke University had confirmed that Ace Parker would succeed Jack Coombs, who left his baseball coaching job after 24 seasons only because of a university policy making retirement mandatory at age 69. Had policy and immortality permitted, Coombs would have stayed in the game as long as his former manager Connie Mack, who only two years earlier had stopped managing at the age of 87. Besides, chronological age had no effect on the performance of a man who knew enough about the game to write a popular baseball textbook and whose opening practices often attracted 80 or more candidates.

His players had called Coombs the "Old Man" in an affectionate sort of way. Coombs had worn a uniform like everyone else when he first came to Duke, but he eventually followed the lead of Mack and came to the park in civilian clothes. In later seasons, he wore a hat instead of a baseball cap, sported a suit instead of a uniform, and substituted a tie and vest in the place of his Duke lettering. On cold days, he turned to a topcoat instead of a warmup jacket.

With a coaching record like his, Coombs probably could have shown up in swim trunks and kept his job. His teams at Duke won 378 games and lost only 170. He was as good as ever in his final season. With Dick Groat at shortstop, the Blue Devils finished with a 31–7 record and captured the Southern Conference championship.

Coombs never pitched a game in the minors. He starred at Colby College in Maine and went straight to the Philadelphia Athletics after signing a contract in 1906 for what was regarded as a high sum: $2,400. The six-foot righthander won 158 games in 14 seasons, more than two-thirds of them before he nearly died in 1913 after being stricken during spring training in San Antonio, Texas, with typhoid fever that settled in his spine.

A 31-game winner in 1910 and five for five in three World Series, Coombs relived one of his greatest games in 1950 with the radio re-creation of his 1911 World Series victory over Christy Mathewson and the New York Giants. He borrowed an FM radio to hear a modern version of the 11-inning, 3-2 affair that was spoiled only by Liberty Network announcer Gordon McLendon repeatedly referring to him as a lefthander.

Although Coombs planned to become a chemist after his retirement from baseball in 1920, he ended up as the head baseball coach at Williams College. He headed for Princeton four years later and then was lured by Duke in 1929 as the university recruited top coaches to help build a national reputation.

Coombs would spend springs and falls at Duke, winters at his home in Palestine, Texas, and summers on a 210-acre farm in his native Kennebunk, Maine. He and his wife, Mary, had no children but enjoyed campus life and the connection with students. "What more could I want?" he once asked.

Coombs produced a long line of future major leaguers at Duke, most of whom would play under Mack at Philadelphia. Mack and Coombs were close friends, but not close enough that Mack would repay his debt on the baseball field. In April of 1939, the Athletics, with four former Duke players on the roster, stopped in Durham on their way north from spring training and destroyed Coombs' Blue Devil team 19-2.

Mack, who was in his forty-second of 53 seasons as a manager, would not be as fortunate in his regular season travels. He became ill on a train to Boston in June and followed the rest of the seventh-place season from his bedside radio as his son, Earle, ran the team for the final 90 games.

In addition to Ace Parker, Coombs' products who played under Mack included infielder Wayne Ambler, outfielder Eric "The Red" Tipton, catcher Hal Wagner, and pitchers Alfred "Chubby" Dean, Bill McCahan, Pete Naktenis, and Dave Smith (a Durham Bull in 1949). Three other Coombs' players—infielders Dick Groat and Bill Werber and outfielder Ron Northey—reached the majors without a Mack connection.

Coombs also coached Mack's son, Connie Mack, Jr., a pitcher who spent most of his one varsity season in 1934 as the team's third-base coach. The 6-5 Mack, who earned a letter in basketball, left school after his sophomore year and, at the age of 22, coached first base for the A's in 1935. He later became the team's treasurer.

Duke's Ambler, a native of Abington, Pennsylvania, revealed how his enrollment at the university was made possible by a "Connie Mack scholarship." Unknown to him, one of his tryouts at Philadelphia's Shibe Park in 1933 took place as Coombs sat in a box seat. Two days later, the 17-year-old prospect took a train to Durham to start the fall semester.

Mack paid him $2,500 over four years to cover his tuition, and Ambler covered his expenses with odd jobs that included waiting on tables and selling football programs. "The minor leagues weren't so good then, and a lot of big league clubs thought we could learn more under coaches like Coombs," said Ambler, who was named to Duke's Hall of Fame in 1989. "At the time, there was nothing illegal about getting payments like that."

A week before graduation, he received a Philadelphia contract in the mail. "I wasn't happy with it, but I wasn't going to turn it down," said Ambler, who estimated that he received $10,000 over three seasons with the A's.

Ambler left Duke halfway through his final exam and took a plane to Washington, D.C., in time to arrive for the second game of a doubleheader. After a 25-hour train ride to St. Louis, he started his first game against the Browns and singled to center his first time up.

Stepping aside after 23 seasons of developing the skills of players such as Ambler, Coombs said he missed familiar faces and felt like a stranger when he returned to the Duke campus after his retirement. He died in his Texas home town of Palestine in 1957. Some, including sports editor Jack Horner, were convinced the cause was a broken heart.

Parker made no attempt to imitate his old coach. He admired and respected Coombs, but considered him too much of an authoritarian at times. "We played at Maryland one time and I skipped breakfast," Parker related. "No one told me there was a rule against that, but Coach Coombs kept me out of the game."

Parker's replacement in left field spent the afternoon chasing balls hit by Maryland's Charlie "King Kong" Keller. "Keller hit three homers that I think I would have stopped," said Parker.

It would be years before Parker had the nerve to approach Coombs about the incident. "I asked him if he remembered the time he cost us the Southern Conference championship," he laughed.

Parker would coach the Blue Devils for 13 seasons. In 1967, after a year as backfield coach at the University of North Carolina, he returned to his native Portsmouth, Virginia, and spent 23 years as a pro football scout. After that, golf took over as his main sports interest as he headed for his favorite course in Portsmouth along a road the city named Ace Parker Drive.

Just as Parker replaced his old mentor, Neville wanted to succeed Parker. In October, Durham assigned his contract to Little Rock.

Although the move apparently was made to discourage other clubs from drafting the lefthander, it also offered one final chance to move up once again in the Detroit organization. But Neville had no interest in playing in the Class AA Southern Association; he wanted to call the shots for an entire team.

# Managing by Numbers

*If you wanted to save the price of admission to a Bulls' game, you could see most of the field from a distant parking lot atop a hill in the block beyond the center field fence. It was something like sitting on the back row of the bleachers in Cleveland and watching a game in Pittsburgh.*

---

Eddie Neville wanted to stay in baseball forever. He hoped his final pitch would be followed by a second career as a manager—an old-professor type with enough knowledge of the game to earn patches on his sleeves.

Circumstances appeared to be on his side. After four years, Ace Parker was leaving the Durham Bulls to become baseball coach at Duke University. Neville felt he would be a natural choice to lead the Bulls. He had played under Parker two years; he would take the same laid-back approach to managing; he, like Parker, was a local hero who could head off a declining interest in Bull baseball.

He skipped winter baseball for the first time and stayed in Durham to sell automobiles. He fully expected Detroit to disclose at the December minor league meeting in Phoenix that he would be Parker's successor. The news never came.

Detroit delayed an announcement in Phoenix, but did inform Durham officials that only experienced managers already in the farm system were being considered. From the Tigers' perspective, Neville—hurt by his low-key personality and the fallout from his Toledo contract squabbles—probably was never under serious consideration.

His support by Durham's front office also was considerably less than Neville expected. Owner Charles Allen, thought by Neville to be his chief backer, admitted that Detroit's ultimate choice had been supported by the Bulls. And Burwell Allen, Charles Allen's brother who served as vice president of the Bulls, recalled that the Durham club expected Detroit to select a manager from its own ranks. Neville said later that Tiger officials told him he had been ruled out because he was a pitcher. It was a reason he refused to accept since Detroit's own manager was former Tiger hurler Fred Hutchinson.

Detroit's decision chewed away at Neville's pride. In January, he threatened to quit and look for a manager's job elsewhere. Neville had been job hunting before, having been a managerial candidate at Tarboro a year earlier before being blocked by his contract with Toledo. He later checked out a manager's opening with the Oshawa semipro club in Canada, only to learn another candidate had been hired.

This time, however, the search never started. His focus was clearly on the game itself by the time he reported to spring training. It would not be until after a frustrating 1954 season that he seriously resumed his efforts to manage.

His stay on the Little Rock roster was brief. Since Tiger minor leaguers in spring training at Lakeland, Florida, wore identical uniforms, only the color of their socks tipped off their team assignment. Long before the clubs broke camp, Neville was wearing the orange socks that labeled him as a Durham Bull.

Neville never really expected to go to Arkansas. Even before his reassignment to the Bulls, he had planned a May wedding in Durham. His engagement had become official in a long-distance telephone conversation at spring training with Janet Goodwin, a Durham native who had neither seen a Bulls' game nor heard of Neville until their chance meeting in a bowling alley the previous October.

Another match also met with Neville's approval. Durham's new manager would be easy-going Marvin Owen, a 47-year-old Californian who had managed nine seasons in the minors, the last at Davenport (Iowa) in the Class B Three-I League. The lanky, likeable Owen had been an outstanding third baseman for Detroit in the 1930s, playing in two World Series for the Tigers and averaging .275 with three clubs over nine seasons.

He was the same Marvin Owen who had been on the receiving end of Joe "Ducky" Medwick's spikes in the seventh game of the 1934 World Series. The St. Louis Cardinals already had run up an 11–0 lead in the top of the sixth when Medwick knocked Owen down with a hard slide after tripling off the right field wall.

Certain he had been spiked deliberately by Medwick, Owen scuffled with the Cardinal outfielder and was kicked in the chest. When Medwick returned to left field in the bottom of the sixth, the Detroit crowd responded with a shower of garbage, bombarding him with fruit, vegetables, ground meat, and anything else that remained in their lunch bags.

The game had been delayed for 15 minutes when Commissioner Kenesaw Mountain Landis called Medwick, Owen, and the two managers to his box seat near first base. Landis had little choice if he wanted the game to continue; he ordered Medwick out of the game even though the future Hall of Famer was just one hit short of tying the World Series record of 12 hits. Owen stayed in and eventually set a World Series record of his own by going hitless in 31 consecutive times at bat in 1934 and 1935.

Owen, according to his son, Skip, of Santa Clara, California, avoided Medwick for the rest of his career. "It was the type of thing where my father would walk on the other side of the street whenever he saw Medwick," explained the younger Owen. Ironically, the rivals came within two years of being opposing managers in the Carolina League. Medwick had managed a third-place team at Raleigh in 1951.

In a 1989 interview that took place before Owen's memory failed, the old Tiger infielder told Dave Anderson of *The New York Times* about a feat the World Series crowd never saw. "I kicked him [Medwick] in the groin," he was quoted as saying. "Anderson was kind," said the son. "Dad didn't say groin."

The Marvin Owen of 1953 was the type of manager who would give his players the shirt off his back. When he learned that his own number seven had been used by Neville for most of his career, Owen switched to 30 and wisely allowed his star pitcher to keep the only single digit number on the team. The move brought him immediate support from the man who had campaigned for the same job.

And rightly so. Seven had been the number of choice for Owen and the number of chance for his wife. Violet Owen had been born on the seventh of January, and their son had been born in the seventh year of their marriage.

Owen would need an ally in Neville since Detroit, in its sixth year of a working agreement with the Bulls, had farmed out a weak supporting cast. With few exceptions, it was a team incapable of developing the fundamentals that Owen was so capable of teaching. No player with the club at the start of the season hit above .264. Shortstop Andy Frazier, one of the 1952 squad's most consistent hitters, would see his average drop 30 points to .233.

Frazier and others should have put themselves in the shoes of Durham's top hitter, Bill Radulovich. The hefty, hawk-nosed first baseman from Detroit joined the team in June, and produced a league-leading .349 batting average with a feet-first approach.

Radulovich felt so uncomfortable in his $26.50 pair of kangaroo leather baseball shoes that he traded them in for the cheapest pair in Jake Woodall's sporting goods store. "I don't think they'll last you very long," Woodall reportedly told Radulovich after reducing the price to $5. "You're a big fellow, and they might come apart on you."

Radulovich wore the shoes for the first time on July 23 and went six for seven in a home doubleheader against Greensboro. "I don't care if they don't last a week," said Radulovich. "They were worth the price last night."

For most of the season, Radulovich's more stylish teammates hit so poorly that two of Jack Coombs' former Duke pitching stars—"Smoky" Joe Lewis and Bob "Diz" Davis—could win only a dozen games between them. A promising 24-year-old righthander from Utica, Michigan, Duane "Duke" Maas, would claim only six victories in 22 decisions despite an impressive 3.03 earned run average.

Once, after suffering through a 3–0 loss that saw the Bulls allow Reidsville two unearned runs, Maas was approached by his manager shortly after the game. "I told Maas he was the first losing pitcher of mine I had ever congratulated," said Owen.

Maas, who had been on the Durham roster briefly in 1949 and 1950 and was attempting a comeback after two years in the service, lost his first seven games when his teammates could push across only five runs in 46 innings. In two of the losses, he was charged with a single earned run.

After the losing streak reached six with young Johnny Sass as the catcher, Owen paired Maas with Ralph Caldwell for the first time. In a scoreless game against Fayetteville in the top of the sixth, the veteran Caldwell dropped a third strike with two outs and threw the ball over the first baseman's head to trigger a two-run rally and a 2–0 Highlander win.

"I can't figure it out," Maas commented on his team's lack of run production. "It's just one of those things that you have to experience in baseball at one time or another. I know the boys are trying to score some runs for me. But that may be just it; they're trying too hard."

As Maas continued to lose, even rival players rose to his defense and described him as a top prospect. "He's the best young pitcher I've seen this year," said veteran Reidsville shortstop Walter "Teapot" Frye. "That kid showed me something I haven't seen all year. He ought to be in the big leagues in a couple of years."

Maas had lost 10 pounds and his weight had dropped to 165 when he attempted to break his seven-game losing streak in a home game against Burlington-Graham. For nine innings, Maas was his usual self—shutting out the Pirates, allowing only three hits, and watching helplessly as the Bulls loaded the bases four times but failed to score against Jim Waugh, an 18-year-old Ohioan who had started the season with the youth-oriented Pittsburgh Pirates.

In the tenth, Maas gave up two singles but retired the side after participating in all three outs. Durham then scored the winning run on an error, two walks, and a single. The run had been unearned, but Maas wasn't complaining. In a moment of optimism, Owen mistakenly predicted that his hard-luck pitcher would win seven in a row.

Maas would go on to post a 45–44 record in six seasons with the

Tigers, Kansas City Athletics, and New York Yankees. His hard luck continued when his career was cut short by an arthritic condition that was a contributing factor to his death in 1976 at the age of 47.

Neville pitched as flawlessly as Maas and with far greater fortune. He kept his earned run average close to two a game and brandished a revived bat that gave life to the lineup when he pitched. On a team described alternately as "spiritless" and "downtrodden," Neville won five of his first six decisions and became the team's only insurance against long losing streaks.

One of his few brushes with bad fortune came the night before his wedding when Owen surprisingly handed him the starting assignment at Fayetteville. He lasted three innings, giving up nine hits and eight runs.

His one-sided battle with Burlington-Graham outfielder Joe Burgess represented an equally frustrating low point. After Neville struck out Burgess four straight times in their first meeting, the left-handed power hitter was benched for Neville's second assignment before striking out a fifth time as a pinch hitter. In their next encounter, Neville ran the strikeout streak to seven, then fell victim to a Burgess double that drove in the winning run in a 1–0 contest.

The Bur-Gra setback took place before a crowd of 1,042, one of three times out of 20 home starts that Neville would pitch before a thousand or more fans. Neville-inspired crowds were down in numbers, but remained large in comparison to the scattering of loyalists who showed up for the rest of the games.

Durham attendance had dropped like a Duncan yo-yo with a broken string as many former fans—like their counterparts across the country—pursued other leisure activities and watched televised major league games on Saturday afternoons in the comfort of air-conditioned homes. The final attendance tally of 53,823 for 1953 would represent an alarming decline of 14,599 from 1952 and 39,943 from 1951.

Turnstiles that had clicked almost automatically in 1949 now just sat there; Ace Parker's battlers had been replaced by a bunch of incompetents who transformed a house of thrills into just another baseball outhouse one block down from the BC headache powder plant.

Most of the talent could be found on other teams. Future Boston Red Sox shortstop Don Buddin batted .300 and hit 25 home runs at Greensboro. Don Blasingame, three years away from succeeding Red Schoendienst at second base for the St. Louis Cardinals, hit .290 at Winston-Salem and struck two of his seven homers off Neville.

Another future major league name showed up near the bottom of the batting averages. Jack McKeon, who later would manage at Kansas City, Oakland, and San Diego, caught for the Burlington-Graham Pirates and

Marvin Owen, left, a former Detroit Tiger infielder who was a popular
manager with Neville, saw his 1953 team finish seventh despite the lefthander's 21 wins. Owen meets here with Herold "Muddy" Ruel, center,
director of Detroit's minor league farm clubs, and Durham owner Charles
Allen. (Courtesy *The Herald-Sun*.)

batted a lowly .181. McKeon, who never reached the top as a player but
capped his career in the majors as San Diego's general manager, returned
to Bur-Gra for 17 games the next season and departed with a .133 average.

The Danville's Leafs' first baseman became the first black to perform
at the league's All-Star game, not as a player but as a participant in the
home run contest. For the season, he would hit .298 with 21 home runs
and 84 runs batted in. His name: Bill White, a future St. Louis Cardinal
star who in 1989 became the thirteenth president of the National League
and the highest-ranking black executive in professional sports.

The league's color line had been broken the season before when

Danville started a pair of infielders from Cuba: second baseman Luis Morales and shortstop Juan Delis. Both players were from Santiago on Cuba's southwest tip and had learned the game on a field built with money donated by Washington Senator owner Clark Griffith. Delis had a brief stay with the Senators in 1955, but he was hardly major league material.

Delis and Morales endured the usual catcalls, but found acceptance from teammates and Manager Morris "Smut" Aderholt. "All the boys like 'em," Aderholt said. "They can hit, run, and field. And they want to play ball. They're helping us win games, too."

Not all Carolina League integration was that pleasant. When Kinston fielded its first two black players later in the 1950s, jeering fans in Durham discovered they could provoke the players enough to be greeted every inning by two extended middle fingers. Many of the same fans welcomed Durham's first black player in 1957; outfielder Bubba Morton made the All-Star team and later played for Detroit and California.

As Durham celebrated its centennial year, some wags insisted that growing a mustache was more exciting than attending a Bull baseball game. Even 25¢ admission prices for bearded men, men in straw hats, and women in bonnets failed to generate enthusiasm. The fans who did show up sometimes turned on the manager. "Hey, Owen," one of them shouted. "You didn't have that many wrinkles on your face when the season opened. What happened?"

"Is it cool down there in the cellar?" bellowed another fan near the Bull dugout. "Uncomfortably cool," responded Owen.

Some critics blamed Owen's lack of fire for Durham's decline. Herold "Muddy" Ruel, director of Detroit's minor league clubs and a major league catcher for 19 seasons, disagreed. "It's true Marvin doesn't charge out and put on a big show when things don't go to suit him," said Ruel. "He could use a lot of vulgarity, kick up dirt, and fuss with the umpires. But that's not Marvin's nature. He's a student of the game and a teacher. He doesn't use profanity."

Owen, who would manage his last minor league team in 1954 and later would become the Tigers' scouting supervisor, compared his team to a Model T Ford. "You can push the pedal all the way to the floorboard, but she still won't go but 35 miles an hour," he said.

Detroit shuffled in a series of players that pushed the speed above 35 but below 40. The brightest of the newcomers came straight out of college: two from Notre Dame, one from Yale, and one from Colgate. The best was a skinny 18-year-old high school graduate from Elizabeth, New Jersey, oufielder George Alusik. Alusik, one of eight Durham players assigned during the season to play right field, drilled Carolina League pitchers for a .331 average in the final month after his promotion from Jamestown in the Class D Pony League.

Alusik's hitting and a Neville winning streak pumped new life into a club that escaped last place only through the generosity of a weak Fayetteville franchise. When August arrived, Neville had won only 12 games because an overstocked pitching staff had reduced his number of starts over a one-month period to four. With the staff now leaner, he looked for eight more starts before the Labor Day finale.

In two weeks, his victory total reached 15. Neville was asked if he could win 20. "Why not?" he responded. "I'll just have to take the next five."

The spurt came as others claimed Neville had lost his fastball. One Raleigh writer reported that he stayed with his slow stuff in shutting out the Capitals with a three-hitter. "Maybe I haven't got a fastball, but that's about all I threw that night," countered Neville. "I used a few curves against their left-handed batters."

Neville, who built his reputation with a knuckler, was asked to name his best pitch at this stage of his career. "It all depends on the situation," he said. "I might use a curve against one batter in a certain situation, and I might think a knuckler or a screwball will do the job against another hitter."

"Eddie knows he's going to beat you when he goes into a ballgame," explained Ralph Caldwell, who joined Neville on the league's All-Star team for a third time. "He feels in here [his heart] that he's better than you are and he just knows he's going to beat you.

"I suppose Eddie has less stuff than any pitcher in the Carolina League," Caldwell continued. "But he knows how to get the most results out of what he has. If I had just one game that I'd like to win, and had my choice of all the pitchers in the league, I'd take Neville. He'd win it, too."

Neville actually had six more starts, all of them at home. He pitched six straight complete games, including three shutouts, and defeated six different teams by a combined score of 54–9. On the final day, he pitched a three-hit, 10–0 victory over Raleigh, his second straight shutout over the pennant-winning Caps.

He finished the year at 21–8, all in support of a sad seventh-place team that somehow won 15 of its last 22 games and still managed to fall 11 games below the .500 mark. No other Durham pitcher won more than eight. His earned run average was second best in the league at 2.28. He pitched 264 innings, seven more than any other pitcher. He completed 23 of 27 starts to bring his totals since rejoining Durham to 40 of 46. He struck out 138 and walked only 74.

His hitting showed new life as Owen used him frequently as a pinch hitter. For the first time in five seasons, he played right field once as a late-inning replacement. In an unusually high 130 times at bat, he hit .260 with 21 runs batted in and one home run. And when the All-League team was

Neville and catcher Ralph Caldwell, who first were teammates in 1947 when Caldwell was an infielder and outfielder at Tarboro, were veterans of the game in their final season together in 1953. Both players were named to the Carolina League All-Star team three times. (Courtesy Janet Neville.)

named after the season, he and Bill Radulovich were the only Bull repre-
sentatives.

The season was over, Owen looked at Number 7 and realized the
switch made it all worthwhile. "Without you," he said, "we would have
finished six floors under the basement."

"He was one of the finest men I ever knew," Neville said of Owen
years later. The lefthander would not feel the same about his boss in his
final season as a Bull. "If I never see him again," he once wrote of Charlie
Metro, "it will be too soon."

# No More Tomorrows

*Two of the boys from our old Rotary team eventually signed on with the Bulls. Flashlights in hand, they chased down foul balls that flew over the grandstand and headed for the underside of automobiles. To souvenir hunters, they seemed as fast as Pat Haggerty and as tough as Charlie Metro.*

---

The cow chips show up, an old saying goes, once the snow starts to melt. The snow began melting for Eddie Neville in 1954, his best years behind him and his career caught in a summer of discontent. Cow chips surrounded his relationship with his manager, a driven man whose management style made it impossible for the grand old man of Bull baseball to finish out his final season at Durham Athletic Park in the dignity and style and grace that his career had embraced.

Charlie Metro treated Neville like the youngsters who made up the rest of the roster, always pushing, always staring over the shoulder of a man who had not required coaching for years and who had thrived only when he operated in his own independent way. Metro would have none of that, allowing no special privileges for the pitcher who already had won more games than any other in the team's history.

Metro was born Charles Moreskonich in Nanty-Glo, Pennsylvania, a town he left behind after being caught in a coal mine explosion that burned off his hair and singed an elbow and ear. He was 18 when it happened, and he never forgot the moaning and the seven dead and pulling his father through two hours of darkness. His father suffered a broken ankle and a fractured skull. Still, he encouraged his son to test his nerve and return to the mine.

Charles Moreskonich went underground just long enough to prove his manhood, then signed a baseball contract with the St. Louis Browns. The scout suggested he drop his Ukrainian surname and replace it with his father's first name. He became Charlie Metro and started clawing his way through baseball with the same tenacity he used to escape the mine.

In an undistinguished major league career as an outfielder over three wartime seasons with Detroit and the Philadelphia Athletics, Metro had a lifetime batting average of .193 that would have qualified him for an extra lap around the outfield if he had been his own manager. His bravado style brought him instant success as a minor league field boss. In his first eight seasons, he won two pennants and finished lower than third only once.

Out of uniform, Metro was the same decent guy who had fallen in love with a girl he met at Mayfield, Kentucky, in 1939 while playing in the Class D Kitty League. He married Helen Bullock, nicknamed her "Babe," and brought her to Durham with a family that had expanded to three children and two dogs. Babe Metro described her husband, whom she usually called by his formal name of Charles, as a man whose "heart and soul are in this business of baseball." Metro, she said, lived "the game morning until night, the year around. He's so anxious to do a good job that sometimes I wonder if he isn't trying too hard."

Try he did. He protected his players on the field with a vengeance. He had been thrown out of games a dozen times the season before at Montgomery (Alabama) in the Class A South Atlantic League. And in Durham, he was destined to establish an unofficial team record by being tossed out in both games of a doubleheader.

He would chatter from the dugout when his team was in the field, wait for the players to reach the steps once the inning ended, give out words of encouragement, then head for the third-base coaching box for more chatter and more encouragement. He pored through motivational books and demanded a positive approach to the game.

Metro knew the rules as well or better than most umpires, and he insisted they be followed to the letter. He claimed that he once protested a game in support of the opposing team, withdrawing the objection only after the situation no longer had any bearing on the outcome of the game. "I was concerned," he said, "with the principle of the situation."

Despite his intensity, Metro had a sparkle in his eyes and could be a charmer at times. When the team bus arrived at Durham Athletic Park after spring training, Metro, after riding through the city for the first time, praised the "perfectly beautiful" trees and shrubbery and said he liked what he had seen in the few minutes he had been there. "I just hope it [Durham] likes me," he commented.

Detroit had dispatched him from Montgomery to ride herd on a bunch of young Bulls who needed discipline but never expected to be hounded for an entire season. Metro would be tougher than ever; he regarded his new assignment as a demotion and intended to fight his way back up. Far more insecure than his image projected, he later admitted

**Charlie Metro, the controversial manager of the 1954 Durham Bulls, fined Neville after the lefthander refused to take batting practice after a Sunday afternoon loss. The fine likely was never paid. (Courtesy *The Herald-Sun*.)**

that he was concerned about losing his job. The players, however, saw him only as a man obsessed with reaching the top.

"I had one rule when I was managing," recalled Metro. "I would never let a ballplayer reach anything less than his potential. I had a fear of them failing. I was very demanding and I pushed them and pushed them.

But I loved them, too, and I praised them a lot to the front office. They probably never knew that."

Neville, who would be the last of Durham's locally owned players, was only four years younger than Metro and seven years older than the second oldest Bull in camp. He softened the age difference by admitting to only 30 of his 31 years, but he was clearly an anachronism on a team whose opening-day starting lineup excluding Neville averaged under 21.

The Tiger farmhands were so young that one of the players fudged on his age by adding a year rather than subtracting. Larry Osborne, a hard-hitting first baseman from Chattahoochee, Georgia, started the season as a 19-year-old prospect but later admitted he was only 18.

Metro kidded Osborne when he first saw the apple-cheeked son of former major league pitcher Earnest "Tiny" Osborne. Insisting that Osborne needed a shave, Metro was surprised when the 200-pounder admitted to three days of growth. "I couldn't tell there was any beard on his face," Metro laughed. "I was just kidding him because his face looked so slick and clean."

Metro glanced around the camp at Lakeland, Florida, on playing fields laid out on the site of an abandoned airport, and observed a series of Osborne clones. Walt Streuli was only 18, third baseman Steve Demeter and pitcher Bob Shaw just 20.

Only one member of the corps of youngsters could vote: 21-year-old outfielder Dick Camilli. Like Osborne, Camilli had major league bloodlines. His father, Dolph Camilli, played first base for 12 seasons with Brooklyn and three other clubs. His younger brother, Doug Camilli, would catch for the Los Angeles Dodgers and Washington Senators.

Camilli, however, would be demoted to Class D on May 31 and— unlike many of his youthful Durham counterparts—would never see the majors. Shaw would be the most successful, winning 108 games over 11 seasons with five clubs, including 18 victories in 1959 for the pennant-winning Chicago White Sox. Osborne would bat a disappointing .206 over five seasons with Detroit and one with Washington. Streuli would appear in six games for Detroit; Demeter would be in the lineup 14 times for the Tigers and Cleveland.

Four other future major leaguers would join the team after the season started, including pitcher Bob Bruce, who in nine seasons with Detroit, Houston, and Atlanta won 49 games and lost 71; outfielder George Bullard, who would be called up by the Tigers, along with Streuli, at the end of the season; and pitcher Gene Host, a lefty who saw limited duty in two seasons with the Tigers and Kansas City Athletics. George Alusik, a 19-year-old outfielder who lit up the league in the closing weeks of the 1953 season, returned for two more months in Durham before entering the service. Alusik, originally signed for a $10,000 bonus, played briefly with the

**Neville, second from right, stood side by side with Manager Charlie Metro, right, as the Bulls prepared to open the 1954 season, the left-hander's last in Durham. Joining Neville in the starting lineup for the opening game were, left to right, shortstop Frank McElroy, second baseman Bobby Taylor, first baseman Larry Osborne, third baseman Steve Demeter, center fielder Dick Camilli, left fielder Bill Hoffler, right fielder Peter Veteretto, and catcher Walt Streuli. (Courtesy *The Herald-Sun*.)**

Tigers before enjoying modest success with the Kansas City Athletics from 1962–64.

With a blend of young talent and an old pro in Neville, Metro appeared to have a clear shot at first place. But the Bulls fell into oblivion at first, then alternated successes with sputters. It turned out to be a roller coaster of a ride that had many of the players waiting for the end and a chance to jump off.

Neville felt soreness in his arm as early as April 1 at Lakeland. He shrugged it off as a cold symptom and readied himself for a season when he would be hit harder and more often than ever before. For the first time, most of his wins would come in games where he would give up ten or more hits and be forced to work his way out of his own jams.

But worse than that, he would be caught in a baseball boot camp that nibbled away at his independence. It was the Army all over again, only this time Neville was a seven-year veteran with his stripes yanked off. "The pressure was on me to develop young ballplayers," Metro emphasized. "I'd tell the players to get out there and run until I told them to stop. I mean I ran them. Eddie kind of balked at that. He was a tremendous physical athlete and didn't have an ounce of fat on him. But he was set in his ways and didn't like to run. He rebelled a little at some of the things I was doing."

The forced marriage of the lefthander and Metro went smoothly at first. Curtis "Sis" Perry, the Bulls' business manager, let Metro know from the start that Neville was a popular player who attracted extra fans. At first, the manager offered Neville a chance to be something of a sidekick. "I've turned the pitchers over to Eddie," he said, "and the move is working out wonderful. Eddie sits next to the pitcher working the game when he comes to the dugout at the end of each inning, and he gives him the benefit of his advice and experience. Eddie knows a lot about pitching, and I think he can be of great help to our young boys."

Metro envisioned Neville as a pitching instructor once his playing days ended. But the move lasted less than a month as Neville showed more interest at the time in pitching instead of teaching. "I was trying to prolong his career, but he just wasn't very receptive," Metro recalled. "I knew what it was like when I was on my last legs. He probably could have pitched for a lot of years, but the younger players were taking over. He was a good pitcher, though. I wouldn't have kept him if he wasn't."

By sticking, Neville had to endure a manager who wouldn't go away. "The pitchers never took a step without me knowing it," Metro admitted. "I had to have them ready to pitch to the best of their ability when the situation demanded it."

Metro also felt he coddled his pitchers at times. "I always let them hit early in batting practice," he said. "Sometimes I would give them the new balls and let the regulars hit the old ones."

Neville was greeted by 13 hits and nine runs in the opening game at Danville, the victim of two future New York Giants. Third baseman Ozzie Virgil hammered a two-run home run over the center field fence; Curt Barclay pitched a five-hitter.

Three days later, Neville learned that it would be his first Durham season without Ralph Caldwell, who had been assigned to Montgomery (Alabama) but refused to report to the Class A South Atlantic League team and retired from the game. What Caldwell really wanted was a sixth season in Durham, but Detroit's youth movement ruled that out. Instead, Neville was paired with a catcher only a year out of high school and 13 years his junior.

Walt Streuli knew nothing of the lefthander's past and perceived him only as a troublemaking but smart "clubhouse lawyer." "I remember him a super-independent, cocky sort of guy," Streuli said. "Maybe that raised Metro's ire a little more. But I don't think Neville's attitude was any worse than some of the other players."

A Memphis high school star, Streuli had played under Metro as a rookie in 1953. "I couldn't fathom how a relationship between a team and coach could be so bad," he said. "Everybody despised Charlie Metro."

Streuli said his first run-in with the manager came after he and other players went out for beer after a game. "I don't think I had ever had a beer," he said. "I just kind of followed the rest of the guys to the Elks Lodge. When we left the place, Metro was out there taking names. I didn't even know what a curfew was, but we wound up being fined $50 apiece."

Then came Durham. "When I got hooked up with him [Metro] again, I knew it was going to be a miserable, miserable year," Streuli said. "I developed a sort of solid relationship with him by the end of the season, though. Maybe he had mellowed or I had matured and realized baseball was more of a business than a fun sport."

Streuli ended up driving Metro to the manager's home in Montgomery after the season. "I was going back to Memphis and planned to drop Larry Osborne off in Georgia when Metro asked for a ride," said Streuli, who later settled in Greensboro and established a successful building materials business. "We got along fine. But there weren't many others that year who got along with him. Osborne did. Steve Demeter probably did, too."

And, unknown to Streuli, so did second baseman Bobby Taylor. Neville actually struck more fear into Taylor than Metro. "When I played behind Eddie, I always tightened up, at least in the early part of the season," said Taylor. "When he'd look around, to see if the infielders were in position, he'd look right through us. I could be loose with most pitchers and make all the plays. But I thought Eddie didn't like me the way he acted. I got so tight I started making errors.

"Later in the season I realized that's just the way he was," Taylor continued. "He would never show his emotions. He'd get belted, but he'd never get rattled. He was all business. He just wasn't a blow-up type of guy."

The two were never close, but the comfort level increased as the season wore on. "I found out he was a terrific person once I got to know him," explained Taylor. "When you asked his advice, he would be glad to tell you."

Taylor became the team's top clutch hitter as well as a fashion plate. Fans found him easy to spot because of the stylish blue choker that covered his neck on cool nights. His dress code also included freshly shined shoes, socks cut just a little higher than the rest of the players, and a cap perfectly squared at the top. "I didn't want to look like a bum," said Taylor, an Ithaca, New York, native who came to Durham after two years in the service and one year at Jamestown in the Class D Pony League.

Taylor was at his best when the Bulls needed a run. He drove in 53 that year as a left-handed leadoff hitter. "Everybody likes to be a hero," he said. "I don't care what you're doing, you like to come through in the clutch."

Metro showed confidence in his 23-year-old second baseman, and Taylor responded accordingly. "If nothing else, he knew I was trying for him," Taylor said.

Taylor seldom passed up a chance to swing. The next season, Durham catcher Charlie Lau — later to become the batting coach credited with developing George Brett's swing at Kansas City — observed Taylor at the plate and nicknamed him "Rip." "I didn't realize at the time that Charlie knew that much about hitting," Taylor said. "Maybe he could have helped me."

Taylor started the 1955 season at Augusta in the South Atlantic League, but said he felt "jittery" in Class A and his fielding suffered. "I don't know what went wrong," he said. "I just wasn't happy."

The stocky infielder went to his manager, who happened to be Charlie Metro. He asked to be sent down to Durham, where he had met his bride-to-be the season before. "He told me not to go back, that it would kill my chances," Taylor related. "He said he was going to the majors and wanted to take me as his utility man."

Taylor ignored the advice and returned to Durham. He retired from baseball after being released in June of 1956. "Johnny Pesky was the manager that year, and he took me out of the lineup after I didn't go all the way down for a grounder," he recalled. "I know he thought I was 'jaking it,' but my back was killing me. I didn't say anything because once they knew you were hurt you could lose your job."

Taylor was married that November to Patsy Upchurch, a bookstore employee he met in a downtown cafe. After driving a dairy truck and a tractor-trailer, Taylor joined his two sons in starting a Durham-based family business producing decorative wood items.

His most vivid memory of Metro's authority was the fungo bat the manager carried around. "It seemed like he had it in his hand every time I looked at him," Taylor said. "It showed that he was the boss."

Metro admitted the fungo was a status symbol. "I'd have a fungo in my hand and a ball in my pocket all the time," he said. "If I saw a guy standing around in the outfield before the game, I'd start hitting to him."

One night at Danville, after the fans had been set off when Taylor traded punches with a player who tried to spike him, Metro picked up his fungo after the game and instructed each of his players to arm themselves with a bat as they headed toward the locker room. The fans backed off.

Metro's attitude at the start of the 1954 season wasn't helped by losing the first seven games. The streak came to an end in a home game that saw umpire Junius Beck clear the bench after an extended round of heckling.

Metro was allowed to stay and summon players as needed, and he called on Neville in the top of the eighth to save a lead. The lefthander, who had lost his first two games, walked the first batter, picked him off, then retired the final five.

Neville won five of his next seven decisions, including his next start at Burlington-Graham when he pitched a three-hit, 1–0 victory after losing a no-hitter to leadoff batter Brandy Davis in the last of the seventh. Davis, a former Duke outfielder, was thrown out at home after trying to score when the throw to the infield went astray.

The conflict between Neville and Metro likely would have stayed low key if the season had continued as smoothly as that one performance. But when the team veered slightly off track, Metro tightened his grip.

The most serious confrontation came on a humid Sunday afternoon in early June. The Bulls languished in sixth place with four losses in a row when Metro sent Neville to the mound at home against veteran knuckleballer Ken Deal and seventh-place Reidsville. Deal was seldom better; Neville was seldom worse. The lefthander gave up 18 hits as Metro let the old hero endure the humiliation for the full nine innings. Neville still pitched with enough savvy to help end the outrageous affair in only one hour and 48 minutes, walking no one and stranding ten runners on base amid a barrage of 16 singles and two doubles that led to an 8–1 loss.

Metro ordered the Bulls back on the field for an unscheduled batting practice, something he had done on several mornings but never after a game. Neville calmly took a shower and refused to return even after Metro told him he would be fined $25.

"He won't take any $25 out of my pay," Neville insisted. "I just pitched nine innings, and I think that's enough for one day's work." As other players remained silent, Neville continued to fume. "They can give me my release if they fine me," he said.

Metro waited until the next morning to issue a prepared four paragraph statement to the press. Like a politician in a heated race, he never mentioned his opponent by name.

"Yesterday, for the first time, the players didn't do as well as I expected," the statement said. "I called a hitting practice after the game and all of the players, except one, cooperated. That one player is the property of the Durham club and apparently he feels that he is 'too big' or above the rest to take part in extra batting practice workouts.

"I think the showing we made yesterday proves otherwise. None of the other players offered any protests or objections to the workout. In fact, they all responded enthusiastically. Most ballplayers, in my opinion, like to get in batting practice even if it comes at midnight. A manager has the right to call a practice session any time he wishes. He also has the right to fine any player for failure to carry out orders. I do not want any player's money, however."

Neville met privately with Metro, then traveled with the club to Reidsville. Durham's front office maintained the fine would be taken out of Neville's pay, but it probably never was. As a matter of pride, Neville would have quit over any action that questioned his integrity. Burwell Allen, vice president of the Bulls in the Neville era, said the fine likely would have been levied if the decision had been left to Business Manager Curtis "Sis" Perry. "Sis was real conscientious about things like that," Allen said. "Charles [owner Charles Allen] probably said something to him."

Neville's record stood at 5–5 at the time of the run-in. He would win seven more times, but he pitched without heart until the end of the season when fourth place was on the line.

Durham players realized Metro's unscheduled workout had been more punitive than instructional, but the team went on a hitting tear and started a five-game winning streak by blasting 17 hits at Reidsville. Neville made his own contribution in a home game against Winston-Salem when he opened the bottom of the ninth with a double and scored the winning run one out later.

The night before, however, he had raised the workout issue again as the Bulls and Winston-Salem waited out a rain delay. He sought—and received—support from Winston-Salem Manager Herb Brett, who had returned to the league after resigning at Wichita in the Class A Western League several weeks earlier.

"Tell me, Herb, have you ever called a batting drill after a Sunday afternoon ballgame?" he asked.

"Never," replied Brett, who was managing his eleventh and last minor league team. "I might bring a couple of players out to the park in the mornings to work on something, or I might ask the infielders out to show them how I wanted something done. But those morning workouts or after-game drills are just a show for the fans and club owners."

Neville repeated his warning. "What I said still goes," he commented. "They better not take a penny out of my paycheck."

Metro continued to defend his decision. "I'm not fining Neville," he responded. "He fined himself. I don't want his money; I don't want any of my players' money. They fine themselves."

The players stayed out of the feud between Neville and Metro. Hugo Germino, sports editor of Durham's afternoon newspaper, *The Durham Sun,* jumped right in. He supported Metro. "Neville should know better than to balk at such an order," Germino wrote. "He has managerial aspirations himself. How would he feel if players under his direction refused to follow his orders?"

**Jack Horner, left, and Hugo Germino followed Neville's career as sports editors of Durham's two daily newspapers. Germino rapped Neville over the pitcher's feud with Manager Charlie Metro, and Horner was a frequent Metro critic. (Courtesy Hugo Germino.)**

Germino's morning rival, Jack Horner, broke the story on the Neville-Brett conversation but remained neutral. Most of the time, however, he voiced his displeasure with Metro. "There are some who don't believe Manager Metro is getting full mileage of the material at his disposal," wrote Horner. "It's no secret some of the players are in his doghouse, so to speak, and there are some of the younger fellows who can't do their best under Metro's John McGraw type of managerial tactics."

The sharpest disagreement between the two sports editors that season didn't involve Metro. It centered around a scoring decision by Horner. In the first inning of a game at Durham Athletic Park, Horner watched Burlington-Graham shortstop Johnny Richardson just miss a looping fly that bounced off his glove in short left. Horner credited leadoff batter

Bobby Taylor with a hit, then watched Bur-Gra pitcher Don Schultz retire the next 27 batters in a row.

In the seventh inning, Horner had summoned Bur-Gra outfielder Brandy Davis to the press box and asked his version of Richardson's attempt to field Taylor's pop fly. "It bounced out of his glove," said Davis. "He says he should have had it."

When Schultz retired the final Durham batter, Horner reversed the decision and awarded a no-hitter to the 24-year-old pitcher from Prairie du Chien, Wisconsin. "If Richardson hadn't got his glove hand on the ball, it would have been a clean hit and impossible to charge an error," wrote Horner. "But under the circumstances, it wasn't anything out of the ordinary to change a scoring decision."

Germino called the decision "a boner," writing that "waiting until the game is over and changing your mind just isn't cricket." Horner fired back, saying, "I can't help but wonder if Hugo wouldn't have kept his trap shut had Don Schultz pitched for Durham instead of Bur-Gra." He insisted that Germino would "rather be wrong than agree with ol' Horner."

Bobby Taylor sided with Germino, but never admitted that to Horner. "He [Horner] came by after the game and asked me what I thought," recalled Taylor. "I told him in a cocky sort of a way that one hit wasn't going to hurt me; I'd just go out there tomorrow and get me two more. Horner didn't give me any writeups the rest of the year. I still think it was a clean hit."

Disagreements like that gave fans the impression the two sports editors were ready to choke each other, but they remained good friends on the job and later in retirement when they moved to the same Durham neighborhood. "Jack would tell me that our little fights would be good for both of us," said Germino, who knocked out his first sports story in 1937 and continued on the job until retiring in 1972. "He would actually encourage me to take the other side."

Writing for newspapers under the same ownership, the two often roomed together on the road and sometimes shared information. "Both of us tried to get stories first," Germino related, "but there were times after games when we'd tell each other what we were doing so we wouldn't wind up with the same story."

Germino became hooked on sports writing as a teenager after writing a story about a football game involving his neighborhood team in Columbia, South Carolina, the previously unheralded Gasden Street Bulldogs. "I turned in a few paragraphs to *The State* newspaper," he recalled. "That was a pretty big operation even in those days, and it was quite a feeling to see my byline on top of the story."

The Germino family moved to Durham when his Italian immigrant father, a blacksmith, took on work repairing tools for workers crafting marble and stone in the construction of Duke University.

Germino went to Duke two years, dropped out after his father's death, then joined the *Durham Morning Herald* as a police reporter. Four years later, he moved over to *The Durham Sun* and advanced from covering the Gasden Street Bulldogs to following Wallace Wade's Duke Blue Devils.

Germino was set to cover Duke's trip to the 1942 Rose Bowl when the Japanese bombed Pearl Harbor. "Here I was, thinking about California and they switched the game to Durham," he said. "I only had to drive three miles to get there."

Durham fans saw the cigar-smoking Germino everywhere during his tenure as sports editor. His photograph ran atop his "Do You Agree?" column six times a week; he was a frequent bridge player on his way to becoming a life master; he and his brother, Dante, were the lead saxaphonists in a popular dance band.

He also spent a lot of time in the little press box at Durham Athletic Park, but it wasn't always the game that attracted his attention. Instead, he was on the lookout for tidbits with an unusual twist—such as the time play-by-play man C. J. "Woody" Woodhouse became so enamored with a housefly that he pinpointed the insect's position between every pitch.

That was the Germino style: the story behind the story. He was fascinated by Neville's ability to pick off runners, but he was even more fascinated years later when he observed the lefthander's unusual way of putting a golf ball. Neville would stand squarely behind the ball, grip his putter like a croquet mallet, and swing in a pendulum style.

But playing under Charlie Metro, Neville for a time couldn't gain attention even if he threw behind his back and gripped a bat with his teeth. He matched up most of his wins with a loss. At the same time, Bob Bruce won eight of his first 11 decisions and pitched three consecutive shutouts. Lefthander Bob Cruze, who joined the team in May after starting the season at Little Rock in the Class AA Southern Association, became the hottest pitcher in the league as he headed toward a 19–7 season.

The team that couldn't buy a hit in those opening weeks turned into a young murderers' row that would lead the league in hitting with a .281 average and finish second in home runs with 105. As the slugging accelerated, a Durham restaurant cancelled its offer of a free steak dinner to every Bull hitting a homer.

In late June, a ten-game winning streak moved the team into fourth place and the first division for the first time. The streak ended in the brightness of a Sunday afternoon when a two-run Burlington-Graham lead increased to three after Manager Stan Wentzel led off the top of the ninth with a triple and stole home with two outs and his pitcher at bat. The steal gave Bur-Gra a cushion that held up after Durham rallied for two runs in the last of the ninth.

Wentzel had steamed most of the game after Metro refused to lend a pair of sunglasses to one of his outfielders. In mid-May, a Bur-Gra outfielder had borrowed sunglasses owned by the Bulls after losing sight of two fly balls. But this time, Metro turned Wentzel down.

"That's right," admitted Metro. "I told Wentzel that I wouldn't approve one of my players lending his sunglasses to a Bur-Gra player. I just don't believe in helping the other fellow beat you. I'm paid to win ballgames and run a ball club. I just don't go for this fraternizing with the opposition.

"I don't care what the other managers do. I'm not paid to run their clubs. I'd feel the same way if I was playing against my brother. It wouldn't make any difference. I'm out there to win fairly. This buddy-buddy business has no place in baseball."

Metro cited two incidents in his career that shaped his philosophy. In 1943, when he was a rookie trying to beat out Roger "Doc" Cramer for a spot in the Detroit outfield, Cramer refused to lend Metro his sunglasses and kept his job. Four years later, at Bisbee (Arizona) in the Class C Arizona-Texas League, his team broke all but two of its bats. When the El Paso manager refused to lend him bats, Metro supplied his own and his club won the game 33–10. "I'll never forget that score as long as I live," Metro commented.

Metro's refusal to assist Wentzel had the same influence on the Bur-Gra manager. After stealing home and breaking the Durham streak, he vowed never to ask Metro for another favor.

"Tell Metro we've got our own sunglasses now and he needn't worry about us wanting his," Wentzel said when his club returned to Durham three weeks later for another Sunday afternoon affair. "In fact, we've got two pairs of the glasses. I'll tell you what. To show Metro what kind of a guy I am, he can use a pair of ours if he wants them."

Wentzel claimed the move backfired on Metro. "I think Charlie is sorry now that he has had time to think it over," he said. "A couple of nights later at Greensboro, a Durham player was hurt and Metro asked the Greensboro trainer to come over and take a look at the boy. What if Greensboro had refused? That wouldn't have been very sportsmanlike."

Metro fired back once again. "I'm out to win ballgames, and I'll take them any way I can," he emphasized. "Off the playing field I can be friendly and sociable, but once we walk on that field to start a ballgame, friendships cease as far as I'm concerned.

"I'm trying to get ahead in this game," he continued. "I've been in it 17 years, and I want to go higher. I'm not going to help a team beat me if I know it. The only way to get anywhere in baseball is to win, and I'm out to win. I don't see why anyone should hold that against me."

The fans at Burlington-Graham did. "The next time we went over there, they threw all sorts of sunglasses from the stands when I went to the third-base coaching box," Metro recalled.

Most of Metro was dead serious; a small part gave way to grandstanding. "Sometimes I did things just to get people to the games," he admitted. "A lot of times only three or four hundred would come out so I had to do something."

Metro's enemy list continued to mount: Neville, Wentzel, just about every umpire in the league, and other players, including pitcher Bob Shaw, who would say little until the season ended. Even the Durham batboy, Kenny Smith, was on his case.

"Kenny would tell me when to bunt them over, when to put a pitcher in," Metro related. "He was a delight. One time I told him if he was trying to run the team, then I was going to knock the hell out of him."

Smith also hounded the players. "He was a real smart kid who thought he could teach all of us dumb ballplayers at least one thing before the season was over," said Walt Streuli. "He had me learning all the state capitals."

Metro landed in the middle of still another controversy when he was ejected from a home game in late July. This time, he had the full support of everyone but umpire Ike Reeder, who had the Bulls' fans and players on edge after a series of disputed calls in a contest against Danville.

Metro was thrown out after protesting Reeder's call of two consecutive balls to Danville's Ozzie Virgil. Virgil then lifted a short fly to center and Danville's Bob Reich appeared to have been an easy victim at home when he tagged up at third and attempted to score the tie-breaking run.

When Reeder called Reich safe, three Durham players—Bob Bruce, George Bullard, and Walt Streuli—engaged in a bitter argument with the umpire and followed Metro to the locker room.

Reeder had lost control of the players and the entire park. As he stood between home and first, 25 to 30 fans poured through the gate next to the Bulls' first-base dugout and charged onto the field. Several crowded around the umpire; one grabbed his elbow before Reeder pulled away.

Danville Manager Andy Gilbert, who would become one of the minors' most highly respected managers in winning 2,009 games over 27 seasons, instructed his players to circle Reeder in a protective ring. Bruce, who minutes earlier had to be restrained from charging Reeder, returned to the field and started pulling spectators away from the umpire.

Several police officers arrived on the scene five minutes later to help restore order. Reeder, later released by the league office, left the field after the game under a police escort. The officers escorted the two umpires to the city limits, and a State Highway Patrol car followed them until their safety was assured.

The attack against the umpire continued the next day. "I have been taught that umpires, like everyone else, make mistakes," said Business Manager Curtis "Sis" Perry. "I also have been taught that umpires should be supported by men in baseball. But last night was the worst exhibition of umpiring I ever have seen. It was lousy. I never have been so disgusted in my whole life."

"I think all the credit for preventing a real mess belongs to Andy Gilbert," said Carolina League President Glenn E. "Ted" Mann. "When they paraded onto the field, along with some of the Durham players, I think the fans knew to leave the umpire alone. It was the worst demonstration I have ever seen by Durham players and fans."

Every time Metro was tossed from a game, he turned to pitcher Bob Cruze to run the team. Cruze was shocked when he saw one fan come on the field with a brick. "I know I had a winning record in the games where I replaced Charlie, but that night was something else," he said.

Cruze was neutral on Metro. Like most players, he tolerated the manager's hell-for-leather style. "Most of us would listen to what he had to say, and then we would just go on and do what we wanted to do," he said.

"Charlie was trying to treat everybody just like a kid," he continued. "Eddie wouldn't go for it; he just wasn't made that way. He probably knew just as much as Charlie and had been around just about as long. It was just a personality clash."

Although he was eight years younger than Neville, Cruze was the second most experienced player on the team. An earlier season as a Bull, in 1950, brought him both a no-hitter and a bride. "We were rained out one night and Tommy Martin [a Bull who had been at Raleigh the year before] and I went over to Raleigh," Cruze recalled. He met Annie Ruth Young at a skating rink that night, and by October the two were married.

Cruze would not play with Neville until 1954, but he was familiar with the other half of Durham's longtime battery. He asked catcher Ralph Caldwell to be his best man.

The Ohio native later discovered that Neville watched his pitches as closely as Caldwell. "Eddie would give me hell if I walked somebody," laughed Cruze, who continued to post numbers after baseball as a state tax auditor in Raleigh and later in Morehead City, North Carolina. "He told me he couldn't learn anything from that."

Cruze eventually won 46 games over three Durham seasons, but his best summer of all couldn't stop a July and August downslide that saw the league's worst fielding team lose 22 of 33 games to drop into sixth place.

Bob Bruce slumped, losing seven games in a row. Bob Shaw threw hard, but never demonstrated the talent that would carry him to the majors three seasons later. "Things just weren't right," Shaw would say after his 6–13 season. "I know I should have won 20 games, but too often we didn't care. It was a season of confusion. We could have done better."

Neville pitched less and less as the season wore on as Metro went with his younger players. The exile started after he failed to last four innings in two consecutive starts. He won only one game—and that was in a relief role—over a 58-day period after defeating Reidsville on June 24, the eighth win in Durham's ten-game streak.

For a time, he seemed to show as much interest in golf as baseball. He lost in relief at Winston-Salem one night, won an amateur golf tournament match the next morning, mopped up in seven innings of relief that night, then carried his next golf match to the final hole before being eliminated.

Neville's start at High Point–Thomasville on August 21 was only his fourth since the Reidsville win. He gave up ten hits before being relieved in the seventh, but received credit for the win and evened his record at 10–10. He lost in relief at Reidsville three days later, and Durham remained in sixth place, five games back of fourth-place Danville.

On August 28, the roller coaster that had gone down, then up, then down again, raced uphill one final time. The Bulls took three in a row, lost one, then pocketed two more before Neville received another starting assignment. This time, he pulled the Bulls to within one-half game of Danville and fourth place by pitching an 11-inning, 3–2 home victory over High Point–Thomasville.

By the final day of the season, Durham had moved to a half-game lead over Danville and needed a sweep of a day-night Memorial Day doubleheader against first-place Fayetteville to assure a playoff spot. The opening game, played in 103-degree heat at Durham, went to the bottom of the twelfth before Bobby Taylor continued his clutch hitting and singled in the winning run with the bases loaded and one out.

Just as he had done in the season opener, Metro turned to Neville as his starter in the nightcap. All the misery between those starts became insignificant as the lefthander took the mound at Fayetteville's Pittman Stadium in what was a "must" contest since Danville also had won that afternoon.

Neville's last regular season appearance in the Carolina League was as successful as his first one five years earlier. Supported by five straight hits by third baseman Steve Demeter, he went the distance in a nine-hit, no-walk affair that pushed his record to 12–11 and sent the Bulls into the playoffs.

Demeter took his .307 batting average and other credits to Buffalo of the International League the next season. Before retiring in 1972, he became a Class AAA fixture over ten International League seasons at Rochester, Syracuse, Toronto, and Buffalo.

Demeter was so highly regarded in the minors that Rochester's management protested vigorously when the Baltimore Orioles failed to protect him from the 1968 minor league draft and the New York Yankees acquired him. Despite 272 home runs and a lifetime minor league batting average of .290 in 8,452 official trips to the plate, he reached the majors only briefly at Detroit in 1959 and Cleveland in 1960.

Durham finished sixteen and one-half games behind pennant winner and playoff opponent Fayetteville, an independent club loaded with veteran players such as 36-year-old catcher Aaron Robinson, the Coastal Plain League rookie of long ago who had wrapped up his major league career in 1951.

The Bulls surprised the Highlanders in the opener at Fayetteville, then lost the next three by a combined score of 27–10. In the fourth and final game at Durham, the Bulls faced the same knuckleballer whose mastery of the team in June had inspired Metro to call for a postgame batting practice. Ken Deal, who had started the season at Reidsville, hooked up in a 3–3 deadlock with Bob Cruze before Fayetteville scored three in the ninth.

Metro pulled Cruze with one out and summoned Neville for what would be his final appearance at Durham Athletic Park. The lefthander, who had been routed in the third playoff game, retired the only two batters he faced and left the mound for the last time. Those remaining in the small crowd of 846 hardly noticed.

Metro's fiery manner and ability to win would lead to two managing jobs in the majors. In 1962, when the Chicago Cubs were experimenting with an ill-fated coaching system, he was fired as head coach at the end of an eighth-place season.

Owner P. K. Wrigley refused to give a reason for the firing. Three days later, Metro pulled a pack of Wrigley spearmint gum out of his pocket, showed it to a reporter, and smiled. He agreed the next day to become the head scout for the Chicago White Sox.

In 1970, the Kansas City Royals proudly pointed to Metro's three pennants and four playoff championships in 15 seasons and appointed him to succeed Manager Joe Gordon after he had served as Kansas City's director of scouting and instruction for a year and a half. "I know I have a Simon Legree tag, but I think it's overrated," said the man who once worked out his Twin Falls, Idaho, club in the desert moonlight after the team bus had a flat tire at three o'clock in the morning.

Metro lasted until June 9. After a 1–8 road trip, he was replaced by easy-going Bob Lemon, the club's pitching coach. He would never manage again. "I probably never should have taken that job," he admitted. "I had a bleeding ulcer just before spring training. My weight dropped from 188 to 160 after an operation. I had one hell of a time."

"He was simply too much of an authoritarian," wrote Joe Falls in the *Detroit Free Press.* "He ran his team as a schoolmaster would run his class, and that just doesn't go anymore. If you've got a winning team, you might get away with it because when a team is winning, all of the little picky things are overlooked. But when you try to run a losing team with the methods of a Charlie Metro . . . well, it's kind of like trying to whip a mule through the homestretch at Churchill Downs. It looks impressive but you're not going anywhere, and pretty soon the mule is going to throw you."

Metro disagreed with Falls. "I could manage," he said. "I outmanaged a hell of a lot of guys. I just never had the connections, the angel guy who would help me out. I had to scrounge and fight my way up."

Metro found his niche later as one of baseball's most highly regarded scouts. He retired from baseball in 1984 after spending the season with the Los Angeles Dodgers as an "eye in the sky" scouting opposing teams from the upper deck.

In Golden, Colorado, the coal miner's son concentrated on another sport: breeding and racing quarter horses. He named his prize stallion, "Six for Six," in memory of his playing days in Detroit. "I had six hits in six months." he laughed.

Metro never knew it, but he continued to haunt Neville the rest of his life. "Even when Eddie was having problems with his memory, he would point out Metro in a team picture at our souvenir store," said Miles Wolff, president of the Bulls from 1980 until selling the club in 1991. "He said he just couldn't stand the man."

Neville, who posted a 75-38 record in four seasons with the Bulls, had no intention of quitting the game after completing what he perceived as a season of humiliation. He had given up winter baseball because of his marriage, but when spring came—even though there no longer was a place for locally owned players in the Detroit farm system—he planned to put on a uniform and go to work.

He received little encouragement when he questioned the Tigers about managing in the minor leagues. When he applied for the manager's job at Fayetteville, he was told the club needed an everyday player to cut costs.

In February, he signed to pitch for Albany in the Eastern League. He was back in Class A, but just barely.

Only weeks before he signed, baseball in New York's state capital remained on the doubtful list after the Boston Red Sox severed ties and shifted their Class A franchise to Montgomery (Alabama) in the South Atlantic League to fill a spot vacated by the Tigers. Owner Tom Mc-Caffrey, in a last-minute scramble, signed free agents to supplement players supplied by several major league clubs, but the team that gathered for spring training in St. Augustine, Florida, was of questionable caliber.

McCaffrey had been so short of players that the opening of camp had been delayed until April 1, giving other clubs a three-week jump on the

Senators. As other players struggled to catch up, Neville made an immediate impression on Dick Walsh, sports editor of Albany's *Times-Union*. Neville, wrote Walsh, had "what appears to be a rubber arm" and "is probably farther advanced than any pitcher in camp, simply because he did quite a bit of throwing before leaving his Durham, N.C., home to report here."

Besides Neville, the talk of the camp was young Johnny Sitts, who only a year earlier had been the team's batboy. Albany obviously had nothing in mind for the 135-pound Sitts except as a body for practice, but the former American Legion outfielder took his mission seriously.

When Sitts was asked to catch in an intrasquad game, he picked up his fielder's glove and went behind the plate—an extremely awkward position since he threw with his left hand. Sitts, as expected, would fail to make the squad, but at least he could tell his Albany friends that he singled off Neville in his first time at bat.

Sitts was not alone in lacking experience. First-year Manager Bert Haas, a former infielder for Cincinnati and three other major league clubs, arrived in St. Augustine after taking a cram course from Birdie Tebbetts at the Reds' training camp in Tampa. With only 13 days to prepare his club for the trip north, Haas often worked his players out twice a day in sessions that ran as long as three and a half hours. Haas was not afraid of work. He had been an aggressive player with a good batting eye but little power, a page-two type who seldom made headlines.

Haas was once on the fringe of an eye-catching story when the Reds were involved in a controversial scoring decision in a 1942 game at Pittsburgh. When he fielded a grounder at first and threw it to second for a force play, second baseman Eddie Joost failed to cover and the ball headed for center field.

Scorer Tom Swope gave the error to Joost. Haas escaped the scoring call as well as the headlines. Joost, who insisted no play was possible at second, woke up the next day to read that he was the "Player Given An Error Though He Doesn't Touch Ball."

Haas was familiar with Neville, having faced him as a first baseman at Minneapolis in 1950. After watching the lefthander pitch seven shutout innings in two exhibition games, Haas knew he had his starter for Albany's season opener. The decision was hardly surprising; in five previous serasons when Neville had been both activated and healthy on opening day, he had been tapped as the first game starter three times.

Neville allowed 11 hits in the opener against Schenectady, but only one counted—a ninth-inning home run with the bases empty. Thanks to five double plays and some heroics by four former Durham players, Neville picked up a 3–1 victory. The ex-Bulls had accounted for all three runs: Emil Restaino homered with Johnny Sass on first, and Pat O'Neill singled after a Dick Eaton triple. Ironically, all but Sass would be released within a month.

Neville never won another game after that. The arm described as rubber in Florida turned to clay in New York. Neville failed to last his next five starts. He lost in a homecoming of sorts at Williamsport, then fell again at Wilkes-Barre. He was chased without decisions in home games against Williamsport and Binghamton.

He was caught in a downhill slide on a going-nowhere team that even Governor Averill Harriman failed to save. Fans applauded Harriman's move to provide free parking in a state-owned lot outside Hawkins Stadium, but the takers were few since the Senators continued to charge for games that offered little entertainment value.

The final game of Neville's career came on a Friday night at Schenectady Stadium. He left the mound after giving up six hits and four runs. He retired only four batters in a game that Albany would lose by 11 runs.

Carl Linhart was in right field that night of May 20. Johnny Sass was the catcher. Both had seen the lefthander in better times in Durham, Linhart when he won 25 times in 1949, Sass when he won 21 four years later.

The Neville they saw that night was the same competitor with the same heart. His age, however, was not the same; there was no longer a place for a 32-year-old pitcher whose pay matched his past but exceeded his potential.

His first minor league victory had come eight years earlier against Class D players such as Hendershot and Munday and May. He had tacked on another 133 after that, plus 50 more in the winter leagues. With 97 losses in year-round play, he had fallen just short of taking two out of every three decisions.

He had thrown his first professional pitch in the Canal Zone 2,448 innings ago. From that windy afternoon in Cristobol until his last pitch under the lights in upstate New York, he had completed three out of every four starts and had given up less than three earned runs a game.

Seventy-two hours after the loss at Schenectady, Albany brought in a pitcher who stood six-foot-three and was eight years younger than the one-time kid from Baltimore. Eddie Neville was smart enough to know he would be out of baseball the very next day.

# Shattered Memories

*Time, like an ever-rolling stream,*
*Bears all its sons away;*
*They fly forgotten, as a dream*
*Dies at the opening day.*
—Protestant hymn

---

Janet Neville had looked forward to a summer in Albany when the telegram arrived. Her husband of two years, a simple yet complex man of very private emotions, had paid Western Union to deliver the news. He was coming home.

Janet had married the man, not the baseball player, but in reality the two identities were inseparable. The paper Neville signed at Albany had booted him out of the game, but no paper or person could take the game out of him. Inside the man would always be the boy who hit the home run at Oriole Park.

When he came home, Janet looked for a spark that was no longer there, the spark she noticed when they first met in a setting that was hardly romantic. Amid the clatter generated by strikes and spares, Neville had spotted his bride-to-be just one lane away. It was a league night on October 15, 1952, at the Center Bowling Alleys in downtown Durham when he introduced himself to a perky 22-year-old with shoulder-length brunette hair.

Janet Goodwin, an office clerk at Watts Hospital, had never heard of the local baseball hero when he leaned over and remarked that the settings in their rings had identical blue stones. There was, however, one major difference. Janet's Sam Houston State Teachers College ring had strips of tape so it would fit her finger. It belonged to a soldier at Fort Bragg, a husky, blond Texan whose next ring, Janet hoped, would symbolize their engagement.

Neville, undeterred, perhaps even challenged, called the next day.

**Neville and his fiancee, Janet Goodwin, exchange admiring looks shortly after his return from spring training in 1953. (Courtesy Janet Neville.)**

"I'm going to teach you to bowl," he said. "I already know how," she said. Still, she agreed to a date, and he showed up that night in his cream-colored Studebaker with a red top, the back seat piled high with his scrap-books. They bowled, drank milk shakes, and browsed through the clip-pings that confirmed he was not your ordinary 30-year-old guy.

The scrapbooks aside, Janet liked her suitor's style. He was quiet and confident at the same time. "And, boy," thought Janet, "is he good looking."

They went to a Durham High School football game the very next night, watching the Bulldogs battle it out on the same field where Neville had pitched for two summers. They sat in the same bleachers where Janet had cheered the team as a student. They stood when the band struck up the school fight song to the tune of "On Wisconsin."

They continued to see each other, enjoying more Durham High games, more milk shakes, movies, a walk in Duke Gardens, and window shopping. Within three weeks, they were on the same mixed doubles bowling team. By Thanksgiving, they were in Baltimore seated at the dinner table on West Mulberry Street as Helen Neville insisted that Janet stuff herself with pumpkin pie.

They visited Tarboro the next weekend, taking a tour of the little town where the pitcher enjoyed some of his greatest moments, then joining a Catholic priest for lunch. Neville, exploring the menu, recommended the filet mignon. "I don't think I want any fish," Janet replied. There were no further suggestions.

For Neville, the winter promised to be even better than the six he had spent in the Canal Zone and Panama. He had given up the trip this time, hoping to land a job as manager of the Bulls and wanting to be available if and when the Detroit Tigers made the announcement. So he stayed in Durham and switched from his usual uniform to the sport coat and bow tie that he wore as an automobile salesman.

He and Janet continued to do the same things the lefthander did when he waited between games, simple pleasures shared by the two of them. Washing the car on a Saturday afternoon. Tossing a baseball on a lazy Sunday at Janet's house. Enjoying a laugh when Janet raved over a "pretty little hammer" in the window of a hardware store.

On Christmas Day, with Neville at home in Baltimore, Janet opened one of his gifts and found the hammer decorated with a red ribbon. On New Year's Eve, both of them stayed at home with the flu.

January arrived and—for the first time since 1947—Neville discontinued his daily diary entries. He never recorded that Janet accepted an engagement ring but returned it three weeks later after expressing uncertainty over the relationship.

Neville received more bad news that same month. The Tigers, planning to send a young team to Durham, turned to an experienced manager within their organization. Instead of appointing Neville, they tapped Marvin Owen, a former Tiger infielder, who had managed in the minors for nine seasons. Neville retreated to his room at the YMCA. Janet heard nothing for two days, then called to make sure he was all right.

They continued to date almost every night until Neville left for spring training. He drove 200 miles a day for three days to reach the Tigertown training camp in Lakeland, Florida, following U.S. 301 through the Carolinas and Georgia and sending Janet a postcard from the two stopovers he made. First came a card proclaiming the good life in Manning, South Carolina. Then came another with a shot of the pink stucco Mimosa Restaurant and Gift Shop in Jesup, Georgia, a billboard on the roof promoting rotisserie chicken as two Atlantic gas pumps sat out front awaiting passing motorists. "You could get lost in the gift shop," wrote Neville.

Next came more cards from Lakeland followed by letters that said romantic things he could never express in person. Janet realized she had made a mistake and said as much when she called one night in early April. "Set the date," said the pitcher. She picked May 9, 1953.

When you marry a baseball player in May, the wedding is akin to an exhibition game wedged into the regular season schedule. Neville's teammates, looking a little uncertain in their seldom-worn suits, sat quietly in the Immaculate Conception Church that morning as the couple exchanged vows in a traditional Catholic ceremony. After a breakfast for the wedding party at the Goodwin family home, the newlyweds drove 55 miles for a one-night honeymoon in Greensboro. Neville would suit up for the Bulls the very next day.

They stayed at a cabin-style motel and played miniature golf instead of drinking champagne. They arose early the next morning, went to mass, then drove to Memorial Stadium. Neville was decked out in a suit that had been handmade in Panama. He added a red boutonniere to go with his red tie and red socks. His bride was far more subdued with a purple orchid pinned to her white linen dress, her outfit accented by a black sash and black hat.

Janet was embarrassed like any bride would be when the team bus pulled up alongside their car. She waited until the players left for the dressing room, then picked out what she thought would be an inconspicuous seat in the grandstand. She was certain no one would recognize her as a newlywed, but the public-address announcer refused to cooperate. "Ladies and gentlemen," he said, "Eddie Neville just got married and his wife is sitting..."

They set up house in a three-room, second-floor apartment just four blocks from the entrance to Durham Athletic Park. Janet attended most of the Bulls' games and sat behind the visitors' dugout on the third-base side of the grandstand. While most of the other wives sat behind the Bulls, Janet realized her seat was the best spot to see her new husband in the dugout and bullpen. She recalls going to one game with her grandmother, Kizzie Sykes. "What," asked the grandmother, "is that pile of dirt doing in the middle of the field?" Janet, fast becoming an expert, explained that it was a pitcher's mound.

The simple pleasures continued as Neville wolfed down chocolate pie at the Little Acorn Restaurant and Janet enjoyed the fried dough he had learned to cook from his mother. Neville was comfortable with a life like that, but uncomfortable in other situations. Off the field, he was shy and appeared aloof, even in the presence of his teammates. At a team picnic late one Sunday afternoon, Janet brought some records and became a favorite dancing partner with several players. Neville slipped away from the picnic shelter unnoticed, left a note in the car, and walked home. It was their first big league argument.

In late November, they left on what would be Neville's final trip to Panama. They drove to Charleston, South Carolina, boarded a steamship, and headed for a second honeymoon, this one lasting 90 days. It was one of those special times that can happen only once. Manager Al Kubski recently had married, as had infielder Ziggy Jazinski. Together, the three couples, along with Ray and Joan Dabek, enjoyed a winter of picnics at the beach and lazy afternoons at the pool.

One afternoon, after the players had left for a game, the wives slipped into a spare set of Carta Vieja uniforms and staged a contest of their own. They took on the appearance of baseball clowns in baggy pants, Janet sliding into home just under the tag of Marie Jazinski. Even before her baseball "debut," Neville had affectionately nicknamed Janet "Number 34," a reference to her bust size.

Neville made Janet laugh when he pronounced outfielder Johnny Kropf's name with a Sylvester Pussycat lisp. The laugh was on Janet when she was lured into a day of tarpon fishing. She had never caught a perch, much less a large game fish. So when she felt a tug on her line, the excitement mounted as the players cheered her on. "They asked me if I could see its eyes," she recalled. "I kept saying, 'yeah, yeah.'" The enthusiasm continued until she learned the line had been rigged.

The wives had planned to accompany the players to the Caribbean Series in Puerto Rico, but with extra seats on the flight taken by sports writers, Janet boarded a steamship to New York and returned to Durham by train. Panama had indeed been a land of romance. When she arrived home, she was two months pregnant.

After the Caribbean Series, Neville went to Florida for spring training. He had been there only a short time when Janet suffered a miscarriage. They reunited at Durham Athletic Park when the team bus arrived from spring training on Easter Sunday. Janet remembered that day as one of the most discouraging times of her life.

Neville was discouraged as well, not only by the miscarriage but also by his running feud with a demanding manager, Charlie Metro. The independent Neville had never required strong direction, but Metro remained dictatorial. Neville would continue pitching, but he no longer thought his career was worthy of a scrapbook.

He signed with Albany the next season. As the bus moved north from spring training in Florida, Janet joined him at Fayetteville, North Carolina, for a one-night stopover. It was the last time she would see her husband as a professional baseball player.

Janet had her bags packed for Albany when the telegram came. Neville returned home, then made one final effort to stay in the game. He contacted the Faribault Lakers of the semipro Southern Minnesota League, a team that had offered him $850 a month the season before. Ed Pfeiffer, business manager of the team, sent a two-page handwritten letter by air mail. He wanted Neville, but for a cheaper price. "Let me know what you would have to have for salary," he wrote. "Our attendance is off over last year but not that bad."

The less-than-enthusiastic letter helped Neville make a decision. He stashed away his glove for good. He took a temporary job as a milkman with a local dairy, rising at four in the morning and delivering milk products to stores and homes. In the fall, he joined a local beer distributorship run by Glenn E. "Ted" Mann, who also served as president of the Carolina League and sports publicity director at Duke University. He started as a route salesman, later moving inside to run the business office. He stayed there just over five years before taking an assembly line job at a new Westinghouse plant in Baltimore.

Less than four months later, he received the telephone call he had waited for since retiring from baseball. The Los Angeles Dodgers, through Baltimore native and eastern scouting supervisor John Carey, offered him a job as a scout covering North and South Carolina. He and Janet returned to Durham in early 1961, and he headed immediately for the Dodgertown training complex in Vero Beach, Florida. In spare moments, he shot home movies of many of the Dodgers who would be playing their final season in the Los Angeles Coliseum.

It seemed an ideal match, the ex-pitcher on the road again evaluating minor league players and searching for talented youngsters. Neville loved the $5,000-a-year job, taking a particular interest in discovering pitchers who reminded him of himself 15 years earlier.

He signed Nicky Warren, a Durham boy who attracted considerable attention as a highly competitive fastballer for the University of North Carolina Tar Heels. Warren struck out more than a batter an inning in his first two seasons, but was released after a poor start in 1963 at Great Falls (Montana) in the Class A Pioneer League.

It was one of the happiest times of their married lives, Neville back in baseball and Janet devoting her time to raising a two-year-old son she thought she would never have. Despite difficult pregnancies, she was to give birth to two other children: a daughter in 1962 and another son in 1966.

On October 31, 1962, the Dodgers released Neville, claiming their scouting system was being streamlined in conjunction with a change in draft rules that would cut scout quotas in half. He would never return to the game in any capacity on a fulltime basis, hurt by his limiting scouting experience and a reputation as a perfectionist who recommended players only if they were of absolute star quality.

Neville had filed his final scouting report on September 15 after following the Boston Red Sox farm club in Winston-Salem for ten days. The player who impressed him the most was a shortstop with a good bat, excellent range, and a strong arm.

"Has one glaring fault in field," Neville wrote on the back of a blue form. "Even in practice, he has trouble finding the handle with the bare hand, more than often using a second grab to get possession. Elimination of this fault and he'd have a chance."

His deficiency corrected, the young shortstop from Brooklyn broke into Boston's starting lineup three years later and anchored the Red Sox infield for more than a decade. His name: Americo Peter Petrocelli, known to the fans of Fenway as Rico.

"Eddie just knew so much about baseball," said Janet. "It was a loss to the game not to have him."

Life went on, and Neville stayed in the game by umpiring after returning to his job at the beer distributorship. When he called Atlantic Coast Conference games in the spring, fellow umpires were surprised when the old lefthander, ever the perfectionist, narrowed the strike zone. But Rusty Herring, a Durham umpire who made game assignments, said that no one questioned Neville's consistency and knowledge of the rules.

By the fall of 1966, Neville had tired of bookkeeping work and resigned to look for a more challenging position. In November, Duke University hired him as a buyer in the purchasing department, a job he would hold for 20 years. He enjoyed his work at Duke, refreshed himself every spring for 19 years as a college umpire, and satisfied his competitive urges on the golf course.

To the American Red Cross, he was a local hero all over again. He took an active role in the Red Cross blood program at Duke and over a 15-year period donated more blood—86 pints—than any other person in Durham. In the eight years Neville spearheaded the blood drive at Duke, university employees responded by donating 3,516 pints.

As the years passed, the three Neville children moved through the Durham school system, each demonstrating athletic skills before graduating from Durham High School. Mike, the oldest, caught for the Durham High varsity before dropping sports and taking after-hours work

**Neville, at 57, bears down as Umpire Lou Bello looks on in a 1980 Old-Timers' game at Durham. (Courtesy *The News and Observer*, Raleigh, N.C.)**

to finance his education at the University of North Carolina at Chapel Hill. Pat, the only daughter, was a champion swimmer as a teenager and became a varsity cheerleader in high school. Tony, blessed with the same athletic body as his father, was an outstanding pitcher at Durham High but showed little interest in pursuing the sport as a pro.

Neville never lost touch with baseball. When he attended youth league games, umpires often asked him to interpret rules. He also voiced opinions on pitching greats without being asked. As a Dodger scout, he had found fault with Sandy Koufax's fielding. As a fan, he wrote a letter of advice to the Cincinnati Reds' Tom Seaver.

For several years starting in the late 1970s, he monitored the progress of players on two fronts. He joined Kansas City as an associate scout, a part-time position that paid a fee each time a recommended prospect was signed, then tacked on bonuses for each promotion in the Royal farm system. When he coached Babe Ruth and American Legion baseball, he armed his pitchers with his personal list of 63 typewritten tips.

He became a fixture at Old-Timers' games. His competitive fire returned as soon as he removed his black-rimmed glasses and covered his balding head with a white cap circled by three red stripes. His broad chest continued to threaten the buttons on his gray wool shirt.

In a 1980 Old-Timers' game at Durham, Neville came to the plate against Tommy Byrne, a fellow Baltimore native who as a New York Yankee had beaten the Brooklyn Dodgers 4–2 in the second game of the 1955 World Series. After stepping back from an inside pitch, Neville drove the ball to deep center. He trotted into second and paused to hitch up his ill-fitting pants. It would be the longest hit of the night.

But life began unraveling for Neville a year later. He became depressed easily. He showed frustration over the slightest change in his daily routine. Twelve years earlier, he had suffered a mild stroke. His jaw became slack and the side of his face drawn. The physical effects of the stroke were undetectable after six months, but Janet noticed a slight change in his personality as he showed signs of distraction and occasional memory lapses.

Starting in early 1982, he underwent periodic psychiatric exams at the Duke University Medical Center. Over the next seven years, his proud body and mind would be destroyed as his memory and ability to think slipped away day by day.

Janet suspected Alzheimer's disease, but doctors diagnosed his illness as multi-infarct dementia, a condition caused by a series of small strokes. The result would be the same as Alzheimer's: a frightening mental and physical debilitation.

Janet was instructed to keep everything the same at home: the same schedule, the same table setting, his clothes laid out in the same place. Any break in the routine, she learned, would confuse and anger him. "If we had fish patties one day, he would want them every day," said Janet. "He was keeping everyone around him on edge with things like that."

He was often sleepy in the morning and reluctant to go to work. He retreated into the past as he thumbed through his old press clippings and typed lengthy letters to friends when he spotted items that revived his memory.

In 1984, Janet found him sitting alone in the living room, a sobbing, angry man who acknowledged his decline to her for the first time. "I can't remember the words," he said. "I can't remember the words."

In February of 1985, the Hot Stove League of Raleigh honored Neville for his 18-inning, 1–0 victory over Greensboro in 1952. The presiding officer at the Hot Stove banquet was none other than former Carolina Leaguer Willie Duke, who 36 years earlier had insisted at first that Neville was "not so hot."

As Duke and North Carolina Governor Jim Martin looked on, Neville received the award from Add Penfield, who had broadcast the game for a Greensboro radio station. The old hero stood before an appreciative audience filled with North Carolina baseball greats and gave a four-word speech before returning to his seat. "The ballgame," he said, "is over."

In October, Neville expected to receive another award when he attended the forty-fifth anniversary reunion of his graduating class at Mount St. Joseph High School in Baltimore. After being nominated to the school's Hall of Fame two consecutive years, he had become convinced that he would be inducted during the reunion banquet. A year earlier, after his first nomination, he had written of plans to give the school a souvenir baseball from the 1940 championship game.

His brother-in-law, Charles Dixon, knew the Hall of Fame induction ceremony had taken place in the spring, but said nothing. He drove Neville to the campus, let him out of the car, and searched for a parking space. Several anxious minutes later, Dixon found Neville appearing to be lost as he wandered around the campus. He would never understand why he wasn't inducted that night.

(Although he was nominated several times, it would not be until December 17, 1992, that Neville was elected to the Mount St. Joe Hall of Fame—a process slowed by a procedure that gave top priority to athletes who, unlike the lefthander, played more than one varsity sport.)

After his return to Durham, Janet struggled to keep him from being institutionalized. "I knew he would be destroyed if he ever left home," she said. "It was all he had."

Duke University expressed its appreciation to Neville by keeping him on the payroll until he qualified for his pension after 20 years. He then was granted a medical leave.

He would spend many of his days strolling the Duke Golf Course and looking for lost balls in the piney woods that lined the fairways. In time, he would fill several chest drawers with used golf balls.

He drove himself to the course until his license was suspended after a minor wreck in 1987. He was taken home by a policeman after being unable to provide information on his car registration and insurance.

Janet continued the routine. She would drive him to the golf course as she headed for work at the Department of Social Services, leaving him with a note listing her phone number and telling him she would return at one o'clock. One afternoon, when he appeared particularly confused and had collected only a handful of balls and tees, Janet knew he would never return.

He had continued to follow the Durham Bulls, occupying a seat in the left field bleachers of Durham Athletic Park and wearing a team cap and souvenir T-shirt. Few of those around him realized this lonely, confused man had won more games than any pitcher in the club's history. Miles Wolff, president of the Bulls, instructed the club's personnel to keep a close eye on the old lefthander as his time at the park ticked away.

Neville treasured that final link to the past. One cold January day, when he became worried the Bulls were leaving Durham, Janet drove him to the park and assured him the team would be there in the spring. He smiled that day, and he smiled again when they returned in April to see the team working out.

The impact of his illness touched everyone in his family. Tony Neville, still at home, witnessed his father's decline and was devastated. He wavered between compassion and frustration.

Ultimately, the father would become the child. Every other day, Janet would hand him two $1 bills and a quarter to purchase a half gallon of milk at a neighborhood convenience store. Just going out for milk became one of the most important events in his life.

Shortly after he left on one of his walks to the store, Janet heard a siren from a police car. "I thought it was Eddie," she recalled, "but he walked through the doorway just about that time. I grabbed him and hugged him and told him how glad I was to see him." Neville looked at his wife and replied, "It's okay; it's okay."

Times like that, when goodness could be found in the least little thing, became less and less frequent as his condition continued to worsen. For nourishment, he became obsessed with corn flakes and milk. He would eat nothing else three times a day. He could neither tell time nor count money. He forgot how to take off his own shoes, and Janet had to remove his clothes and lead him to the bathroom. Once he was in the bathtub, he refused to let Janet touch him. He still could remember how to bathe himself.

By the summer of 1988, Neville had become lost in his own house. He called his wife of 35 years "woman." Everything he had ever known or ever done had bolted from his mind forever.

One night, as she heard her husband pacing in the dark, the house sweltering in a late summer heat wave, Janet realized the time had come. "I hated to turn him loose, but I knew I had to," she said.

Neville walked around the house the entire night. When Janet returned from work the next day, she found him with his pants soiled by his own waste. He was angrier and more frustrated than ever. She tried to remove his pants but couldn't. Out of answers, she led him to the car, buckled his seat belt, and drove him to the Duke University Medical Center. This time it was not the red and cream Studebaker and the handsome athlete with the scrapbooks in back and a craving for milk shakes. It was a different form of love in a different time. Even as his illness had devastated their lives, it had, in its own strange way, strengthened their bonds.

It took two security men and a nurse to lead Neville into the hospital. As he struggled, he looked back at Janet, held out an arm, and shouted in desperation, "Lady, lady." The hospital attendants ushered him into a room, cut off his clothes, fitted him with a hospital gown, and confined him to the violent ward for two weeks.

That was in August. In October, he was transferred to the nearby Veterans Administration Medical Center. He grew worse by the day; the only reminder that he had a past of greatness was the old Bulls souvenir cap that he sometimes wore as he lay in bed. He had lost more than half his body weight; his once bulky thighs had been reduced to the size of Janet's forearms. He would scream at night, repeating "Hit, Victor" over and over as a game in a far distant past floated through his mind.

When Veterans Administration regulations required that he be transferred to a nursing home, Janet received financial assistance after word of Neville's plight reached the Association of Professional Baseball Players of America. His stay in a Raleigh nursing home abruptly ended after ten days when Janet expressed outrage after finding him tied to a chair, his head hanging between his knees and his pajamas soaked in urine. Fighting her husband's last battle, she cut through red tape and had him re-admitted to the VA Medical Center to spend his final weeks.

The end came on January 29, 1989. Eddie Neville, husband, father, and an extraordinary baseball player in his time, died late that morning in his sleep. He was 66 years old.

# Epilogue

*Only little boys with middle-aged faces really give a damn about yesterday's town heroes. But in minor league towns from Medicine Hat to Modesto, the cycle starts all over again as other Eddie Nevilles sign balls that other boys somehow lose. My souvenir disappeared several summers after he mailed it from spring training. I don't guess I ever told him that.*

As the tobacco town of Eddie Neville's era was swallowed up by urban growth and a new economic base combining medicine, research, and education, many of the qualities that gave Durham its blue-collar flavor disappeared at the same time.

Although the nickname still appears in signs of businesses that peddle bicycles and submarine sandwiches and sound equipment, the colorful "Bull City" has vanished forever. In its place stands the "City of Medicine," a key link in a sprawling metropolitan area known as the Research Triangle.

Raleigh, once the home of the hated Capitals, is now a partner in the Triangle—as well as the headquarters of the Bulls' corporate owner, Capitol Broadcasting, Inc. Ironically, the company's president, James Goodmon, is a grandson of the late Ray Goodmon, the Coastal Plain League president who once fined Neville five dollars for throwing his bat.

Another Durham asset was claimed by Reidsville, which dropped out of the Carolina League after the 1955 season but gained one final victory when American Tobacco Company shifted its entire Durham production there in 1987.

Even with the closing of American, tobacco had become such a diminishing part of Durham's everyday life that the immediate impact on the city was regarded as slight. Truth is, one of Leo "Muscle" Shoals' 1949 blasts for the Reidsville Luckies probably hurt more—at least until the area felt the impact of a national recession.

187

More changes are inevitable. Durham Athletic Park—its left and center field fences mercifully shorter—remains the home of the Class A Bulls, but it faces a finite future as a professional baseball facility. The grand old park, its 5,400 seats wedged into every available space, has become too small and too inaccessible to accommodate a population large enough to support a Triple A franchise.

The team that started playing in Durham in 1902 at the modest George Lyon Ball Park is scheduled to move into a new stadium in 1994, and for a time it appeared the facility would be located in a proposed suburban sports complex on the Raleigh side of the Research Triangle. That was the site originally favored by Goodmon, whose company bought the franchise from Miles Wolff in 1991 for a reported $2 million.

Wolff had been discouraged by the failure of voters to support a bond issue financing a new stadium, but in 1992 the Durham City Council approved an outlay of more than $11 million once it became obvious that part of the city's heritage was in danger of being lost to neighboring Wake County. The new facility, whose designers include architects from the same firm that created Baltimore's Oriole Park at Camden Yards, will adjoin the abandoned American Tobacco Company complex that includes the original Bull Durham plant.

As the countdown continues for Durham Athletic Park, my old neighborhood ages gracefully in the city's historic Trinity Park section. It looks almost the same along Englewood and Dollar over four decades after Neville threw his first Durham pitch, but everyone in the street gang I knew has been gone for more than a quarter of a century.

Youngsters occasionally emerge in the yards, but no one swats tennis balls in the street. It is just as well, for only grounders would be possible under the umbrella of aging trees that blanks out most of the sun.

The front stoop is still there at my old house on Englewood, but the single occupant is a professional woman with a career instead of children. Her front-door screen is intact; bushes no longer grow where the first and third bases of my imagination once stood.

Most of the people have never heard of Joe Holloway, the boy next door whose attack of diarrhea forced my midget league coach to play me at first base for four innings I'll never forget.

Joe, who died of cancer in 1990, was a holy terror who was the heart and soul of our neighborhood, a blond-haired kid with an open grin and a mind that plotted all sorts of things. When an exasperated neighbor wasn't putting a hammerlock on him and trying to force a confession for his latest misdeed, Joe starred in the street and on the empty lot that he and I had named Vaughan Field.

In a nearby part of the city, Janet Neville often walks through another

**Janet Neville's favorite photograph: her husband as a Durham Bull in 1949. (Courtesy *The Herald-Sun*.)**

of our playgrounds of long ago—a public park where I once tossed twigs into a creek and watched them race toward a designated finish line.

Janet typically walks four miles in the morning and two more in the afternoon. In the autumn of her life, "Number 34" follows a conditioning

plan as ambitious as the one once prescribed by Toledo Manager Eddie
Mayo.

As I joined her one winter afternoon, Janet walked and talked in
rapid-fire fashion as we headed toward my in-laws' house where Eddie had
returned my two boyhood letters. She laughed at my Slippery Rock sweat-
shirt, recalling that Eddie always looked for the football score of the school
with the funny name. She remembered the ugly mutt of a dog that Bull
fan "Ma" Gregory had given them shortly after their marriage.

More memories would emerge after my wife, Ann, and I presented
Janet with her favorite photograph of Eddie, one that had been stored in
newspaper files after being published in his first season as a Bull. Janet took
one look and described him as "pretty"—this pitcher from Baltimore who
peered from beneath his Durham cap with the same smile that one day
would win her over.

He was 26 then, and I was 8. It was 1949.

I fired one final fastball toward the stoop. I smelled the aging tobacco
as we approached the park. I heard Jack Horner call out the starting lineup
on the public-address system. And I saw Ace Parker lumber over to the little pitcher leaning forward on the dugout bench.

"Danville's coming to town, lefthander," Parker might have said.
"It's your turn tomorrow."

# APPENDIX: EDDIE NEVILLE'S PITCHING STATISTICS

*Minor Leagues*

| Year | Club | League | G | GS | CG | IP | W | L | PCT | H | R | ER | SO | BB | ERA |
|---|---|---|---|---|---|---|---|---|---|---|---|---|---|---|---|
| 1947 | Tarboro | Coastal Plain | 43 | 32 | 28 | 304 | 28 | 9 | .757 | 269 | 122 | 78 | 172 | 89 | 2.31 |
| 1948 | Tarboro | Coastal Plain | 25 | 19 | 17 | 176 | 15 | 4 | .789 | 204 | 82 | 63 | 59 | 53 | 3.22 |
| 1949 | Durham | Carolina | 40 | 31 | 25 | 274 | 25 | 10 | .714 | 252 | 112 | 79 | 154 | 69 | 2.59 |
| 1950 | Toledo | A.A. | 35 | 20 | 11 | 174 | 6 | 15 | .286 | 181 | 98 | 80 | 72 | 94 | 4.14 |
| 1951 | Toledo | A.A. | 6 | 1 | 0 | 16 | 2 | 0 | 1.000 | 19 | 8 | 5 | 5 | 7 | 2.81 |
| 1951 | Williamsport | Eastern | 32 | 18 | 9 | 162 | 7 | 11 | .389 | 176 | 77 | 61 | 95 | 73 | 3.39 |
| 1952 | Durham | Carolina | 30 | 19 | 17 | 215 | 17 | 9 | .654 | 186 | 53 | 41 | 95 | 61 | 1.72 |
| 1953 | Durham | Carolina | 41 | 27 | 23 | 264 | 21 | 8 | .724 | 243 | 99 | 67 | 138 | 74 | 2.28 |
| 1954 | Durham | Carolina | 43 | 23 | 10 | 216 | 12 | 11 | .522 | 267 | 128 | 92 | 119 | 52 | 3.83 |
| 1955 | Albany | Eastern | 6 | 6 | 1 | 35 | 1 | 3 | .250 | 49 | 24 | 18 | 24 | 14 | 4.63 |
| Minor League Totals | | | 301 | 196 | 141 | 1836 | 134 | 80 | .626 | 1846 | 803 | 584 | 933 | 586 | 2.86 |

*Winter Leagues*

| Year | Club | League | G | GS | CG | IP | W | L | PCT | H | R | ER | SO | BB | ERA |
|---|---|---|---|---|---|---|---|---|---|---|---|---|---|---|---|
| 1946–47 | Cristobol | Canal Zone | 14 | 10 | 9 | 93 | 9 | 1 | .900 | 79 | 30 | 20 | 52 | 39 | 1.98 |
| 1947–48 | Cristobol | Canal Zone | 17 | 9 | 6 | 91 | 5 | 4 | .556 | 96 | 48 | 35 | 32 | 34 | 3.46 |
| 1948–49 | Cristobol | Canal Zone | 16 | 12 | 11 | 118 | 11 | 3 | .786 | 98 | 43 | 33 | 35 | 38 | 2.52 |
| 1949–50 | Cristobol | Canal Zone | 16 | 12 | 12 | 112 | 12 | 2 | .857 | 79 | 33 | 25 | 45 | 48 | 2.01 |
| 1950–51 | Cristobol | Canal Zone | 7 | 5 | 4 | 48 | 3 | 1 | .750 | 50 | 28 | 21 | 19 | 20 | 3.93 |
| 1951–52 | Carta Vieja | Panama | 9 | 9 | 6 | 72 | 5 | 3 | .625 | 57 | 23 | 20 | 25 | 21 | 3.50 |
| 1953–54 | Carta Vieja | Panama | 14 | 10 | 4 | 78 | 5 | 3 | .625 | 84 | 44 | 32 | 28 | 21 | 3.71 |
| Winter League Totals | | | 93 | 67 | 52 | 612 | 50 | 17 | .746 | 543 | 249 | 186 | 236 | 221 | 2.74 |
| Career Totals | | | 394 | 263 | 193 | 2448 | 184 | 97 | .655 | 2389 | 1052 | 770 | 1169 | 807 | 2.83 |

# Bibliography

Much of the information in *Eddie Neville of the Durham Bulls* is based on newspaper research, interviews, and the memorabilia of Eddie Neville. In addition to microfilm at public libraries, newspaper material came from two other sources: clippings in Neville's scrapbooks and the player files at the National Baseball Library in Cooperstown, New York.

In order to give a complete account of Neville's career, newspaper research included virtually every professional game he appeared in, his early years in Baltimore, and day-by-day coverage of each professional season. Newspapers used extensively for their coverage of Neville's career in organized baseball included the *Durham* (N.C.) *Morning Herald, The Durham Sun,* the *Daily Southerner* of Tarboro, N.C., the *Toledo Blade,* the *Toledo Times,* the *Albany* (N.Y.) *Times-Union,* the *Butler* (Pa.) *Eagle,* the *Williamsport* (Pa.) *Gazette-Bulletin,* the *Williamsport* (Pa.) *Sun,* and the *Wilmington* (Del.) *Morning News. The Panama American* and the *Star & Herald* of Panama City, Panama, two English language newspapers no longer in existence, were the primary sources of game information spanning Neville's seven seasons in the winter leagues. *The Sun* of Baltimore, Md., was the major source of information on Neville's days as an amateur and as a member of the Baltimore Oriole organization.

Because Neville's teams played more than 1,300 games during his professional career, only the most significant articles from that period are listed. Newspaper articles of historical significance also are included, as are a number of articles used as sources of information on other players and managers in the Neville era.

Anderson, Dave. "Once 0 for 31, Now He Roots for Canseco." *New York Times,* October 29, 1990.
Anderson, Jean Bradley. *Durham County.* Durham, N.C.: Duke University Press, 1990.
Angel, Lu. "What Was and Will Be." *The News and Observer* (Raleigh, N.C.), August 9, 1980.

"Ball Park and Warehouse Burn." *The Durham* (N.C.) *Herald-Sun,* June 18, 1939.

*The Baseball Blue Book.* Fort Wayne, In.: Heilbroner Baseball Bureau. Numerous editions.

*Baseball Guide and Record Book.* St. Louis, Mo.: The Sporting News Publishing Co. Numerous editions.

*Baseball Register.* St. Louis, Mo.: The Sporting News Publishing Co. Numerous editions.

"Baseball Royals Win Over All-Stars, 25–7." Article published during Jackie Robinson's Canal Zone tour with Dodgers. *The Gazette* (Montreal), March 22, 1947.

Beck, Walter "Boom Boom." Obituary, *The Sporting News,* April 25, 1987.

Benson, Michael. *Ballparks of North America.* Jefferson, N.C.: McFarland, 1989.

Biederman, Les. "'A Future Dean,' Detore's Tag on Strikeout King." Article on Ron Necciai. *The Sporting News,* May 21, 1952.

_____. "Murry Promises to Worry Contenders Down Stretch." Includes Ron Necciai's Pittsburgh pitching debut. *The Sporting News,* August 20, 1952.

*Biographical Dictionary of American Sports. Baseball.* Edited by David L. Porter. New York: Greenwood, 1987.

*Bird's Eye View of the Panama Canal and Map of Panama.* Panama: I. L. Maduro, Jr. Undated.

Blackman, Herman. "Neville, Too Tiny as Gardener, Stands High on Tarboro's Hill." *The Sporting News,* September 3, 1947.

Browning, Wilt. "Neville Finally Honored in Appropriate Manner." *Greensboro* (N.C.) *News & Record,* February 26, 1985.

*Bulletin, National Association of Professional Baseball Leagues.* Columbus, Ohio, and Durham, N.C. Numerous issues.

*Canal Zone League Official Records.* Edited by Leo Eberenz. 1946–47 season.

*Canal Zone League Official Score Book.* 1947–48 season.

*Carolina League Record Book.* Edited by Jack Horner. Carolina League Office, Durham, N.C. 1948–55 editions.

*Carolina League Media Guide and Record Book.* Edited by Mickey McLean. Carolina League Office, Greensboro, N.C., 1992.

Casey, Elton. "Casey at the Bat." Column on Neville's Durham career. *The Durham* (N.C.) *Sun,* April 23, 1953.

_____. "Neville Balks at Metro's Order of After-Game Batting Workout." *The Durham Sun,* June 7, 1954.

_____. "Ordinarily Charlie Metro Is a Charitable Sort of a Guy." *The Durham Sun,* July 1, 1954.

_____. "Ted Mann Scorns Actions of Durham Players, Fans." *The Durham Sun,* July 23, 1954.

_____. "Loved Baseball Fan 'Ma' Gregory Dies." *Durham* (N.C.) *Morning Herald,* January 5, 1969.

_____. "S. C. (Sis) Perry." *Durham Morning Herald,* May 27, 1971.

_____. "Where Are You? Durham's Eddie Neville Still Talking Baseball." *Durham Morning Herald,* December 9, 1973.

Centennial Edition. *Durham Morning Herald,* April 26, 1953.

*Century of Achievement—1876–1976.* History of Mt. St. Joseph High School, Baltimore, Md. Edited by Richard Bostwick. Cambridge, Md.: Western Publishing.

Clay, Russell. "On Sixth Day, the Verdict." *Durham Morning Herald,* September 18, 1960.

Cope, Myron. "Can Dick Groat Fire Up the Pirates Again?" *Sport,* April 1961.

"Council Awards Contract for Ball Park Stands." *Durham Morning Herald.* October 20, 1939.

Creamer, Robert W. *Babe: The Legend Comes to Life.* New York: Simon and Schuster, 1974.

"Crowd Would Be Tribute to Bulls." *The Durham Herald-Sun,* June 18, 1939.

Dacsenzo, Frank. *Groat: I Hit and Ran.* Durham, N.C.: Moore, 1979.

Daniel, Dan. "Crowds Force Landis to Put Medwick Out." *World-Telegram* (New York), October 10, 1934.

*Dickson Baseball Dictionary.* Edited and compiled by Paul Dickson. New York: Facts on File, 1989.

Dixon, Wyatt T. "Baseball's Beginnings." *The Durham Sun,* September 3, 1943.

_____. "Pro Ball Comes to Durham." *The Durham Sun,* May 18, 1979.

Duane F. "Duke" Maas obituary. *The Sporting News,* December 25, 1976.

Dula, S. C., and Simpson, A. C. *Durham and Her People,* Durham, N.C.: The Citizens Press, 1951.

*The Durham Architectural and Historic Inventory.* Claudia P. Roberts, principal investigator. Sponsored by the City of Durham, N.C., and the Historic Preservation Society of Durham, 1982.

"Durham Opens New Park This Afternoon." *Durham Morning Herald,* July 7, 1926.

"El Toro Field Scene of Dedication Ceremonies Today." *Durham Morning Herald,* July 26, 1926.

Falls, Joe. "Metro's Ideas Gone Up in Smoke." *Detroit Free Press,* June 10, 1970.

Fox, John. Column on Walter "Boom Boom" Beck. *Binghamton* (N.Y.) *News,* June 25, 1964.

Germino, Hugo. "After the Fire." *The Durham Sun,* July 3, 1939.

_____. "Boner by Official Scorer." *The Durham Sun,* June 5, 1954.

_____. "Three Cheers for Charlie Metro." *The Durham Sun,* June 12, 1954.

Gibbs, C. M. "Old Oriole Park Was Called Prep School for Ball Stars." *The* (Baltimore) *Sun,* July 5, 1944.

Godwin, John. "Happy 50th, DAP!" *Bulls Illustrated, The Magazine of the Durham Bulls,* April–May 1988.

Haraway, Frank. "Bounced Metro Lands on Feet—Nabs Scout Job." *The Sporting News,* November 24, 1962.

Harris, Maurice "Mickey." Obituary, *The Sporting News,* May 1, 1971.

*Hill's Durham* (N.C.) *City Directory.* Richmond, Va.: Hill Directory Co. Numerous editions.

"Hills Turn Over El Toro Park to City." *Durham Morning Herald,* November 25, 1922.

Horner, Jack. "Eddie Neville Looks Like Sure Winner for Bulls." *Durham Morning Herald,* March 31, 1949.

_____. "Wee Willie Says It'll Be Different Story Next Time." *Durham Morning Herald,* May 3, 1949.

_____. "Neville Makes Headlines with Great Performances." *Durham Morning Herald,* July 1, 1950.

_____. "Fans Will Turn Out to See Eddie Neville Pitch." *Durham Morning Herald,* May 29, 1952.

_____. "18-Inning Thriller Wasn't Neville's Biggest Thrill." *Durham Morning Herald,* August 31, 1952.

_____. "Neville Sets Sight on 20 Victories." *Durham Morning Herald,* August 16, 1953.

————. "Scorers Changing Decisions Nothing New." *Durham Morning Herald,* June 7, 1954.

————. "Unhappy Bulls Didn't Play Best for Metro." *Durham Morning Herald,* September 12, 1954.

Hufford, Tom. "Leo (Muscle) Shoals." *Baseball Historical Review.* The Society for American Baseball Research, 1981.

Kerkhoff, Blake. "When Eddie Neville Pitched All Night." *The Raleigh* (N.C.) *Times,* August 9, 1980.

King, Joe. "Player Given an Error Though He Doesn't Touch Ball." *World-Telegram* (New York), June 14, 1942.

Landwehr, Hazel. *Home Court—Fifty Years of Cameron Indoor Stadium.* Durham, N.C.: Phoenix Communications, 1989.

Lieb, Frederick G. "Schoolboy Rowe, Ace Tiger Twirler in '30s, Dies at 51." *The Sporting News,* January 18, 1961.

Lin Weber, Ralph E. "Chronicle History of Toledo Mud Hens." Article published by the Toledo Mud Hens, undated.

*Los Angeles Dodgers Souvenir Yearbook,* 1962.

Lowry, Philip J. *Green Cathedrals.* The Society for American Baseball Research, 1986.

McGowen, Roscoe. "Dodgers Play Tie with Royals, 1–1. Robinson Makes Two Hits and Stars Afield in Initial Start at First Base." *New York Times,* March 18, 1947.

"Manager Bear Fined $25." *Durham Daily Sun.* May 17, 1902.

Marthey, Larry. "Hurler Ed Neville Takes His Vacation on Mound." *Toledo Blade,* March 23, 1950.

————. "Hens' Kid Chuckers Goose-Egg Specialists. Late-Starter Eddie Neville Seen as Best Prospect Among Promising Trio." *The Sporting News,* June 7, 1950.

Martin, Gerald. "Fernando and Kid Might Learn from Neville." *The News and Observer* (Raleigh, N.C.), July 12, 1984.

Meany, Tom. "Tigers' Mayo Clinic Steadied Eddie." *The Sporting News,* June 14, 1945.

Miller, James Edward. *The Baseball Business.* Chapel Hill, N.C.: University of North Carolina Press, 1990.

*Minor League Baseball Stars, Volumes 1 and 2.* The Society for American Baseball Research, 1978, 1985.

*Minor League Digest.* Fort Wayne, In.: Heilbroner Baseball Bureau. Numerous editions.

Mitchell, Edward V. "Crowd Could Be Tribute to Bulls." *The Durham Herald-Sun,* July 2, 1939.

————. "Minor League Headquarters a Beehive of Detail Work." *The Sporting News,* November 30, 1939.

————. "Jack Coombs Finds Fountain of Youth at Duke." *The Sporting News,* April 20, 1944.

Morris, Ron. "Eddie Neville—Smart, Gutsy Pitcher Bulls' Top Attraction." *Durham Morning Herald,* March 30, 1980.

"Necciai Whiffs 24 in Final Game Before Buc Move-up." *The Sporting News,* May 28, 1952.

"No Matter How They Tell Jackie's Story, Fleet Was First." *The Sporting News,* October 29, 1990.

"Notables in Durham for Dedication of New Athletic Park." *Durham Morning Herald,* July 27, 1926.

Objoski, Robert. *Bush League.* New York: Macmillan, 1975.

———. "Baseball Latin Style." *Baseball Research Journal.* The Society for American Baseball Research, 1977.

*The Official 1947 Coastal Plain League Record Book.* Edited by J. Gaskill McDaniel. New Bern, N.C.: Owen G. Dunn, 1947.

"Orioles Plan Stadium Use for Present." *The* (Baltimore) *Sun,* July 5, 1944.

Pozar, Stephen M., and Jean B. Purvis. *Butler: A Pictorial History.* Virginia Beach, Va.: Donning, 1980.

*The Quill.* Student Annual of Mt. St. Joseph High School, Baltimore, Md., 1939–41.

"Ray Pitched No Hit Game." *The Morning Herald* (Durham, N.C.), April 29, 1913.

Robert J. "Bob" Bowman obituary. *The Sporting News,* April 9, 1984.

"Robinson Hailed in Bribe Attempt." United Press International, September 25, 1959.

Rose, Karen. "A Collector's Glove Affair." *Sports Illustrated,* June 24, 1991.

Salsinger, H. G. "Tiger Lemon Toledo Gets Cut-Rate Tag." *The Sporting News,* September 26, 1951.

Schultz, Scott, et al. "An Early History of the Professional Baseball Teams in Toledo." Article published by the Toledo Mud Hens. Undated.

Sculley, Francis X. "House of David Revisited." *The Sunday Rutland* (Vt.) *Herald and The Sunday Times Argus,* July 10, 1977.

Senn, Jack. "Ed Neville Gets More Than Casual Glance." *Toledo Times,* March 21, 1950.

Smith, Leverett T. "Minor League Baseball in Rocky Mount." *Baseball Research Journal.* The Society for American Baseball Research, 1978.

Sobol, Ken. *Babe Ruth & the American Dream.* New York: Random House, 1974.

*Spaldings Official Base Ball Guide.* New York: American Sports Publishing, 1903.

Spink, J. G. Taylor. "Motor City Sparkplug and Hex Machine, Too." Feature on Eddie Mayo. *The Sporting News,* October 4, 1945.

Stargell, Willie, and Tom Bird. *Willie Stargell: An Autobiography.* New York: Harper and Row, 1984.

Sullivan, Neil J. *The Minors.* New York: St. Martin's, 1990.

Taylor, Craig E. "Mount St. Joe Defeats City, 5 to 1, for State Scholastic Baseball Title." *The* (Baltimore) *Sun,* June 1, 1940.

Terrell, Roy. "Head Man in a Hurry." Article on Dick Groat. *Sports Illustrated,* August 6, 1980.

"Umpire Proud Assaulted." *The Morning Herald,* May 17, 1902.

Walter "Boom Boom" Beck obituary. *The Sporting News,* April 25, 1987.

Ward, Gene. "Ward to the Wise." Column on Clarence "Ace" Parker. *Daily News* (New York), February 15, 1972.

Weirich, Frank. "Necciai Whiffs 27 in Bristol No-Hitter." *The Sporting News,* May 21, 1952.

Wilkinson, Jack. "Does He or Doesn't He?" Feature on Mike Caldwell. *Daily News* (New York), April 25, 1979.

Wolff, Miles. "Eddie Neville Was Much More Than Just a Minor League Pitcher." *Bulls Illustrated, The Magazine of the Durham Bulls,* April–May 1989.

Wolff, Rick, et al. *The Baseball Encyclopedia.* New York: MacMillan, 1990.

Wynn, Early. "Wynn's Better-Late-Than-Never 300th." *New York Times,* May 5, 1982.

Youngs, Rick. "Professional Baseball in Toledo." Article published by the Toledo Mud Hens, 1987. Updated 1988.

# Index

Homeland Investment Co. 71
Homestead Grays 62
Horner, Jack xiv, 92–94, 98, 114,
   141, 163, 164, 190
Host, Gene 156
House of David 81–82, 133
Houston Astros 156
Houtteman, Art xv
Howard, Dot 66
Hubbell, Carl 122
Huntington Avenue Baseball
   Grounds 74
Hutchinson, Fred 126


Immaculate Conception Church 177
Indianapolis Indians 111, 113, 115,
   137
International League 5, 6, 18, 26,
   30, 53, 83, 106, 108, 121, 169
Inter-State League 9, 31, 108
Isthmian Championship 19, 22, 42


Jablonski, Ray 74
Jackson, Shoeless Joe 14, 71
Jacobs, Forrest "Spook" 48
James, Lacy 101
Jamestown baseball club 149, 159
Jansen, Larry 125
Jarlett, Al 17
Jazinski, Marie 178
Jazinski, Ziggy 178
Jeffries, Bill 33, 34, 65, 66, 68
Jersey City baseball club 6
Joe Palooka comic books xii
John, Brother Martin 4
John Heisman Club 108
Johnson, Earl 121
Johnson, H. I. 66
Johnson City baseball club 90, 128
Jones, Bob 65
Joost, Eddie 172
Junior World Series 9


Kalin, Frank 111
Kaline, Al 1
Kansas City Athletics 12, 43, 46,
   47, 107, 147, 156, 157
Kansas City Blues 118, 119
Kansas City Royals 44, 49, 147,
   160, 170, 181
Kardash, Mike 26

Karlik, Emil 126, 127, 133, 134–35,
   136
Kavanaugh, Jerry 29
Kehn, Chet 16
Keller, Charlie "King Kong" 29, 141
Kelly, Pat 102
Kendrick, James 123
Kennedy, Bill 30, 36
Kennedy, Roy 21, 22–23, 28, 31–32,
   53, 67, 68
Kiker Stadium 138
King, Charles "Chick" 126, 127,
   133, 134, 135, 136
Kingsport baseball club 91, 128
Kinston Eagles 29, 30, 31, 35, 36,
   37, 57, 59, 61, 65, 66
Kirkland, Ann 190
Kirkland, Bill xi–xv, 1, 14, 24, 38,
   50, 69, 187–90
Kirkland, Buck xiv
Kirkland, Kirk xiv, xv
Kitty League 154
Klein, Lou 47
Klippstein, Johnny 74
Knickerbocker, Austin 106, 110
Komanecky, Ray 29, 31, 53, 56, 58,
   64, 68
Korean War 39, 127, 135
Kornegay, Jim 123
Koshorek, Clem 46, 47, 48
Koufax, Sandy 181
Koy, Ernie 81
Kraus, Jack 81
Kropf, Johnny 178
Kubski, Al 16–18, 21, 22, 39, 42,
   43, 44, 45–46, 47, 48–49, 50–51,
   178
Kubski, Gil 49
Kyser, Kay 30


Lafayette baseball club 85
LaGrange, Ga. 26, 31, 52, 63
Lakeland, Fl. (spring training
   camp) 109, 144, 156, 157, 177
Lamar Tech 97
Landis, Kenesaw Mountain 71,
   144–45
Lane, Frank 79
LaPalme, Paul 111, 114
LaRue, Lash 79
Lasorda, Tommy 43, 47
Lau, Charlie 160
Lavagetto, Cookie 14

League Park 95
Leaksville Triplets 74, 82–83, 87
Lee, Jack 59
Lemon, Bob 7, 170
Leonard, Walter "Buck" 62
Lerchen, "Dutch" 106
Lerchen, George 106, 107, 111, 113, 114
Lewis, "Smoky" Joe 146
Liberty Network 104, 140
Lillis, Bob 119
Liggett & Myers 75
Lincoln baseball club 22
Lincoln Hotel 113
Linhart, Carl 85, 100, 102, 173
Little Acorn Restaurant 178
Little Rock baseball club 115, 119, 135, 141, 144, 165
Lockamy, Glenn 102
Logan, Johnny 110
Lombardi, Vic 81
Lone Star League 18, 22
"The Lone Ranger" 121
Lopat, Eddie 88
Lopez, Al 113, 114, 115
Lopez, Hector 45–46
Lord Calvert whiskey 20–21
Los Angeles (Pacific Coast League) 105
Los Angeles Coliseum 9, 179
Los Angeles Dodgers 9, 30, 44, 79, 156, 171, 179, 180, 181
Louisville Colonels 9, 104, 110, 115, 116
Lucas, Ramona 85
Lucky Strike cigarettes 76
Lumberton baseball club 63
Lund, Don 106, 114
Luszcynski, Eddie 58
Luzinski, Greg 70
Lynch, Dale 48

Maas, Duane "Duke" 146–47
MacArthur, Gen. Douglas 6
McCaffrey, Tom 171
McCahan, Bill 140
McCormick, Frank 79, 81
McDonogh baseball club 5
McElroy, Frank 157
McGowen, Roscoe 16
Mack, Connie 6, 30, 139, 140–41
Mack, Connie Jr. 140
Mack, Earle 140

McKeon, Jack 147–48
McLawhorn, Sam 37
McLean, Gov. Angus 71
McLendon, Gordon 104, 140
McManus, Joe 101
McMillan, Roy 18
McNay, Charles 29
McPadden, John "Mickey" 81–82, 101, 127, 133
Main, Forrest 111
Malbourne Hotel 82
Maloney, Phyllis 19
Malzone, Frank 119
Mancuso, Frank 115
Mangum, Leo "Blackie" 80
Manila baseball club 11
Mankiewicz, Felix 9
Mann, Glenn E. "Ted" 168, 179
Manning, Brother Bertin 4
Mantle, Mickey 119
Maranville, Walter "Rabbit" 126
Markham, Jerry 132
Markos, Steve 58
Marlowe, Dick 106
Marthey, Larry 105, 113
Martin, Gov. Jim 182
Martin, Jim 127, 128, 130, 135
Martin, Tommy 84, 132, 168
Martin and Lewis 77
Martinsville Athletics 74, 97, 137
Maryland Amateur Baseball Association 6, 13
Maryland Scholastic Association 1
Maryland, University of 29, 141
Mashburn, Clara Ruth 66
Masterson, Walt 57
Mathewson, Christy 140
Mauch, Gene 79, 81
Mavis, Bobby 113, 115
May, Merrill 81
Maynard, James "Buster" 126, 127, 130, 136
Mayo, Eddie 104, 105, 107, 113, 115, 116, 190
Mays, Willie 118
Meadows, Lee 80, 81
Medwick, Joe "Ducky" 29–30, 144–45
Menendez, Danny 122, 123
Metro, Charlie 152–56, 157–58, 159, 160–63, 165–67, 168, 169, 170–71, 178
Metro, Helen 154
Middle Atlantic League 10